Modern Critical Views

Modern Critical Views

Modern Critical Views

FRANZ KAFKA

Edited and with an introduction by

Harold Bloom
Sterling Professor of the Humanities
Yale University

CHELSEA HOUSE PUBLISHERS
New York ◇ Philadelphia

© 1986 by Chelsea House Publishers, a division of
Main Line Book Co.

Introduction © 1986 by Harold Bloom

Printed and bound in the United States of America

10   9   8   7   6   5   4

∞   The paper used in this publication meets the minimum
requirements of the American National Standard for Permanence
of paper for Printed Library Materials, Z39.48-1984.

Library of Congress Cataloging-in-Publication Data
Main entry under title:

Franz Kafka.

    (Modern critical views)
    Bibliography: p.
    Includes index.
    1. Kafka, Franz, 1883-1924—Criticism and
interpretation—Addresses, essays, lectures.   I. Bloom,
Harold.   II. Series.
PT2621.A26Z7166   1986   833'.912   85-27005
ISBN 0-87754-724-6

Contents

Editor's Note

This volume gathers together what its editor judges to be a representative selection of the best criticism yet devoted to the writings of Franz Kafka. The editor is grateful to Marijke Rijsberman for her erudition and intelligence in helping to locate and evaluate these essays. They are arranged here in the chronological order of their publication.

The editor's introduction attempts to explain Kafka's curious authority as *the* Jewish writer, neither normative nor quite Gnostic, yet inescapably central to Jewish spirituality in this century. Among the brief stories and parables analyzed are "The Hunter Gracchus," "The Cares of a Family Man," "The Problem of Our Laws," and the more ambitious "Josephine the Singer and the Mouse Folk," which is read as being Kafka's testament.

Walter Benjamin, Kafka's most eminent critic, necessarily begins the chronological sequence here. In Benjamin's subtle formulation, Kafka is seen as having taken the necessary step beyond wisdom literature, into a realm of hope, "but not for us."

The scholar Heinz Politzer, writing on *The Castle,* centers upon Kafka's tone of "knowing despair," which naturalizes *The Castle* in the Western tradition of the grotesque. In Mark Spilka's oxymoronic reading of *Amerika*, the influence and analogue of Dickens is invoked to illuminate Kafka's tenacity in holding on to a desperate sense of what might be called "innocence." Another deeply oxymoronic analysis is offered in Martin Greenberg's reflections upon Kafka's curious "literalism," with its uncanny mixture of a Messianic hope in human possibility and a rationalistic and skeptical stance towards that hope.

Peter Heller's acute meditation upon Kafkan incongruities makes a definitive argument against the existence of any positive rhetoric of values anywhere in the writings. The great Frankfurt cultural philosopher, Theodor W. Adorno, also urges a careful literalism in reading Kafka, while attempting to contextualize the narratives in relevant social and political history.

Dorrit Cohn's exegesis of "A Country Doctor" offers a useful explana-tion of Kafka's characteristic mode of first-person narration in the present tense. In the reading of "The Burrow" by Heinrich Henel, a cogent rejection of allegorical interpretations of Kafka relies upon a sense of dissonance between cognition and figuration in the story.

A more thematic approach that achieves parallel conclusions is repre-sented by Erich Heller's influential account of *The Castle*, which allows for some allegorical elements but essentially gives a Gnostic reading, in which "no comfort can be found *within* this world." Alwin L. Baum, exploring the dialectical relations of parable, paradox, and story in Kafka, presents an analogous realization by assigning Kafka's way of interpretation to Kabbalis-tic tradition. The advanced discussion by Walter H. Sokel of the vexed relations between language and truth in Kafka culminates many previous critical recognitions, Benjamin's in particular, when it states that Kafka's "idea of a purely allusive language establishes the otherness of language in regard to truth." However, this otherness is no defect, but a necessary condition for Kafka's idiosyncratic art.

A final group of more recent essays begins with David Grossvogel's shrewd analysis of *The Trial* as a mystery story, and as a parable of human exile. David Eggenschwiler's discussion of *The Metamorphosis* splendidly acknowledges the Kafkan evasions of interpretation as being themselves the parabolic quest Kafka would have us undertake. This book ends fittingly with Laura Quinney's previously unpublished essay on Kafka's "frail and tenuous" sense of his own appearance in our world, which is represented in his work by figures and images of tenuous intensity. Quinney's admirable mediation between personal and rhetorical criticism is both an instance of a true response to Kafka, and a presage of much criticism still to come.

Introduction

In her obituary for her lover, Franz Kafka, Milena Jesenská sketched a modern Gnostic, a writer whose vision was of the *kenoma*, the cosmic emptiness into which we have been thrown:

> He was a hermit, a man of insight who was frightened by life. . . . He saw the world as being full of invisible demons which assail and destroy defenseless man. . . . All his works describe the terror of mysterious misconceptions and guiltless guilt in human beings.

Milena—brilliant, fearless, and loving—may have subtly distorted Kafka's beautifully evasive slidings between normative Jewish and Jewish Gnostic stances. Max Brod, responding to Kafka's now-famous remark— "We are nihilistic thoughts that came into God's head"—explained to his friend the Gnostic notion that the Demiurge had made this world both sinful and evil. "No," Kafka replied, "I believe we are not such a radical relapse of God's, only one of His bad moods. He had a bad day." Playing straight man, the faithful Brod asked if this meant there was hope outside our cosmos. Kafka smiled, and charmingly said: "Plenty of hope—for God—no end of hope—only not for us."

Kafka, despite Gershom Scholem's authoritative attempts to claim him for Jewish Gnosticism, is both more and less than a Gnostic, as we might expect. Yahweh can be saved, and the divine degradation that is fundamental to Gnosticism is not an element in Kafka's world. But we were fashioned out of the clay during one of Yahweh's bad moods; perhaps there was divine dyspepsia, or sultry weather in the garden that Yahweh had planted in the East. Yahweh is hope, and we are hopeless. We are the jackdaws or crows, the kafkas (since that is what the name means, in Czech) whose impossibility is what the heavens signify: "The crows maintain that a single crow could

1

destroy the heavens. Doubtless that is so, but it proves nothing against the heavens, for the heavens signify simply: the impossibility of crows."

In Gnosticism, there is an alien, wholly transcendent God, and the adept, after considerable difficulties, can find the way back to presence and fullness. Gnosticism therefore is a religion of salvation, though the most negative of all such saving visions. Kafkan spirituality offers no hope of salvation, and so is not Gnostic. But Milena Jesenská certainly was right to emphasize the Kafkan terror that is akin to Gnosticism's dread of the *kenoma*, which is the world governed by the Archons. Kafka takes the impossible step beyond Gnosticism, by denying that there is hope for us anywhere at all.

In the aphorisms that Brod rather misleadingly entitled "Reflections on Sin, Pain, Hope and The True Way," Kafka wrote: "What is laid upon us is to accomplish the negative; the positive is already given." How much Kabbalah Kafka knew is not clear. Since he wrote a new Kabbalah, the question of Jewish Gnostic sources can be set aside. Indeed, by what seems a charming oddity (but I would call it yet another instance of Blake's insistence that forms of worship are chosen from poetic tales), our understanding of Kabbalah is Kafkan anyway, since Kafka profoundly influenced Gershom Scholem, and no one will be able to get beyond Scholem's creative or strong misreading of Kabbalah for decades to come. I repeat this point to emphasize its shock value: we read Kabbalah, via Scholem, from a Kafkan perspective, even as we read human personality and its mimetic possibilities by way of Shakespeare's perspectives, since essentially Freud mediates Shakespeare for us, yet relies upon him nevertheless. A Kafkan facticity or contingency now governs our awareness of whatever in Jewish cultural tradition is other than normative.

In his diaries for 1922, Kafka meditated, on January 16, upon "something very like a breakdown," in which it was "impossible to sleep, impossible to stay awake, impossible to endure life, or, more exactly, the course of life." The vessels were breaking for him as his demoniac, writerly inner world and the outer life "split apart, and they do split apart, or at least clash in a fearful manner." Late in the evening, K. arrives at the village, which is deep in snow. The Castle is in front of him, but even the hill upon which it stands is veiled in mist and darkness, and there is not a single light visible to show that the Castle was there. K. stands a long time on a wooden bridge that leads from the main road to the village, while gazing, not at the village, but "into the illusory emptiness above him," where the Castle should be. He does not know what he will always refuse to learn, which is that the emptiness is "illusory" in every possible sense, since he does gaze at the *kenoma*, which resulted initially from the breaking of the vessels, the splitting apart of every world, inner and outer.

Writing the vision of K., Kafka counts the costs of his confirmation, in a passage prophetic of Scholem, but with a difference that Scholem sought to negate by combining Zionism and Kabbalah for himself. Kafka knew better, perhaps only for himself, but perhaps for others as well:

> Second: This pursuit, originating in the midst of men, carries one in a direction away from them. The solitude that for the most part has been forced on me, in part voluntarily sought by me— but what was this if not compulsion too?—is now losing all its ambiguity and approaches its denouement. Where is it leading? The strongest likelihood is that it may lead to madness; there is nothing more to say, the pursuit goes right through me and rends me asunder. Or I can—can I?—manage to keep my feet somewhat and be carried along in the wild pursuit. Where, then, shall I be brought? "Pursuit," indeed, is only a metaphor. I can also say, "assault on the last earthly frontier," an assault, moreover, launched from below, from mankind, and since this too is a metaphor, I can replace it by the metaphor of an assault from above, aimed at me from above.
>
> All such writing is an assault on the frontiers; if Zionism had not intervened, it might easily have developed into a new secret doctrine, a Kabbalah. There are intimations of this. Though of course it would require genius of an unimaginable kind to strike root again in the old centuries, or create the old centuries anew and not spend itself withal, but only then begin to flower forth.

Consider Kafka's three metaphors, which he so knowingly substitutes for one another. The pursuit is of ideas, in that mode of introspection which is Kafka's writing. Yet this metaphor of pursuit is also a piercing "right through me" and a breaking apart of the self. For "pursuit," Kafka then substitutes mankind's assault, from below, on the last earthly frontier. What is that frontier? It must lie between us and the heavens. Kafka, the crow or jackdaw, by writing, transgresses the frontier and implicitly maintains that he could destroy the heavens. By another substitution, the metaphor changes to "an assault from above, aimed at me from above," the aim simply being the signifying function of the heavens, which is to mean the impossibility of Kafkas or crows. The heavens assault Kafka *through his writing*; "all such writing is an assault on the frontiers," and these must now be Kafka's own frontiers. One thinks of Freud's most complex "frontier concept," more complex even than the drive: the bodily ego. The heavens assault Kafka's bodily ego, *but only through his own writing*. Certainly such an assault is not un-Jewish, and has as much to do with normative as with esoteric Jewish tradition.

Yet, according to Kafka, his own writing, were it not for the intervention of Zionism, might easily have developed into a new Kabbalah. How are we to understand that curious statement about Zionism as the blocking agent that prevents Franz Kafka from becoming another Isaac Luria? Kafka darkly and immodestly writes: "There are intimations of this." Our teacher Gershom Scholem governs our interpretation here, of necessity. Those intimations belong to Kafka alone, or perhaps to a select few in his immediate circle. They cannot be conveyed to Jewry, even to its elite, because Zionism has taken the place of Messianic Kabbalah, including presumably the heretical Kabbalah of Nathan of Gaza, prophet of Sabbatai Zvi and of all his followers down to the blasphemous Jacob Frank. Kafka's influence upon Scholem is decisive here, for Kafka already has arrived at Scholem's central thesis of the link between the Kabbalah of Isaac Luria, the Messianism of the Sabbatarians and Frankists, and the political Zionism that gave rebirth to Israel.

Kafka goes on, most remarkably, to disown the idea that he possesses "genius of an unimaginable kind," one that either would strike root again in archaic Judaism, presumably of the esoteric sort, or more astonishingly "create the old centuries anew," which Scholem insisted Kafka had done. But can we speak, as Scholem tried to speak, of the Kabbalah of Franz Kafka? Is there a new secret doctrine in the superb stories and the extraordinary parables and paradoxes, or did not Kafka spend his genius in the act of new creation of the old Jewish centuries? Kafka certainly would have judged himself harshly as one spent withal, rather than as a writer who "only then began to flower forth."

Kafka died only two and a half years after this meditative moment, died, alas, just before his forty-first birthday. Yet as the propounder of a new Kabbalah, he had gone very probably as far as he (or anyone else) could go. No Kabbalah, be it that of Moses de Leon, Isaac Luria, Moses Cordovero, Nathan of Gaza or Gershom Scholem, is exactly easy to interpret, but Kafka's secret doctrine, if it exists at all, is designedly uninterpretable. My working principle in reading Kafka is to observe that he did everything possible to evade interpretation, which only means that what most needs and demands interpretation in Kafka's writing is its perversely deliberate evasion of interpretation. Erich Heller's formula for getting at this evasion is: "Ambiguity has never been considered an elemental force; it is precisely this in the stories of Franz Kafka." Perhaps, but evasiveness is not the same literary quality as ambiguity.

Evasiveness is purposive; it writes between the lines, to borrow a fine trope from Leo Strauss. What does it mean when a quester for a new Negative, or perhaps rather a revisionist of an old Negative, resorts to the evasion of every possible interpretation as his central topic or theme? Kafka does not doubt guilt, but wishes to make it "possible for men to enjoy sin without guilt, almost without guilt," by reading Kafka. To enjoy sin almost without guilt is to evade interpretation, in exactly the dominant Jewish sense of interpretation. Jewish tradition, whether normative or esoteric, never teaches you to ask Nietzsche's question: "Who is the interpreter, and what power does he seek to gain over the text?" Instead, Jewish tradition asks: "Is the interpreter in the line of those who seek to build a hedge about the Torah in every age?" Kafka's power of evasiveness is not a power over his own text, and it does build a hedge about the Torah in our age. Yet no one before Kafka built up that hedge wholly out of evasiveness, not even Maimonides or Judah Halevi or even Spinoza. Subtlest and most evasive of all writers, Kafka remains the severest and most harassing of the belated sages of what will yet become the Jewish cultural tradition of the future.

II

The jackdaw or crow or Kafka is also the weird figure of the great hunter Gracchus (whose Latin name also means a crow), who is not alive but dead, yet who floats, like one living, on his death-bark forever. When the fussy Burgomaster of Riva knits his brow, asking: "And you have no part in the other world (*das Jenseits*)?", the Hunter replies, with grand defensive irony:

> I am forever on the great stair that leads up to it. On that
> infinitely wide and spacious stair I clamber about, sometimes up,
> sometimes down, sometimes on the right, sometimes on the left,
> always in motion. The Hunter has been turned into a butterfly.
> Do not laugh.

Like the Burgomaster, we do not laugh. Being a single crow, Gracchus would be enough to destroy the heavens, but he will never get there. Instead, the heavens signify his impossibility, the absence of crows or hunters, and so he has been turned into another butterfly, which is all we can be, from the perspective of the heavens. And we bear no blame for that:

> "I had been glad to live and I was glad to die. Before I stepped
> aboard, I joyfully flung away my wretched load of ammunition,
> my knapsack, my hunting rifle that I had always been proud to

carry, and I slipped into my winding sheet like a girl into her marriage dress. I lay and waited. Then came the mishap."

"A terrible fate," said the Burgomaster, raising his hand defensively. "And you bear no blame for it?"

"None," said the hunter. "I was a hunter; was there any sin in that? I followed my calling as a hunter in the Black Forest, where there were still wolves in those days. I lay in ambush, shot, hit my mark, flayed the skin from my victims: was there any sin in that? My labors were blessed. 'The Great Hunter of Black Forest' was the name I was given. Was there any sin in that?"

"I am not called upon to decide that," said the Burgomaster, "but to me also there seems to be no sin in such things. But then, whose is the guilt?"

"The boatman's," said the Hunter. "Nobody will read what I say here, no one will come to help me; even if all the people were commanded to help me, every door and window would remain shut, everybody would take to bed and draw the bedclothes over his head, the whole earth would become an inn for the night. And there is sense in that, for nobody knows of me, and if anyone knew he would not know where I could be found, and if he knew where I could be found, he would not know how to deal with me, he would not know how to help me. The thought of helping me is an illness that has to be cured by taking to one's bed."

How admirable Gracchus is, even when compared to the Homeric heroes! They know, or think they know, that to be alive, however miserable, is preferable to being the foremost among the dead. But Gracchus wished only to be himself, happy to be a hunter when alive, joyful to be a corpse when dead: "I slipped into my winding sheet like a girl into her marriage dress." So long as everything happened in good order, Gracchus was more than content. The guilt must be the boatman's, and may not exceed mere incompetence. Being dead and yet still articulate, Gracchus is beyond help: "The thought of helping me is an illness that has to be cured by taking to one's bed."

When he gives the striking trope of the whole earth closing down like an inn for the night, with the bedclothes drawn over everybody's head, Gracchus renders the judgment: "And there is sense in that." There is sense in that only because in Kafka's world as in Freud's, or in Scholem's, or in any world deeply informed by Jewish memory, there is necessarily sense in everything, total sense, even though Kafka refuses to aid you in getting at or close to it.

But what kind of a world is that, where there is sense in everything, where everything seems to demand interpretation? There can be sense in everything, as J. H. Van den Berg once wrote against Freud's theory of repression, only if everything is already in the past and there never again can be anything wholly new. That is certainly the world of the great normative rabbis of the second century of the Common Era, and consequently it has been the world of most Jews ever since. Torah has been given, Talmud has risen to complement and interpret it, other interpretations in the chain of tradition are freshly forged in each generation, but the limits of Creation and of Revelation are fixed in Jewish memory. There is sense in everything because all sense is present already in the Hebrew Bible, which by definition must be totally intelligible, even if its fullest intelligibility will not shine forth until the Messiah comes.

Gracchus, hunter and jackdaw, is Kafka, pursuer of ideas and jackdaw, and the endless, hopeless voyage of Gracchus is Kafka's passage, only partly through a language not his own, and largely through a life not much his own. Kafka was studying Hebrew intensively while he wrote "The Hunter Gracchus," early in 1917, and I think we may call the voyages of the dead but never-buried Gracchus a trope for Kafka's belated study of his ancestral language. He was still studying Hebrew in the spring of 1923, with his tuberculosis well advanced, and down to nearly the end he longed for Zion, dreaming of recovering his health and firmly grounding his identity by journeying to Palestine. Like Gracchus, he experienced life-in-death, though unlike Gracchus he achieved the release of total death.

"The Hunter Gracchus" as a story or extended parable is not the narrative of a Wandering Jew or Flying Dutchman, because Kafka's trope for his writing activity is not so much a wandering or even a wavering, but rather a repetition, labyrinthine and burrow-building. His writing repeats, not itself, but a Jewish esoteric interpretation of Torah that Kafka himself scarcely knows, or even needs to know. What this interpretation tells Kafka is that there is no written Torah but only an oral one. However, Kafka has no one to tell him what this Oral Torah is. He substitutes his own writing therefore for the Oral Torah not made available to him. He is precisely in the stance of the Hunter Gracchus, who concludes by saying, " 'I am here, more than that I do not know, further than that I cannot go. My ship has no rudder, and it is driven by the wind that blows in the undermost regions of death.' "

III

"What is the Talmud if not a message from the distance?", Kafka wrote to Robert Klopstock, on December 19, 1923. What was all of Jewish tradition, to Kafka, except a message from an endless distance? That is surely part of the burden of the famous parable, "An Imperial Message," which concludes with you, the reader, sitting at your window when evening falls and dreaming to yourself the parable—that God, in his act of dying, has sent you an individual message. Heinz Politzer read this as a Nietzschean parable, and so fell into the trap set by the Kafkan evasiveness:

> Describing the fate of the parable in a time depleted of meta-physical truths, the imperial message has turned into the subjective fantasy of a dreamer who sits at a window with a view on a darkening world. The only real information imported by this story is the news of the Emperor's death. This news Kafka took over from Nietzsche . . .

No, for even though you dream the parable, the parable conveys truth. The Talmud does exist; it really is an Imperial message from the distance. The distance is too great; it cannot reach you; there is hope, but not for you. Nor is it so clear that God is dead. He is always dying, yet always whispers a message into the angel's ear. It is said to you that: "Nobody could fight his way through here even with a message from a dead man," but the Emperor actually does not die in the text of the parable.

Distance is part of Kafka's crucial notion of the Negative, which is not a Hegelian nor a Heideggerian Negative, but is very close to Freud's Negation and also to the Negative imaging carried out by Scholem's Kabbalists. But I want to postpone Kafka's Jewish version of the Negative until later. "The Hunter Gracchus" is an extraordinary text, but it is not wholly characteristic of Kafka at his strongest, at his uncanniest or most sublime.

When he is most himself, Kafka gives us a continuous inventiveness and originality that rivals Dante, and truly challenges Proust and Joyce as that of the dominant Western author of our century, setting Freud aside, since Freud ostensibly is science and not narrative or mythmaking, though if you believe that, then you can be persuaded of anything. Kafka's beast fables are rightly celebrated, but his most remarkable fabulistic being is neither animal nor human, but is little Odradek, in the curious sketch, less than a page and a half long, "The Cares of a Family Man," where the title might have been translated: "The Sorrows of a Paterfamilias." The family man

narrates these five paragraphs, each a dialectical lyric in itself, beginning
with one that worries the meaning of the name:

> Some say the word Odradek is of Slavonic origin, and try to
> account for it on that basis. Others again believe it to be of
> German origin, only influenced by Slavonic. The uncertainty of
> both interpretations allows one to assume with justice that
> neither is accurate, especially as neither of them provides an
> intelligent meaning of the word.

This evasiveness was overcome by the scholar Wilhelm Emrich, who
traced the name Odradek to the Czech word *odraditi*, meaning to dissuade
anyone from doing anything. Like Edward Gorey's Doubtful Guest,
Odradek is uninvited yet will not leave, since implicitly he dissuades you
from doing anything about his presence, or rather something about his very
uncanniness advises you to let him alone:

> No one, of course, would occupy himself with such studies if
> there were not a creature called Odradek. At first glance it looks
> like a flat star-shaped spool for thread, and indeed it docs seem to
> have thread wound upon it; to be sure, they are only old,
> broken-off bits of thread, knotted and tangled together, of the
> most varied sorts and colors. But it is not only a spool, for a small
> wooden crossbar sticks out of the middle of the star, and another
> small rod is joined to that at a right angle. By means of this latter
> rod on one side and one of the points of the star on the other, the
> whole thing can stand upright as if on two legs.

Is Odradek a "thing," as the bemused family man begins by calling
him, or is he not a childlike creature, a daemon at home in the world of
children? Odradek clearly was made by an inventive and humorous child,
rather in the spirit of the making of Adam out of the moistened red clay by
the J writer's Yahweh. It is difficult not to read Odradek's creation as a
deliberate parody when we are told that "the whole thing can stand upright
as if on two legs," and again when the suggestion is ventured that Odradek,
like Adam, "once had some sort of intelligible shape and is now only a
broken-down remnant." If Odradek is fallen, he is still quite jaunty, and
cannot be closely scrutinized, since he "is extraordinarily nimble and can
never be laid hold of," like the story in which he appears. Odradek not only
advises you not to do anything about him, but in some clear sense he is yet
another figure by means of whom Kafka advises you against interpreting
Kafka.

One of the loveliest moments in all of Kafka comes when you, the paterfamilias, encounter Odradek leaning directly beneath you against the banisters. Being inclined to speak to him, as you would to a child, you receive a surprise: "'Well, what's your name?' you ask him. 'Odradek,' he says. 'And where do you live?' 'No fixed abode,' he says and laughs; but it is only the kind of laughter that has no lungs behind it. It sounds rather like the rustling of fallen leaves."

"The 'I' is another," Rimbaud once wrote, adding: "So much the worse for the wood that finds it is a violin." So much the worse for the wood that finds it is Odradek. He laughs at being a vagrant, if only by the bourgeois definition of having "no fixed abode," but the laughter, not being human, is uncanny. And so he provokes the family man to an uncanny reflection, which may be a Kafkan parody of Freud's death drive beyond the pleasure principle:

> I ask myself, to no purpose, what is likely to happen to him? Can he possibly die? Anything that dies has had some kind of aim in life, some kind of activity, which has worn out; but that does not apply to Odradek. Am I to suppose, then, that he will always be rolling down the stairs, with ends of thread trailing after him, right before the feet of my children? He does no harm to anyone that I can see, but the idea that he is likely to survive me I find almost painful.

The aim of life, Freud says, is death, is the return of the organic to the inorganic, supposedly our earlier state of being. Our activity wears out, and so we die because, in an uncanny sense, we wish to die. But Odradek, harmless and charming, is a child's creation, aimless, and so not subject to the death drive. Odradek is immortal, being daemonic, and he represents also a Freudian return of the repressed, of something repressed in the *paterfamilias*, something from which the family man is in perpetual flight. Little Odradek is precisely what Freud calls a cognitive return of the repressed, while (even as) a complete affective repression is maintained. The family man introjects Odradek intellectually, but totally projects him affectively. Odradek, I now suggest, is best understood as Kafka's synecdoche for *Verneinung*; Kafka's version (not altogether un-Freudian) of Jewish Negation, a version I hope to adumbrate in what follows.

IV

Why does Kafka have so unique a spiritual authority? Perhaps the question should be rephrased. What kind of spiritual authority does Kafka have for us, or why are we moved or compelled to read him as one who has such authority? Why invoke the question of authority at all? Literary authority, however we define it, has no necessary relation to spiritual authority, and to speak of a spiritual authority in Jewish writing anyway always has been to speak rather dubiously. Authority is not a Jewish concept but a Roman one, and so makes perfect contemporary sense in the context of the Roman Catholic Church, but little sense in Jewish matters, despite the squalors of Israeli politics and the flaccid pieties of American Jewish nostalgias. There is no authority without hierarchy, and hierarchy is not a very Jewish concept either. We do not want the rabbis, or anyone else, to tell us what or who is or is not Jewish. The masks of the normative conceal not only the eclecticism of Judaism and of Jewish culture, but also the nature of the J writer's Yahweh himself. It is absurd to think of Yahweh as having mere authority. He is no Roman godling who augments human activities, nor a Homeric god helping to constitute an audience for human heroism.

Yahweh is neither a founder nor an onlooker, though sometimes he can be mistaken for either or both. His essential trope is fatherhood rather than foundation, and his interventions are those of a covenanter rather than of a spectator. You cannot found an authority upon him, because his benignity is manifested not through augmentation but through creation. He does not write; he speaks, and he is heard, in time, and what he continues to create by his speaking is *olam*, time without boundaries, which is more than just an augmentation. More of anything else can come through authority, but more life is the blessing itself, and comes, beyond authority, to Abraham, to Jacob, and to David. No more than Yahweh, do any of them have mere authority. Yet Kafka certainly does have literary authority, and in a troubled way his literary authority is now spiritual also, particularly in Jewish contexts. I do not think that this is a post-Holocaust phenomenon, though Jewish Gnosticism, oxymoronic as it may or may not be, certainly seems appropriate to our time, to many among us. Literary Gnosticism does not seem to me a time-bound phenomenon, anyway. Kafka's *The Castle*, as Erich Heller has argued, is clearly more Gnostic than normative in its spiritual temper, but then so is Shakespeare's *Macbeth*, and Blake's *The Four Zoas*, and Carlyle's *Sartor Resartus*. We sense a Jewish element in Kafka's apparent Gnosticism, even if we are less prepared than Scholem was to name it as a new Kabbalah. In his 1922 Diaries, Kafka subtly insinuated that even his espousal of the Negative was dialectical:

> The Negative alone, however strong it may be, cannot suffice, as in my unhappiest moments I believe it can. For if I have gone the tiniest step upward, won any, be it the most dubious kind of security for myself, I then stretch out on my step and wait for the

Negative, not to climb up to me, indeed, but to drag me down
from it. Hence it is a defensive instinct in me that won't tolerate
my having the slightest degree of lasting ease and smashes the
marriage bed, for example, even before it has been set up.

What is the Kafkan Negative, whether in this passage or elsewhere? Let
us begin by dismissing the Gallic notion that there is anything Hegelian
about it, any more than there is anything Hegelian about the Freudian
Verneinung. Kafka's Negative, unlike Freud's, is uneasily and remotely descended from the ancient tradition of negative theology, and perhaps even
from that most negative of ancient theologies, Gnosticism, and yet Kafka,
despite his yearnings for transcendence, joins Freud in accepting the ultimate authority of the fact. The given suffers no destruction in Kafka or in
Freud, and this given essentially is the way things are, for everyone, and for
the Jews in particular. If fact is supreme, then the mediation of the Hegelian
Negative becomes an absurdity, and no destructive use of such a Negative is
possible, which is to say that Heidegger becomes impossible, and Derrida,
who is a strong misreading of Heidegger, becomes quite unnecessary.

The Kafkan Negative most simply is his Judaism, which is to say the
spiritual form of Kafka's self-conscious Jewishness, as exemplified in that
extraordinary aphorism: "What is laid upon us is to accomplish the negative;
the positive is already given." The positive here is the Law or normative
Judaism; the negative is not so much Kafka's new Kabbalah, as it is that
which is still laid upon us: the Judaism of the Negative, of the future as it is
always rushing towards us.

His best biographer to date, Ernst Pawel, emphasizes Kafka's consciousness "of his identity as a Jew, not in the religious, but in the national
sense." Still, Kafka was not a Zionist, and perhaps he longed not so much for
Zion as for a Jewish language, be it Yiddish or Hebrew. He could not see
that his astonishing stylistic purity in German was precisely his way of *not*
betraying his self-identity as a Jew. In his final phase, Kafka thought of
going to Jerusalem, and again intensified his study of Hebrew. Had he lived,
he would probably have gone to Zion, perfected a vernacular Hebrew, and
given us the bewilderment of Kafkan parables and stories in the language of
the J writer and of Judah Halevi.

V

What calls out for interpretation in Kafka is his refusal to be interpreted, his evasiveness even in the realm of his own Negative. Two of his

most beautifully enigmatical performances, both late, are the parable, "The Problem of Our Laws," and the story or testament "Josephine the Singer and the Mouse Folk." Each allows a cognitive return of Jewish cultural memory, while refusing the affective identification that would make either parable or tale specifically Jewish in either historical or contemporary identification. "The Problem of Our Laws" is set as a problem in the parable's first paragraph:

> Our laws are not generally known; they are kept secret by the small group of nobles who rule us. We are convinced that these ancient laws are scrupulously administered; nevertheless it is an extremely painful thing to be ruled by laws that one does not know. I am not thinking of possible discrepancies that may arise in the interpretation of the laws, or of the disadvantages involved when only a few and not the whole people are allowed to have a say in their interpretation. These disadvantages are perhaps of no great importance. For the laws are very ancient; their interpretation has been the work of centuries, and has itself doubtless acquired the status of law; and though there is still a possible freedom of interpretation left, it has now become very restricted. Moreover the nobles have obviously no cause to be influenced in their interpretation by personal interests inimical to us, for the laws were made to the advantage of the nobles from the very beginning, they themselves stand above the laws, and that seems to be why the laws were entrusted exclusively into their hands. Of course, there is wisdom in that—who doubts the wisdom of the ancient laws?—but also hardship for us; probably that is unavoidable.

In Judaism, the Law is precisely what is generally known, proclaimed, and taught by the normative sages. The Kabbalah was secret doctrine, but increasingly was guarded not by the normative rabbis, but by Gnostic sectaries, Sabbatarians, and Frankists, all of them ideologically descended from Nathan of Gaza, Sabbatai Zvi's prophet. Kafka twists askew the relation between normative and esoteric Judaism, again making a synecdochal representation impossible. It is not the rabbis or normative sages who stand above the Torah but the *minim*, the heretics from Elisha Ben Abuyah through to Jacob Frank, and in some sense, Gershom Scholem as well. To these Jewish Gnostics, as the parable goes on to insinuate: "The Law is whatever the nobles do." So radical a definition tells us "that the tradition is far from complete," and that a kind of Messianic expectation is therefore necessary.

> This view, so comfortless as far as the present is concerned, is lightened only by the belief that a time will eventually come when the tradition and our research into it will jointly reach their conclusion, and as it were gain a breathing space, when everything will have become clear, the law will belong to the people, and the nobility will vanish.

If the parable at this point were to be translated into early Christian terms, then "the nobility" would be the Pharisees, and "the people" would be the Christian believers. But Kafka moves rapidly to stop such a translation: "This is not maintained in any spirit of hatred against the nobility; not at all, and by no one. We are more inclined to hate ourselves, because we have not yet shown ourselves worthy of being entrusted with the laws."

"We" here cannot be either Christians or Jews. Who then are those who "have not yet shown ourselves worthy of being entrusted with the laws"? They would appear to be the crows or jackdaws again, a Kafka or a Hunter Gracchus, wandering about in a state perhaps vulnerable to self-hatred or self-distrust, waiting for a Torah that will not be revealed. Audaciously, Kafka then concludes with overt paradox:

> Actually one can express the problem only in a sort of paradox: Any party that would repudiate not only all belief in the laws, but the nobility as well, would have the whole people behind it; yet no such party can come into existence, for nobody would dare to repudiate the nobility. We live on this razor's edge. A writer once summed the matter up in this way: The sole visible and indubitable law that is imposed upon us is the nobility, and must we ourselves deprive ourselves of that one law?

Why would no one dare to repudiate the nobility, whether we read them as normative Pharisees, Jewish Gnostic heresiarchs, or whatever? Though imposed upon us, the sages *or* the *minim* are the only visible evidence of law that we have. Who are we then? How is the parable's final question, whether open or rhetorical, to be answered? "Must we ourselves deprive ourselves of that one law?" Blake's answer, in *The Marriage of Heaven and Hell*, was: "One Law for the Lion and the Ox is Oppression." But what is one law for the crows? Kafka will not tell us whether it is oppression or not.

Josephine the singer also is a crow or Kafka, rather than a mouse, and the folk may be interpreted as an entire nation of jackdaws. The spirit of the

Negative, dominant if uneasy in "The Problem of our Laws," is loosed into a terrible freedom in Kafka's testamentary story. That is to say: in the parable, the laws could not be Torah, though that analogue flickered near. But in Josephine's story, the mouse folk simultaneously are *and* are not the Jewish people, and Franz Kafka both is *and* is not their curious singer. Cognitively the identifications are possible, as though returned from forgetfulness, but affectively they certainly are not, unless we can assume that crucial aspects making up the identifications have been purposefully, if other than consciously, forgotten. Josephine's piping *is* Kafka's story, and yet Kafka's story is hardly Josephine's piping.

Can there be a mode of negation neither conscious nor unconscious, neither Hegelian nor Freudian? Kafka's genius provides one, exposing many shades between consciousness and the work of repression, many demarcations far ghostlier than we could have imagined without him. Perhaps the ghostliest come at the end of the story:

> Josephine's road, however, must go downhill. The time will soon come when her last notes sound and die into silence. She is a small episode in the eternal history of our people, and the people will get over the loss of her. Not that it will be easy for us; how can our gatherings take place in utter silence? Still, were they not silent even when Josephine was present? Was her actual piping notably louder and more alive than the memory of it will be? Was it even in her lifetime more than a simple memory? Was it not rather because Josephine's singing was already past losing in this way that our people in their wisdom prized it so highly?
>
> So perhaps we shall not miss so very much after all, while Josephine, redeemed from the earthly sorrows which to her thinking lay in wait for all chosen spirits, will happily lose herself in the numberless throng of the heroes of our people, and soon, since we are no historians, will rise to the heights of redemption and be forgotten like all her brothers.

"I am a Memory come alive," Kafka wrote in the Diaries. Whether or not he intended it, he was Jewish memory come alive. "Was it even in her lifetime more than a simple memory?" Kafka asks, knowing that he too was past losing. The Jews are no historians, in some sense, because Jewish memory, as Yosef Yerushalmi has demonstrated, is a normative mode and not a historical one. Kafka, if he could have prayed, might have prayed to rise to the heights of redemption and be forgotten like most of his brothers and sisters. But his prayer would not have been answered. When we think of *the* Catholic writer, we think of Dante, who nevertheless had the audacity to enshrine his Beatrice in the hierarchy of Paradise. If we think of *the* Protestant writer, we think of Milton, a party or sect of one, who believed that the soul was mortal, and would be resurrected only in conjunction with the body. Think of *the* Jewish writer, and you must think of Kafka, who evaded his own audacity, and believed nothing, and trusted only in the Covenant of being a writer.

WALTER BENJAMIN

Some Reflections on Kafka

It is related that Potemkin suffered from states of depression which recurred more or less regularly. At such times no one was allowed to go near him, and access to his room was strictly forbidden. This malady was never mentioned at court, and in particular it was known that any allusion to it incurred the disfavor of Empress Catherine. One of the Chancellor's depressions lasted for an extraordinary length of time and brought about serious difficulties; in the offices documents piled up that required Potemkin's signature, and the Empress pressed for their completion. The high officials were at their wits' end. One day an unimportant little clerk named Shuvalkin happened to enter the anteroom of the Chancellor's palace and found the councillors of state assembled there, moaning and groaning as usual. "What is the matter, Your Excellencies?" asked the obliging Shuvalkin. They explained things to him and regretted that they could not use his services. "If that's all it is," said Shuvalkin, "I beg you to let me have those papers." Having nothing to lose, the councillors of state let themselves be persuaded to do so, and with the sheaf of documents under his arm, Shuvalkin set out, through galleries and corridors, for Potemkin's bedroom. Without stopping or bothering to knock, he turned the door-handle; the room was not locked. In semidarkness Potemkin was sitting on his bed in a threadbare nightshirt, biting his nails. Shuvalkin stepped up to the writing desk, dipped a pen in ink, and without saying a word pressed it into Potemkin's hand while putting one of the documents on his knees. Potemkin gave the intruder a vacant stare; then, as though in his sleep, he started to sign—first one paper, then a second, finally all of them. When the last signature had been affixed, Shuvalkin took the papers under his arm and left the room without further ado, just as he had entered it. Waving the papers triumphantly, he stepped into the ante-room. The councillors of state rushed toward him and tore the documents out of his hands. Breathlessly they bent over them. No one spoke a word; the whole group seemed paralyzed. Again Shuvalkin came close and solicitously asked why the gentlemen seemed so upset. At that point he noticed the signatures. One document after another was signed Shuvalkin . . . Shuvalkin . . . Shuvalkin. . . .

This story is like a herald racing two hundred years ahead of Kafka's work. The enigma which beclouds it is Kafka's enigma. The world of offices and registries, of musty, shabby, dark rooms, is Kafka's world. The obliging Shuvalkin, who makes light of everything and is finally left empty-handed, is Kafka's K. Potemkin, who vegetates, somnolent and unkempt, in a remote, inaccessible room, is an ancestor of those holders of power in Kafka's works who live in the attics as judges or in the castle as secretaries; no matter how highly placed they may be, they are always fallen or falling men, although even the lowest and seediest of them, the doorkeepers and the decrepit officials, may abruptly and strikingly appear in the fullness of their power. Why do they vegetate? Could they be the descendants of the figures of Atlas that support globes with their shoulders? Perhaps that is why each has his head "so deep on his chest that one can hardly see his eyes," like the Castellan in his portrait, or Klamm when he is alone. But it is not the globe they are carrying; it is just that even the most commonplace things have their weight. "His fatigue is that of the gladiator after the fight; his job was the whitewashing of a corner in the office!" Georg Lukács once said that in order to make a decent table nowadays, a man must have the architectural genius of a Michelangelo. If Lukács thinks in terms of ages, Kafka thinks in terms of cosmic epochs. The man who whitewashes has epochs to move, even in his most insignificant movement. On many occasions and often for strange reasons Kafka's figures clap their hands. Once, the casual remark is made that these hands are "really steam hammers."

We encounter these holders of power in constant, slow movement, rising or falling. But they are at their most terrible when they rise from the deepest decay—from the fathers. The son calms his spiritless, senile father whom he has just gently put to bed:

> "Don't worry, you are well covered up." "No," cried his father, cutting short the answer, threw the blanket off with such strength that it unfolded fully as it flew, and stood up in bed. Only one

hand lightly touched the ceiling to steady him. "You wanted to cover me up, I know, my little scamp, but I'm not all covered up yet. And even if this is all the strength I have left, it's enough for you, too much for you. . . . But thank goodness a father does not need to be taught how to see through his son." . . . And he stood up quite unsupported and kicked his legs out. He beamed with insight. . . . "So now you know what else there was in the world besides yourself; until now you have known only about yourself! It is true, you were an innocent child, but it is even more true that you have been a devilish person!"

As the father throws off the burden of the blanket, he also throws off a cosmic burden. He has to set cosmic ages in motion in order to turn the age-old father-son relationship into a living and consequential thing. But what consequences! He sentences his son to death by drowning. The father is the one who punishes; guilt attracts him as it does the court officials. There is much to indicate that the world of the officials and the world of the fathers are the same to Kafka. The similarity does not redound to this world's credit; it consists of dullness, decay, and dirt. The father's uniform is stained all over; his underwear is dirty. Filth is the element of the officials. "She could not understand why there were office hours for the public in the first place. 'To get some dirt on the front staircase'—this is how her question was once answered by an official, who was probably annoyed, but it made a lot of sense to her." Uncleanness is so much the attribute of officials that one could almost regard them as enormous parasites. This, of course, does not refer to the economic context, but to the forces of reason and humanity from which this clan makes a living. In the same way the fathers in Kafka's strange families batten on their sons, lying on top of them like giant parasites. They not only prey upon their strength, but gnaw away at the sons' right to exist. The fathers punish, but they are at the same time the accusers. The sin of which they accuse their sons seems to be a kind of original sin. The definition of it which Kafka has given applies to the sons more than to anyone else: "Original sin, the old injustice committed by man, consists in the complaint unceasingly made by man that he has been the victim of an injustice, the victim of original sin." But who is accused of this inherited sin—the sin of having produced an heir—if not the father by the son? Accordingly the son would be the sinner. But one must not conclude from Kafka's definition that the accusation is sinful because it is false. Nowhere does Kafka say that it is made wrongfully. A never-ending process is at work here, and no cause can appear in a worse light than the one for which the father enlists the aid of these officials and court offices. A boundless corruptibility is not their worst feature, for their essence is such that their venality is the only hope held out to the human spirit facing them. The courts, to be sure, have lawbooks at their disposal, but people are not allowed to see them. "It is characteristic of this legal system," conjectures K., "that one is sentenced not only in innocence but also in ignorance." Laws and definite norms remain unwritten in the prehistoric world. A man can transgress them without suspecting it and thus become subject to atonement. But no matter how hard it may hit the unsuspecting, the transgression in the sense of the law is not accidental but fated, a destiny which appears here in all its ambiguity. In a cursory investigation of the idea of fate in antiquity Hermann Cohen came to a "conclusion that becomes inescapable": "the very rules of fate seem to be what causes and brings about the breaking away from them, the defection." It is the same way with the legal authorities whose proceedings are directed against K. It takes us back far beyond the time of the giving of the Law on twelve tablets to a prehistoric world, written law being one of the first victories scored over this world. In Kafka the written law is contained in books, but these are secret; by basing itself on them the prehistoric world exerts its rule all the more ruthlessly.

In Kafka's works, the conditions in offices and in families have multifarious points of contact. In the village at the foot of Castle Hill people use an illuminating saying. " 'We have a saying here that you may be familiar with: Official decisions are as shy as young girls.' 'That's a sound observation,' said K., 'a sound observation. Decisions may have even other characteristics in common with girls.' " The most remarkable of these qualities is the willingness to lend oneself to anything, like the shy girls whom K. meets in *The Castle* and *The Trial*, girls who indulge in unchastity in the bosom of their family as they would in a bed. He encounters them at every turn; the rest give him as little trouble as the conquest of the barmaid.

> They embraced each other; her little body burned in K.'s hands; in a state of unconsciousness which K. tried to master constantly but fruitlessly, they rolled a little way, hit Klamm's door with a thud, and then lay in the little puddles of beer and the other refuse that littered the floor. Hours passed . . . in which K. constantly had the feeling that he was losing his way or that he had wandered farther than anyone had ever wandered before, to a place where even the air had nothing in common with his native air, where all this strangeness might choke one, yet a place so insanely enchanting that one could not help but go on and lose oneself even further.

We shall have more to say about this strange place. The remarkable thing is that these whorelike women never seem to be beautiful. Rather, beauty appears in Kafka's world only in the most obscure places—among the accused persons, for example. "This, to be sure, is a strange phenomenon, a natural law, as it were. . . . It cannot be guilt that makes them attractive . . . nor can it be the just punishment which makes them attractive in anticipation . . . so it must be the mere charges brought against them that somehow show on them."

From *The Trial* it may be seen that these proceedings usually are hopeless for those accused—hopeless even when they have hopes of being acquitted. It may be this hopelessness that brings out the beauty in them—the only creatures in Kafka thus favored. At least this would be very much in keeping with a conversation which Max Brod has related. "I remember," Brod writes,

> a conversation with Kafka which began with present-day Europe and the decline of the human race. "We are nihilistic thoughts, suicidal thoughts that come into God's head," Kafka said. This reminded me at first of the Gnostic view of life: God as the evil demiurge, the world as his Fall. "Oh no," said Kafka, "our world is only a bad mood of God, a bad day of his." "Then there is hope outside this manifestation of the world that we know." He smiled. "Oh, plenty of hope, an infinite amount of hope—but not for us."

These words provide a bridge to those extremely strange figures in Kafka, the only ones who have escaped from the family circle and for whom there may be hope. These are not the animals, not even those hybrids or imaginary creatures like the Cat Lamb or Odradek; they all still live under the spell of the family. It is no accident that Gregor Samsa wakes up as a bug in his parental home and not somewhere else, and that the peculiar animal which is half kitten, half lamb, is inherited from the father; Odradek likewise is the concern of the father of the family. The "assistants," however, are outside this circle.

These assistants belong to a group of figures which recurs through Kafka's entire work. Their tribe includes the confidence man who is unmasked in "Meditation"; the student who appears on the balcony at night as Karl Rossmann's neighbor; and the fools who live in that town in the south and never get tired. The twilight in which they exist is reminiscent of the uncertain light in which the figures in the short prose pieces of Robert Walser appear [the author of *Der Gehülfe*, The Assistant, a novel Kafka was very fond of]. In Indian mythology there are the *gandharvas*, celestial creatures, beings in an unfinished state. Kafka's assistants are of that kind: neither members of, nor strangers to, any of the other groups of figures, but, rather, messengers from one to the other. Kafka tells us that they resemble Barnabas, who is a messenger. They have not yet been completely released from the womb of nature, and that is why they have "settled down on two old women's skirts on the floor in a corner. It was . . . their ambition . . . to use up as little space as possible. To that end they kept making various experiments, folding their arms and legs, huddling close together; in the darkness all one could see in their corner was one big ball." It is for them and their kind, the unfinished and the bunglers, that there is hope.

What may be discerned, subtly and informally, in the activities of these messengers is law, in an oppressive and gloomy way, for this whole group of beings. None has a firm place in the world, firm, inalienable outlines. There is not one that is not either rising or falling, none that is not trading qualities with its enemy or neighbor, none that has not completed its period of time and yet is unripe, none that is not deeply exhausted and yet is only at the beginning of a long existence. To speak of any order or hierarchy is impossible here. Even the world of myth of which we think in this context is incomparably younger than Kafka's world, which has been promised redemption by the myth. But if we can be sure of one thing, it is this: Kafka did not succumb to its temptation. A latter-day Ulysses, he let the Sirens go by "his gaze which was fixed on the distance, the Sirens disappeared as it were before his determination, and at the very moment when he was closest to them he was no longer aware of them." Among Kafka's ancestors in the ancient world, the Jews and the Chinese, whom we shall encounter later, this Greek one should not be forgotten. Ulysses, after all, stands at the dividing line between myth and fairy tale. Reason and cunning have inserted tricks into myths; their forces cease to be invincible. Fairy tales are the traditional stories about victory over these forces, and fairy tales for dialecticians are what Kafka wrote when he went to work on legends. He inserted little tricks into them; then he used them as proof "that inadequate, even childish measures may also serve to rescue one." With these words he begins his story about the "Silence of the Sirens." For Kafka's Sirens are silent; they have "an even more terrible weapon than their song . . . their silence." This they used on Ulysses. But he, so Kafka tells us, "was so full of guile, was such a fox that not even the goddess of fate could pierce his armor. Perhaps he had really noticed, although here the human understanding is beyond its depths, that the Sirens were silent, and opposed the afore-mentioned pretense to them and the gods merely as a sort of shield."

Kafka's Sirens are silent. Perhaps because for Kafka music and singing are an expression or at least a token of escape, a token of hope which comes to us from that intermediate world—at once unfinished and commonplace, comforting and silly—in which the assistants are at home. Kafka is like the lad who set out to learn what fear was. He has got into Potemkin's palace and finally, in the depths of its cellar, has encountered Josephine, the singing mouse, whose tune he describes: "Something of our poor, brief childhood is in it, something of lost happiness which can never be found again, but also something of active present-day life, of its small gaieties, unaccountable and yet real and unquenchable."

THE LITTLE HUNCHBACK

Some time ago it became known that Knut Hamsun was in the habit of expressing his views in an occasional letter to the editor of the local paper in the small town near which he lived. Years ago that town was the scene of the jury trial of a maid who had killed her infant child. She was sentenced to a prison term. Soon thereafter the local paper printed a letter from Hamsun in which he announced his intention of leaving a town which did not visit the supreme punishment on a mother who killed her newborn child—the gallows, or at least a life term of hard labor. A few years passed. *Growth of the Soil* appeared, and it contained the story of a maid who committed the same crime, suffered the same punishment, and, as is made clear to the reader, surely deserved no more severe one.

Kafka's posthumous reflections, which are contained in *The Great Wall of China*, recall this to mind. Hardly had this volume appeared when the reflections served as the basis for a Kafka criticism which concentrated on an interpretation of these reflections to the neglect of his real works. There are two ways to miss the point of Kafka's works. One is to interpret them naturally, the other is the supernatural interpretation. Both the psychoanalytic and the theological interpretations equally miss the essential points. The first kind is represented by Hellmuth Kaiser; the second, by numerous writers, such as H. J. Schoeps, Bernhard Rang, and Bernhard Groethuysen. To these last also belong Willy Haas, although he has made revealing comments on Kafka in other contexts which we shall discuss later; such insights did not prevent him from interpreting Kafka's work after a theological pattern. "The powers above, the realm of grace," so Haas writes, "Kafka has depicted in his great novel *The Castle*; the powers below, the realm of the courts and of damnation, he has dealt with in his equally great novel *The Trial*. The earth between the two, earthly fate and its arduous demands, he

attempted to present in strictly stylized form in a third novel, *Amerika*." The
first third of this interpretation has, since Brod, become the common property of Kafka criticism. Bernhard Rang writes in a similar vein: "To the
extent that one may regard the Castle as the seat of grace, precisely these vain
efforts and attempts mean, theologically speaking, that God's grace cannot
be attained or forced by man at will and deliberately. Unrest and impatience
only impede and confound the exalted stillness of the divine." This interpretation is a convenient one; but the further it is carried, the clearer it becomes
that it is untenable. This is perhaps seen most clearly in a statement by
Willy Haas. "Kafka goes back . . . to Kierkegaard as well as to Pascal; one
may call him the only legitimate heir of these two. In all three there is an
excruciatingly harsh basic religious theme: man is always in the wrong before
God. . . . Kafka's upper world, his so-called Castle, with its immense,
complex staff of petty and rather lecherous officials, his strange heaven plays
a horrible game with people . . . and yet man is very much in the wrong
even before this god." This theology falls far behind the doctrine of justification of St. Anselm of Canterbury into barbaric speculations which do not
even seem consistent with the text of Kafka's works. "Can an individual
official forgive?" we read in *The Castle*. "This could only be a matter for the
over-all authorities, but even they can probably not forgive but only judge."
This road has soon led into a blind alley. "All this," says Denis de Rouge-
mont, "is not the wretched situation of man without a god, but the wretched
state of a man who is bound to a god he does not know, because he does not
know Christ."

It is easier to draw speculative conclusions from Kafka's posthumous
collection of notes than to explore even one of the motifs that appear in his
stories and novels. Yet only these give some clue to the prehistoric forces that
dominated Kafka's creativeness, forces which, to be sure, may justifiably be
regarded as belonging to our world as well. Who can say under what names
they appeared to Kafka himself? Only this much is certain: he did not know
them and failed to get his bearings among them. In the mirror which the
prehistoric world held before him in the form of guilt he merely saw the
future emerging in the form of judgment. Kafka, however, did not say what
it was like. Was it not the Last Judgment? Does it not turn the judge into
the defendant? Is the trial not the punishment? Kafka gave no answer. Did
he expect anything of this punishment? Or was he not rather concerned to
postpone it? In the stories which Kafka left us, narrative art regains the
significance it had in the mouth of Scheherazade: to postpone the future. In
The Trial postponement is the hope of the accused man only if the proceedings do not gradually turn into the judgment. The patriarch himself is to

benefit by postponement, even though he may have to trade his place in tradition for it.

> I could conceive of another Abraham—to be sure, he would never get to be a patriarch or even an old-clothes dealer—an Abraham who would be prepared to satisfy the demand for a sacrifice immediately, with the promptness of a waiter, but would be unable to bring it off because he cannot get away, being indispensable; the household needs him, there is always something or other to take care of, the house is never ready; but without having his house ready, without having something to fall back on, he cannot leave—this the Bible also realized, for it says: "He set his house in order."

This Abraham appears "with the promptness of a waiter." Kafka could understand things only in the form of a *gestus*, and this *gestus* which he did not understand constitutes the cloudy part of the parables. Kafka's writings emanate from it. The way he withheld them is well known. His testament orders their destruction. This document, which no one interested in Kafka can disregard, says that the writings did not satisfy their author, that he regarded his efforts as failures, that he counted himself among those who were bound to fail. He did fail in his grandiose attempt to convert poetry into doctrine, to turn it into a parable and restore to it that stability and unpretentiousness which, in the face of reason, seemed to him to be the only appropriate thing for it. No other writer has obeyed the commandment "Thou shalt not make unto thee a graven image" so faithfully.

"It was as if the shame of it was to outlive him." With these words *The Trial* ends. Corresponding as it does to his "elemental purity of feeling," shame is Kafka's strongest gesture. It has a dual aspect, however. Shame is an intimate human reaction, but at the same time it has social pretensions. Shame is not only shame in the presence of others, but can also be shame one feels for them. Kafka's shame, then, is no more personal than the life and thought which govern it and which he has described thus: "He does not live for the sake of his own life, he does not think for the sake of his own thought. He feels as though he were living and thinking under the constraint of a family. . . . Because of this unknown family . . . he cannot be released." We do not know the make-up of this unknown family, which is composed of human beings and animals. But this much is clear: it is this family that forces Kafka to move cosmic ages in his writings. Doing this family's bidding, he moves the mass of historical happenings as Sisyphus rolled the stone. As he does so, its nether side comes to light; it is not a pleasant sight, but Kafka is capable of bearing it. "To believe in progress is not to believe that progress has already taken place. That would be no belief." Kafka did not consider the age in which he lived as an advance over the beginnings of time. His novels are set in a swamp world. In his works, created things appear at the stage which Bachofen has termed the hetaeric stage. The fact that it is now forgotten does not mean that it does not extend into the present. On the contrary: it is actual by virtue of this very oblivion. An experience deeper than that of an average person can make contact with it. "I have experience," we read in one of Kafka's earliest notes, "and I am not joking when I say that it is a seasickness on dry land." It is no accident that the first "Meditation" was made on a swing. And Kafka does not tire of expressing himself on the fluctuating nature of experiences. Each gives way and mingles with its opposite. "It was summer, a hot day," so begins "The Knock at the Manor Gate." "With my sister I was passing the gate of a great house on our way home. I don't remember whether she knocked on the gate out of mischief or in a fit of absentmindedness, or merely shook her fist at it and did not knock at all." The very possibility of the third alternative puts the other two, which at first seemed harmless, in a different light. It is from the swampy soil of such experiences that Kafka's female characters rise. They are swamp creatures like Leni, "who stretches out the middle and ring fingers of her right hand between which the connecting web of skin reached almost to the top joint, short as the fingers were." "Fine times," so the ambivalent Frieda reminisces about her earlier life; "you never asked me about my past." This past takes us back to the dark, deep womb, the scene of the mating "whose untrammeled voluptuousness," to quote Bachofen, "is hateful to the pure forces of heavenly light and which justifies the term used by Arnobius, *luteae voluptates* [dirty voluptuousness]."

Only from this vantage point can the technique of Kafka the storyteller be comprehended. Whenever figures in the novels have anything to say to K., no matter how important or surprising it may be, they do so casually and with the implication that he must really have known it all along. It is as though nothing new was being imparted, as though the hero was just being subtly invited to recall to mind something that he had forgotten. This is how Willy Haas has interpreted the course of events in *The Trial*, and justifiably so. "The object of the trial," he writes, "indeed, the real hero of this incredible book is forgetting, whose main characteristic is the forgetting of itself. . . . Here it has actually become a mute figure in the shape of the accused man, a figure of the most striking intensity." It probably cannot be denied that "this mysterious center . . . derives from the Jewish religion." "Memory plays a very mysterious role as piousness. It is not an ordinary, but

. . . the most profound quality of Jehovah that he remembers, that he retains an infallible memory 'to the third and fourth, even to the hundredth generation.' The most sacred . . . act of the . . . ritual is the erasing of sins from the book of memory."

What has been forgotten—and this insight affords us yet another avenue of access to Kafka's work—is never something purely individual. Everything forgotten mingles with what has been forgotten of the prehistoric world, forms countless, uncertain, changing compounds, yielding a constant flow of new, strange products. Oblivion is the container from which the inexhaustible intermediate world in Kafka's stories presses toward the light.

> Here the very fullness of the world is considered as the only reality. All spirit must be concrete, particularized in order to have its place and *raison d'être*. The spiritual, if it plays a role at all, turns into spirits. These spirits become definite individuals, with names and a very special connection with the name of the worshiper. . . . Without any scruples their fullness is crammed into the fullness of the world. . . . The crowd of spirits is swelled without any concern . . . new ones are constantly added to the old ones, and all are distinguished from the others by their own names.

All this does not refer to Kafka, but to—China. This is how Franz Rosenzweig describes the Chinese ancestor cult in his *Star of Redemption*. To Kafka, the world of his ancestors was as unfathomable as the world of realities was important for him, and we may be sure that, like the totem poles of primitive peoples, the world of ancestors took him down to the animals. Incidentally, Kafka is not the only writer for whom animals are the receptacles of the forgotten. In Tieck's profound story "Fair Eckbert," the forgotten name of a little dog, Strohmi, stands for a mysterious guilt. One can understand, then, that Kafka did not tire of picking up the forgotten from animals. They are not the goal, to be sure, but one cannot do without them. A case in point is the "hunger artist," who, "strictly speaking, was only an impediment on the way to the menagerie." Can one not see the animals in "The Burrow" or "The Giant Mole" ponder as they dig in? And yet this thinking is extremely flighty. Irresolutely it flits from one worry to the next, it nibbles at every anxiety with the fickleness of despair. Thus there are butterflies in Kafka, too. The guilt-ridden "Hunter Gracchus," who refuses to acknowledge his guilt, "has turned into a butterfly." "Don't laugh," says the hunter Gracchus. This much is certain; of all of Kafka's creatures, the animals have the greatest opportunity for reflection. What corruption is in the law, anxiety is in their thinking. It messes a situation up, yet it is the only hopeful thing about it. However, because the most forgotten alien land is one's own body, one can understand why Kafka called the cough that erupted from within him "the animal." It was the most advanced outpost of the great herd.

The strangest bastard which the prehistoric world has begotten with guilt in Kafka is Odradek [in "The Cares of a Family Man"]. "At first sight it looks like a flat, star-shaped spool for thread, and it really seems to have thread wound around it; to be sure, they probably are only old, broken-off bits of thread that are knotted and tangled together, of all sorts and colors. But it is not just a spool, for a small wooden cross-bar sticks out of the middle of the star, and another small rod is joined to it at a right angle. With the aid of this latter rod on one side and one of the extensions of the star on the other, the whole thing can stand upright as if on two legs." Odradek "stays alternately in the attic, on the staircase, in the corridors, and in the hall." So it prefers the same places as the court of law which investigates guilt. Attics are the places of discarded, forgotten objects. Perhaps the necessity to appear before a court of justice gives rise to a feeling similar to that with which one approaches trunks in the attic which have been locked up for years. One would like to put off this chore till the end of time, just as K. regards his written defense as suitable "for occupying one's senile mind some day during retirement."

Odradek is the form which things assume in oblivion. They are distorted. The "cares of a family man," which no one can identify, are distorted; the bug, of which we know all too well that it represents Gregor Samsa, is distorted; the big animal, half lamb, half kitten, for which "the butcher's knife" might be "a release," is distorted. These Kafka figures are connected by a long series of figures with the prototype of distortion, the hunchback. Among the images in Kafka's stories, none is more frequent than that of the man who bows his head far down on his chest: the fatigue of the court officials, the noise affecting the doormen in the hotel, the low ceiling facing the visitors in the gallery. In the "Penal Colony" those in power use an archaic apparatus which engraves letters with curlicues on the backs of guilty men, multiplying the stabs and piling up the ornaments to the point where the back of the guilty man becomes clairvoyant and is able to decipher the writing from which he must derive the nature of his unknown guilt. It is the back on which this is incumbent. It was always this way with Kafka. Compare this early diary entry: "In order to be as heavy as possible, which I believe to be an aid to falling asleep, I had crossed my arms and put my hands on my shoulders, so that I lay there like a soldier with his pack." Quite palpably, being loaded down is here equated with forgetting, the forgetting of a sleeping man. The same symbol occurs in the folksong "The Little Hunchback." This little man is at home in distorted life; he will disappear with the coming of the Messiah, of whom a great rabbi once said that he did not wish to change the world by force, but would only make a slight adjustment in it.

> When I come into my room,
> My little bed to make,
> A little hunchback is in there,
> With laughter does he shake.

This is the laughter of Odradek, which is described as sounding "something like the rustling in falling leaves."

> When I kneel upon my stool
> And I want to pray,
> A hunchbacked man is in the room
> And he starts to say:
> My dear child, I beg of you,
> Pray for the little hunchback too.

So ends the folksong. In his depth Kafka touches the ground which neither "mythical divination" nor "existential theology" supplied him with. It is the core of folk tradition, the German as well as the Jewish. Even if Kafka did not pray—and this we do now know—he still possessed in the highest degree what Malebranche called "the natural prayer of the soul": attentiveness. And in this attentiveness he included all living creatures, as saints include them in their prayers. . . .

Kafka's work is an ellipse with foci that are far apart and are determined, on the one hand, by mystical experience (in particular, the experience of tradition) and, on the other, by the experience of the modern big-city dweller. In speaking of the experience of the big-city dweller, I have a variety of things in mind. On the one hand, I think of the modern citizen who knows that he is at the mercy of a vast machinery of officialdom whose functioning is directed by authorities that remain nebulous to the executive organs, let alone to the people they deal with. (It is known that one level of meaning in the novels, particularly in *The Trial*, is encompassed by this.) When I refer to the modern big-city dweller, I am speaking also of the contemporary of today's physicists. If one reads the following passage from Eddington's *The Nature of the Physical World*, one can virtually hear Kafka speak.

I am standing on the threshold about to enter a room. It is a complicated business. In the first place I must shove against an atmosphere pressing with a force of fourteen pounds on every square inch of my body. I must make sure of landing on a plank travelling at twenty miles a second round the sun—a fraction of a second too early or too late, the plank would be miles away. I must do this whilst hanging from a round planet head outward into space, and with a wind of aether blowing at no one knows how many miles a second through every interstice of my body. The plank has no solidity of substance. To step on it is like stepping on a swarm of flies. Shall I not slip through? No, if I make the venture one of the flies hits me and gives a boost up again; I fall again and am knocked upwards by another fly; and so on. I may hope that the net result will be that I remain about steady; but if unfortunately I should slip through the floor or be boosted too violently up to the ceiling, the occurrence would be, not a violation of the laws of Nature, but a rare coincidence. . . .

Verily, it is easier for a camel to pass through the eye of a needle than for a scientific man to pass through a door. And whether the door be barn door or church door it might be wiser that he should consent to be an ordinary man and walk in rather than wait till all the difficulties involved in a really scientific ingress are resolved.

In all of literature I know no passage which has the Kafka stamp to the same extent. Without any effort one could match almost every passage of this physical perplexity with sentences from Kafka's prose pieces, and there is much to indicate that in so doing many of the most "incomprehensible" passages would be accommodated. Therefore, if one says—as I have just said—that there was a tremendous tension between those of Kafka's experiences that correspond to present-day physics and his mystical ones, only a half-truth is stated. What is actually and in a very literal sense wildly incredible in Kafka is that this most recent world of experience was conveyed to him precisely by this mystical tradition. This, of course, could not have happened without devastating processes (to be discussed presently) within this tradition. The long and the short of it is that apparently an appeal had to be made to the forces of this tradition if an individual (by the name of Franz Kafka) was to be confronted with that reality of ours which realizes itself theoretically, for example, in modern physics, and practically in the technology of modern warfare. What I mean to say is that this reality can virtually no longer be experienced by an *individual*, and that Kafka's world, frequently of such playfulness and interlaced with angels, is the exact complement of his era which is preparing to do away with the inhabitants of this planet on a considerable scale. The experience which corresponds to that of Kafka, the private individual, will probably not become accessible to the masses until such time as they are being done away with.

Kafka lies in a *complementary* world. (In this he is closely related to Klee, whose work in painting is just as essentially *solitary* as Kafka's work is in literature.) Kafka offered the complement without being aware of what surrounded him. If one says that he perceived what was to come without perceiving what exists in the present, one should add that he perceived it essentially as an *individual* affected by it. His gestures of terror are given scope by the marvelous *margin* which the catastrophe will not grant us. But his experience was based solely on the tradition to which Kafka surrendered; there was no farsightedness or "prophetic vision." Kafka listened to tradition, and he who listens hard does not see.

The main reason why this listening demands such effort is that only the most indistinct sounds reach the listener. There is no doctrine that one could absorb, no knowledge that one could preserve. The things that want to be caught as they rush by are not meant for anyone's ears. This implies a state of affairs which negatively characterizes Kafka's works with great precision. (Here a negative characterization probably is altogether more fruitful than a positive one.) Kafka's work presents a sickness of tradition. Wisdom has sometimes been defined as the epic side of truth. Such a definition stamps wisdom as inherent in tradition; it is truth in its haggadic consistency.

It is this consistency of truth that has been lost. Kafka was far from being the first to face this situation. Many had accommodated themselves to it, clinging to truth or whatever they happened to regard as truth and, with a more or less heavy heart, foregoing its transmissibility. Kafka's real genius was that he tried something entirely new: he sacrificed truth for the sake of clinging to its transmissibility, it haggadic element. Kafka's writings are by their nature parables. But it is their misery and their beauty that they had to become *more* than parables. They do not modestly lie at the feet of the doctrine, as the Haggadah lies at the feet of the Halakah. Though apparently reduced to submission, they unexpectedly raise a mighty paw against it.

This is why, in regard to Kafka, we can no longer speak of wisdom. Only the products of its decay remain. There are two: one is the rumor about the true things (a sort of theological whispered intelligence dealing with matters discredited and obsolete); the other product of this diathesis is folly—which, to be sure, has utterly squandered the substance of wisdom, but preserves its attractiveness and assurance, which rumor invariably lacks. Folly lies at the heart of Kafka's favorites—from Don Quixote via the assistants to the animals. (Being an animal presumably meant to him only to have given up human form and human wisdom from a kind of shame—as shame may keep a gentleman who finds himself in a disreputable tavern from wiping his glass clean.) This much Kafka was absolutely sure of: first, that someone must be a fool if he is to help; second, that only a fool's help is real help. The only uncertain thing is whether such help can still do a human being any good. It is more likely to help the angels (compare the passage about the angels who get something to do) who could do without help. Thus, as Kafka puts it, there is an infinite amount of hope, but not for us. This statement really contains Kafka's hope; it is the source of his radiant serenity. . . .

To do justice to the figure of Kafka in its purity and its peculiar beauty one must never lose sight of one thing: it is the purity and beauty of a failure. The circumstances of this failure are manifold. One is tempted to say: once he was certain of eventual failure, everything worked out for him *en route* as in a dream. There is nothing more memorable than the fervor with which Kafka emphasized his failure.

HEINZ POLITZER

The Wall of Secrecy:
Kafka's Castle

THE INFORMATION GIVERS

There is only one moment in the narrative when K. comes near to penetrating the wall of secrecy that surrounds the Castle. At this moment the fruitless attempts he has made to communicate with the interior of the offices are suddenly met by the Castle's unexpected attention.

Erlanger, one of Klamm's chief secretaries, wishes to see him before five o'clock in the morning of his sixth day in the village. The place of the meeting is to be the Herrenhof. "Tell him that it is very important that I should speak to him," he commissions Barnabas, the messenger. When Erlanger (whose name means "the one who achieves") finally talks to K., he requests him to send Frieda back to the taproom. This, he makes clear, is not Klamm's wish but a precaution taken by his colleagues to secure the undisturbed progress of their superior's work. However carefully his opponent may hide behind the back of his subordinates, K.'s plan to use Frieda as a kind of hostage seems to have worked at last. The only trouble is that K. is no longer in a position to comply with Erlanger's request: he has found Frieda too indispensable to part from her, he has fallen in love; and more important still, Frieda has left him and returned to the Herrenhof of her own accord, in the dubious company of Jeremias, the assistant. Therefore Erlanger's rather vague offer, "If you show yourself reliable in this trivial affair, it may on some occasion be of use to you in improving your prospects," sounds at best like an ironic echo of K.'s original intention to secure a hold

From *Franz Kafka: Parable and Paradox*. Copyright © 1966 by Cornell University Press. Originally entitled "The Bitter Herb: *The Castle*."

on Klamm by seducing Frieda. It is no more helpful than were Klamm's previous letters.

K.'s moment of truth does not, however, come in the meeting with Erlanger. Before he passes (and almost misses) Erlanger's door, he has been engaged in a completely unexpected nightlong conversation with another official who introduces himself as Bürgel. This Bürgel is, promisingly enough, a "liaison secretary"; yet he is not assigned to Klamm but to a secretary, unknown to K., by the name of Friedrich. Of this Friedrich we learn very little; (one of the deleted fragments mentions that "Bürgel is not even Friedrich's first secretary" and that "Friedrich's glory has greatly declined in recent years"); we can only note that his name, like Frieda's, alludes to a highly ironical *Frieden* ("peace"). As far as Bürgel's own name is concerned, it is, first and foremost, the diminutive of *Burg*, a synonym of Castle; this seems to promise that he belongs to the inner circle of the Castle administration and that his liaison with the interior offices is close and effective. At the same time it points to the smallness and unimportance of his person when it is compared with the immensity of the *Burg*, the Castle which he represents. Moreover, his name is also, as Heller has noted, "a diminutive of *Bürge*, guarantor"; and it is this second meaning to which he seems to refer when he talks about the chance that applicants like K. actually have to force their way into the presence of a secretary. Generally speaking, these chances are nil, "but some nights—for who can guarantee (*bürgen*) for everything?—it *does* happen." While he faces Bürgel, the little guarantor who cannot guarantee anything, K. is confronted with this opportunity.

At first K. gives his name, an introduction which, counter to his expectations, seems "to have a good effect." He is even more astonished when the secretary asks him about his surveying although he has not mentioned his profession. All augurs well. When K. complains that he is not employed as a Land-Surveyor, the official jots down a note immediately. "I am prepared," he assures the applicant, "to follow up this matter further. With us here the things are quite certainly not in such a way that an expert employee should be left unused." Yet he is not only willing to further K.'s cause by using his close relations with the Castle—"at every moment I must be prepared to drive up"—he personally offers help to K. by subjecting him immediately to a night interrogation.

Such an interrogation is admittedly "a very rare possibility or, rather, one that almost never occurs. It consists in the applicant's coming unannounced in the middle of the night." This condition is fulfilled in the case of K. While looking for Erlanger, he has opened a door in the hope of finding an empty sleeping place. There Bürgel greets him with a faint scream. He has indeed appeared uninvited.

The secretaries, Bürgel continues to explain, are, of course, overtired and try to dispose of the applicants one way or the other. Some seem to be so fatigued that they actually fear the interruption of their rest by an untoward applicant. "In any case," Bürgel continues, "it is morbid to be so afraid of him [the applicant] that one hides, say under the quilt." This position, which is, incidentally, also a favorite of the lawyer Huld in *The Trial*, has been relinquished by Bürgel, if only after some hesitation, when K. enters his room: he "pulled the quilt a little off his face, anxiously ready, however, to cover himself up completely if something was not quite all right out there. But then he flung back the quilt without qualms and sat up."

Bürgel goes on enlightening K. The more he describes the resistance offered to the applicants by the other secretaries, the more he seems to emphasize the uniqueness of this one night interrogation which finds him, Bürgel, willing to assist K. To ward off the applicants, Bürgel relates, the officials are accustomed to refer to the system of competences as it is observed by the Castle. (Here Kafka alludes to the efficient defense mechanism Old Austria's bureaucrats devised to protect *their* sleep.) Many an applicant, Bürgel says, "has lost the game because, thinking he was not making enough progress with the competent authority, he tried to slip through by approaching some other, one not competent." Such a train of thought is of course familiar to K.; yet all the circumstances seem to conspire in his favor. He has chanced upon this meeting with Bürgel while he was summoned by a competent authority, Erlanger. However, Bürgel and his chief, Friedrich, may not be so incompetent in the case of the Land-Surveyor as the appearances indicate. For the secret of this Castle administration "lies in the relations regarding competence. The fact is, things are not so constituted . . . that there is only one definite secretary competent to deal with each case." With an expression of deep emotional involvement Bürgel exclaims, "Land-Surveyor, consider the possibility that through some circumstance or other . . . an applicant does, nevertheless, in the middle of the night surprise a secretary who has a certain degree of competence."

At this point Bürgel seems to possess a certain competence. This coincidence opens completely new vistas before K.; the barriers break down and the tables are turned. Now the official speaks of the distribution of duties in his administration, which is such that suddenly everybody seems to be competent for everybody else. His colleagues, normally so intent on repose, burn with impatience to occupy themselves with any case for which they are in the slightest degree responsible; they are filled with a passionate desire to help. However much they may differ in character and rank, this passion is "always the same, always present in full intensity." Apparently Bürgel himself has been enraptured by this heavenly feeling of ardent charity, and his passion is aimed at none other than K., who, as he sits on the edge of the bed, is "the never beheld, always expected applicant, truly thirstingly expected and always reasonably regarded out of reach."

An official, then, has been waiting for K. just as desperately as K. has been waiting for Klamm. Bürgel's eyes are now resting on him with the same feverish longing with which K. has contemplated the Castle for six long days. A mysterious union between official and applicant is under way, an embrace both actual and metaphysical in nature. Bürgel's pronouncement has acquired a hymnlike quality, which reveals a dinstinctly erotic coloration. The applicant's presence in his room invites him, as he says, "to penetrate into his poor life. . . . This invitation in the silent night is beguiling." Although Bürgel retains enough official decorum at the climax of this night scene to classify its mystery strictly as "a misuse of official power," he is also carried away by passion to such an extent that he is able to cry: "Nevertheless, we are happy. How suicidal happiness can be!" This is the language of love. Possessed by love, the official chooses an imagery consistent with his glowing feelings when he describes the hour of this night interrogation as "the official's hour of labor," which in German is "the difficult hour" (*die schwere Stunde*), the hour when a new being is born. With grandiose labor pains a union between previously fighting forces has been established. The abyss between official and applicant has been bridged, and the gate to the interior of the Castle opens. The impossible has become possible after all. Nobody will be able to deny that this scene possesses a pathos of truly cosmic dimensions.

Nobody except K., that is. For "K. was asleep, impervious to all that was happening." In reply to the salvation Bürgel promises him, K. succumbs to sleep. He exchanges the heightened awareness, the ecstasy which is offered to him, for complete unconsciousness.

While we imagine K. lying there on Bürgel's bed, a motionless heap of extinguished humanity, we encounter some difficulties in following Emrich's evaluation of this scene as "tragic." Emrich's question "whether this tragedy will also lead K. to take a turn to catharsis, to the liberation and purification by a higher consciousness," seems to be irrelevant in view of K.'s complete loss of any consciousness. He is, as the German original says, "locked up against everything" (*abgeschlossen gegen alles*). This sleeper does not correspond to the description of a "perishing hero" which Emrich gives of him, and the speculation "whether the tragic antinomies in his mind can be overcome" appears strangely farfetched and out of place. These notions apply more readily to one of the heroes of German idealism—Heinrich von Kleist's romantic Prince of Homburg, for example. Kafka's imagination, however, was nourished from different sources.

In Bürgel we can see the last of Kafka's Information Givers. Once more the writer attempted to answer the questions his heroes have been asking throughout his books. In the Fourth Octavo Notebook he spells out the kind of information he and his protagonists were seeking. The following imaginary dialogue takes place:

> The decisively characteristic thing about this world is its transience. In this sense centuries have no advantage over the present moment. Thus the continuity of transience cannot give any consolation; the fact that new life blossoms among the ruins proves not so much the tenacity of life as that of death. If I wish to fight against this world, I must fight against its decisively characteristic element, that is, its transience. Can I do that in this life, and do it really, not only by means of hope and faith?
>
> So you want to fight against the world, fight it with weapons that are more real than hope and faith. There probably are such weapons, but they can be recognized and used only under certain basic assumptions; I want to see first whether these assumptions apply to you.
>
> Look into it. But if I have not got these qualifications, perhaps I can acquire them.
>
> Certainly, but this is a matter in which I could not help you.
>
> So you can only help me if I have already acquired these qualifications.
>
> Yes. To put it more precisely, I cannot help you at all, for if you had these qualifications, you would have everything already.
>
> If this is how things stand, why then did you want to examine me in the first place?
>
> Not in order to show you what you lack, but that you lack something. I might perhaps have been of a certain use to you in this way, for although you know there is something you lack, you do not believe it.
>
> So, in answer to my original question, all you offer me is the proof that I had to ask the question.
>
> I do offer something more, something that you, in accordance with your present state, are now completely incapable of recognizing precisely. I am offering the proof of the fact that you really ought to have asked the original question differently.
>
> So this means: you either will not or cannot answer me.
>
> "Not answer you"—this is it.

And this faith—this is what you can give.

This minimal insight—the residue of a possible answer—only this kind of information is offered K. And then, it is proffered merely as a chance.

Bürgel, the "little guarantor," is the most sophisticated in the long line of Kafka's doorkeepers. The underporters in the Hotel Occidental, the Information Giver in the Court House, Titorelli, Huld, and even the Prison Chaplain have only been pointing the tortuous way which led to him. Bürgel, too, guards a door, the gate to the interior of the Castle; he, too, deceives K. while informing him; he tempts him with the last, faint opportunity to ask "the original question differently"; he does so by holding a mirror out to K., indeed, by being this mirror himself.

Word by word, image after image, Bürgel shows K. the situation in which he finds himself. Because he mirrors K., he is acquainted with his profession without being told about it. Because he echoes him, he is able to read his innermost thoughts and answer questions which K. never uttered. Thus when K. reminds himself silently not to underestimate the official before him, Bürgel breaks into his reflections with a sudden "no," spoken, as the narrator adds, "as if he were answering a thought of K.'s and were considerately trying to save him the effort of formulating it aloud." The night interrogation and the chance it offers to the applicant appear as K.'s wish dream reflected back to him by the official. This mirage materializes in Bürgel to such an extent that the Information Giver is able to continue his recitation even when K. has withdrawn into sleep. That the dream outlasts the dreamer and the mirrored image is more powerful than the object it mirrors is perhaps the subtlest paradox that the labyrinth of the Castle holds for the reader. Apart from being K.'s mirror, Bürgel is and remains an official; indeed, he is the most hindering helper in the twilight zone of Kafka's intermediaries.

The scene of this night interrogation is set on the threshold of K.'s consciousness. Its time spans the moments between waking and sleep in which unconscious states give way to flashes of insight, reason is submerged and rises to the surface once more, and oblivion alternates with clairvoyance. The six days in the village have readied K. for it: he enters Bürgel's room in a condition of extreme fatigue. In the corridor he had almost sunk down with drowsiness; to make things worse he has emptied to the dregs a little carafe of rum, Frieda's farewell gift. In the room he finds, as a mirror of his own tiredness, Bürgel asleep in his bed. Greedily K. surveys this "voluptuous but unfortunately not empty bed," which is mentioned over and over again during the introductory stages of the interrogation: K. longs to lie down on it; Bürgel invites him to sit on its edge; he accepts and cannot prevent his head from leaning against its post. Words like "cover," "tired," and "sleep" occur with increasing frequency. One has only to listen to Bürgel's seemingly innocent comments on his room to see how he manages to trick K. into falling asleep:

> Well, I had the choice of getting either a completely furnished room with a narrow hotel bed, or this big bed and nothing else. . . . I chose the big bed; after all, in a bedroom the bed is undoubtedly the main thing! Ah, for anyone who could stretch out and sleep soundly, for a sound sleeper, this bed would surely be truly delicious.

This lullaby of lurid suggestiveness is intended to draw the drowsy K. deeper and deeper down the unending coils of half-sleep. Once more K. starts up and in a sudden fit of clearsightedness observes Bürgel smiling "as though he had just succeeded in misleading K. a little."

How far Bürgel succeeds in misleading him we see when K. slips into his own dream vision, a mirage mirrored and duly distorted by the all-encompassing magic of this interrogation. "The tiresome consciousness had gone, he felt free." It is certainly true, his consciousness had receded, but only insofar as it was tiresome; K.'s consciousness of himself, his self-confidence, is rising to unexpected heights. The freedom he feels is but another name for a sudden superiority which he dreams he has gained over his opponent. After all, one of his basic traits is arrogance, the *Anmassung* [arrogance] and *Vermessenheit* [hubris] of the *Land-vermesser* [Land Surveyor]. Once he had prided himself on having conquered death in the churchyard of his home village; now he braves his dream opponent in a similar way:

> And it seemed to him as though . . . he had achieved a great victory . . . and he or someone else raised the champagne glass in honor of this victory. And so that all should know what it was all about, the fight and the victory were repeated once again or perhaps not repeated at all, but only took place now and had already been celebrated earlier and there was no letdown in the celebration, because fortunately the outcome was certain.

K. experiences here the fulfillment of his wishes: his opponent has at long last taken a stand and is prepared to give battle; the mere fact that this battle has come about means victory. Dizzy with dreaming, he does not notice that the time sequences of his vision have been reversed, that the celebration comes before the victory, and the victory precedes the fight. He is beyond space and time, occupied only with the task of asserting himself victoriously. Yet with his time sense his other perspectives have also been reversed: left is right, up is down, truth is lie, and victory, defeat. The phrase "fortunately the outcome was certain" is true if we attribute the conquest to Bürgel, but it is an utter delusion if the victory is claimed by K.

His opponent in the dream is "a secretary, naked, very like the statue of a Greek god." While we can explain the dream image by the sight of "Bürgel's bare chest" in front of K.'s closing eyes, we are surprised that a Greek god should emerge in the thoroughly un-Hellenic imagination of the Land-Surveyor. We suspect that Kafka is taking over from his dreaming hero and creating this spectre as a sign of the absolute incongruity of the scene. He once wrote about the Prometheus legend that it "tries to explain the inexplicable. As it came out of a substratum of truth it had in turn to end in the inexplicable." The substratum of truth in K.'s case, as in that of Prometheus, is the forlornness of man as a result of his presumption.

There is hardly any trace of grandeur in Kafka's treatment of ancient motifs; instead he stressed the nightmarish quality of a thoroughly modern despair by blending it in a mock-heroic fashion with the inevitability of Greek myth. In a letter written to Brod in April 1921 about certain lives which show a "historical development" and others which do not, Kafka said:

> Sometimes I play with the idea of an anonymous Greek who arrives in Troy without ever having had the intention of getting there. He has not yet looked around and is already in the midst of the melee; the gods themselves do not yet know at all what is at stake, but he has already been dragged around the city roped to a Trojan chariot; Homer has not yet started to sing, but he already lies there with his glassy eyes, if not in the dust of Troy then on the cushions of his deck chair. And why? Hecuba, of course, is nothing to him; Helena is not decisive either. Whereas the other Greeks have set out at the bidding of the gods and, protected by the gods, have fought their battles, he has left because of a paternal kick in the pants and has fought under a paternal curse. Fortunately there were other Greeks besides him, or world history would have remained restricted to the two rooms of one's parental apartment and the threshold between them.

In many respects this ingenious *quid pro quo* of Troy and Prague is reminiscent of K.'s drowsy vision of himself: here, too, the sense of time is suspended by a confusion of time sequences; here, too, the result of the heroic mingling with the trivial is an absurd tragicomedy that seems to be mocking itself. The "anonymous Greek" is as untragic, as unheroic, and as locked up in himself as K. Neither figure is allowed any human development, and the mood of grotesque abandonment prevailing in both visions is enhanced by the rational and matter-of-fact tone with which they are reported.

K.'s dream secretary offers him no serious obstacle. "This Greek god squeaked like a girl being tickled." The statue has come to life; the half-naked secretary has almost turned into a young female. K. may remember a saying which is quoted around the Castle and which Olga had told him the night before: "Official decisions are as shy as young girls." "This is a good observation," K. had answered; "the decisions may have other characteristics in common with young girls." Now as an official decision is near, the official himself resembles a girl. The girl even opens her mouth, but only to issue a birdlike and soulless tone. The mechanical sound is the perfect parody of the mystical humming in the telephone with which the Castle had once greeted K. His vision remains sharp and pitiless, although his eyes are closing. Like Joseph K. on the way to his execution, he tries to keep his "intelligence calm and analytical to the end." He finds this scene "very funny."

His "fun" consists in projecting all he has learned about the Castle onto his squeaking god, in approaching him with whatever critical acuteness he still possesses, in ridiculing, humiliating, and denigrating him. Bürgel, on his part, keeps talking. There is a distinct countermovement under way: the more the official is enraptured by his hymnlike peace offer, the more K. opposes it, in the few lucid intervals still permitted to him, with maliciously rational observations. "Clatter, mill, keep clattering," he thinks, "you clatter just for me." Thereby he finally and irrevocably succumbs to the treachery of the labyrinth.

Even in tradition the labyrinth could not be conquered by rational tricks. The more a person tried to find his way through the maze by means of the intellect, the more he was bound to lose himself. The universal nature of the labyrinth reveals itself in the challenge it offers to the *total* existence of man. It is a sign of K.'s arrogance that he mobilizes the forces of his intelligence in the hour of a mystical revelation. Yet so viciously are the circles of this labyrinth constructed that the mystical revelation of its interior is bound to occur in the hour when K. succumbs to his fatigue. Bürgel's droning recitation finally drowns out the last flicker of K.'s reason.

In his dream K. wins out and puts the secretary-turned-god to flight. "And finally he was gone, K. was alone in a large room." Inasmuch as the dream secretary represents Bürgel, the defeat of the former means also the elimination of the chances proferred by the latter. There remain only the splinters of the champagne glass, lying broken on the floor. "K. trampled it to smithereens." The dream is over, the mirror smashed. K. is lost in sleep and Bürgel, his chest still bare, opens his mouth. But instead of a squeak, he utters the promise of K.'s admission into the Castle, a promise which is broken before it is fully made. As K.'s dream contained a declaration of victory before the fight has started, so Bürgel's message of peace is defeated even before it is delivered. The multiple mirrors of the labyrinth have distorted conquest and decline until they form one pernicious glitter, the cutting glitter of the splinters in K.'s dream.

Bürgel talks now about the competence of incompetence, the open gates of the inaccessible, the passion of premeditated deceit. Triumphantly bent over the applicant, the official proves to him that not victory was expected from him but reconciliation. The doors he had tried to force stood open. His inability to be redeemed is confirmed by the announcement that redemption is at hand. There is a shade of poetic justice in the reflection that Bürgel's efforts are also in vain since he preaches to ears deafened by sleep.

Bürgel's "hour of labor" has miscarried. Never will K. be able to "put forward his plea, for which fulfilment is already waiting." He is, in the official's language, an "oddly and quite specially constituted, small, skilful grain" that had almost succeeded in slipping "through the incomparable sieve." More to himself than to the man slumbering before him Bürgel remarks, "You think it cannot happen at all. You are right, it cannot happen at all."

This night interrogation climaxes not only Kafka's *The Castle* but a long series of attempts which European man has undertaken to overcome and exorcize the demonic forces of the universe which throng around him in complete obscurity. The irony of frustration which informs this scene makes it a prime example of grotesque art, its depth and its limitations. As the outcome of Kafka's novel demonstrates, these attempts to penetrate the mystery of the world are bound to end in ultimate failure. Hence Kafka derives the tone of knowing despair which ennobles all truly grotesque representations of human destiny.

JOURNEY'S END?

Brod reports that Kafka once told him the end he had had in mind for *The Castle*:

> The ostensible Land-Surveyor was to find partial satisfaction at least. He was not to relax in his struggle, but was to die worn out

by it. Round his death-bed the villagers were to assemble, and from the Castle itself the word was to come that though K.'s legal claim to live in the village was not valid, yet, taking certain auxiliary circumstances into account, he was to be permitted to live and work there.

Commenting on this plan, Emrich has correctly observed that it offers no more than a repetition of the situation already reached during the night interrogation.

If Kafka had been satisfied with describing K.'s pilgrimage through a modern labyrinth, he could have stopped here, at the end of the eighteenth of twenty chapters. The following scenes do not provide us with any new hints about unexpected turns ahead on K.'s way. The conversation with Erlanger mentioned before, the distribution of the official files in the corridor of the Herrenhof, Pepi's suggestion that K. may follow her to the basement and hibernate in her company, and finally K.'s musings about the landlady's dresses—all this remains, in the end, inconclusive.

To be sure, K. witnesses the destruction of a file which "actually was only . . . a leaf from a note pad," and the suspicion arises in his mind that this file may be his own and that his application may have been dismissed once and for all. On the other hand, the landlady restores his courage in an oblique way by claiming that an uproar which suddenly shakes the Inn is coming from some officials who are shouting for help against K., "whom nothing else would cause to waver." The gentlemen from the Castle seem to have started trembling before the Land-Surveyor. But these are only more new doors leading the hero toward new dead ends disguised by new mirrors. Their effectiveness fades before the impact which was already achieved by the night interrogation. Not only K.'s but Kafka's energies seem to be exhausted on these last pages; eventually the labyrinth succeeded in trapping its own creator.

But the Castle is built of more than mirror effects. Its inner chamber not only shelters nothingness but, combined with it in absolute ambiguity, the promise of total existence. Conversely, K. is not only, like the "anonymous Greek," congenitally deprived of any "historical development," he is also exposed to occasions which might have led his story to quite different conclusions. To trace these possibilities hidden in K.'s nature, we have to change our direction and read the book backward. Moving in a circle, we will still follow the basic design of the novel, the periphery of a labyrinth.

THE MESSENGERS: BARNABAS AND AMALIA

On the evening of the fourth day K. sends Barnabas to the Castle in order to request a personal interview with Klamm. Whatever he does or says during the next day is colored by his expectation of the messenger's return. High hopes and grave doubts alternate in his mind. Barnabas, by delivering favorable messages, has lived up to his name, which, according to the Acts of the Apostles (4:36), means "son of consolation." On the other hand, these messages, K.'s "decree of appointment," and his laudatory citation as a Land-Surveyor, have also turned out to be malicious specimens of Klamm's peculiar sense of humor in spite of the comfort they offered. There are other reasons for distrusting Barnabas. He had introduced himself with words of evangelical simplicity: "Barnabas is my name. . . . A messenger am I," and K. could not help noticing the noble quality of his clothes: "He was dressed all in white; not in silk, of course, . . . but the material he was wearing had the softness and dignity of silk." Yet as soon as he follows Barnabas to his hut, he is disillusioned. He recognizes that "he had been bewitched by Barnabas's close-fitting, silken-gleaming jacket, which, now that it was unbuttoned, . . . displayed a coarse, dirty gray shirt patched all over, and beneath it the huge muscular chest of a farm-laborer." Furthermore, this messenger who looks like a peasant turns out to be a journeyman in the service of Brunswick, the cobbler, and it seems as if he would let this menial work interfere with the errands he undertakes at the behest of K. Barnabas is a cobbler's son and resembles a cobbler much more than a messenger (in Austrian usage the word *Schuster* {"cobbler"} has the connotation of "misfit"); nor does the garment which has drawn K.'s attention by any means represent the livery of an official Castle servant; it was sewn for him by his sister, Amalia. Only a certain duplicity of behavior identifies him as an envoy of Klamm, whose ambiguity seems to have influenced the servant: Barnabas hurries about when carrying out the orders of the Castle but drags his feet when he is supposed to deliver K.'s answer. The Land-Surveyor cannot be blamed for bursting out, "It is very bad for me to have only a messenger like you for important affairs."

It turns out, however, that this ambiguity is inherent only in Barnabas' function as an emissary from the Castle and does not extend to him as a person. When Olga, his second sister, initiates K. into the story of her family, the Land-Surveyor discovers that the messenger's personal intentions toward him are thoroughly honorable. "He did not sleep all night because you were displeased with him yesterday evening," Olga informs K. It is not his fault when the part he plays as Klamm's errand boy arouses K.'s suspicions. The Castle bears the blame, for it makes use of his services without having acknowledged him as its servant. Thus Barnabas finds himself in essentially the same predicament as K. And yet what seems to be an ordeal to the Land-Surveyor is at the same time the fulfillment of the most tender hopes of the messenger and his family. K.'s arrival appears to them as the turning point after three years of misery. Klamm's letters, questionable as they are, have meant to them "the first signs of grace." Barnabas himself is more than willing to serve on sufferance without any right. He is happy like a little boy, "in spite of all the doubts that he had about his capability." "He confined these doubts to himself and me," Olga reveals, "but he felt it a point of honor to look like a real messenger." Nor should K. deny him his sympathy, since it is also his point of honor to be a "real" Land-Surveyor.

In spite of his doubtful appearance Barnabas is really a messenger of hope. The hope he offers is a human hope. When K. hears about Barnabas' true feelings, he has an opportunity to realize that his mere presence is able to raise the spirits of others and to comfort them by supporting their expectations. To see this, he has only to desist from mirroring himself in them and to accept them for what they are, just as he demands to be accepted himself. After Barnabas was entrusted with his first letter, Olga informs K. he "laid his head on my shoulder, and cried for several minutes. He was again the little boy he used to be." K.'s response to her tale, though it was fraught with emotion, is cold: "All of you have made pretences." He dismisses as mere fabrication the messenger's outbreak of joy and does not want to have any part of it.

Although K. is groping desperately for help, he refuses to give it to others. When Olga greets him almost jubilantly, "How fortunate that you have come!" he simply turns away, annoyed at such a display of enthusiasm: "He had not come to bring good fortune to anyone. . . . Nobody should greet him as a bearer of good tidings; whoever did this, was liable to confuse his ways, claiming him for causes for which he was at nobody's disposal under such coercion; with the best of intentions he had to refuse." He is afraid of confusing his ways by being a messenger of good tidings himself. Yet the path before him is already so tortuous that he need not fear to confuse it still further by a simple human response. On the contrary, any kindliness he showed to others might help him along his way. This is one of the passages in *The Castle* where K. actually could have changed his course. But it is no accident that Kafka deleted these sentences in his manuscript; they would have pointed too clearly in a direction neither he nor his hero was prepared to take in their self-inflicted isolation.

Olga is as favorably inclined toward K. as her brother is. It was she who accompanied him on his first walk to the Herrenhof. When she exposes the secret of her family to him in a long night's story, she wants to help him as much as to be helped by him. Her very name may be derived from the

German equivalent of "holy." There are striking similarities between their fates. Like him she hopes to establish "a certain connection with the Castle" by making love with its subordinates. Before K. tumbled down to embrace Frieda on the taproom floor, he observed Olga in a mating dance with a number of villagers, and when he emerged, he saw her again, her clothes torn and her hair deranged. At that time her debauchery had not particularly surprised him. He took it as a sign of simple sexual jealousy, a revenge for his having preferred Frieda to her. But now he learns that Olga's villagers were in actual fact servants of the Castle: "For more than two years, at least twice a week, I have spent the night with them in the stable." Olga's promiscuity differs from K.'s lovemaking in one decisive aspect: she does not surrender to the Castle in this indirect and unpromising way to further her own ends. She sacrifices herself to atone for Amalia.

Amalia's story is a novella in its own right, connected to the rest of the narrative by the remarks which K. makes about it. Since he mirrors himself in Amalia, he cannot perceive the true stature of this woman who towers over the village in silent grandeur. One feels that she is present throughout Olga's tale, although she exits from the scene before Olga begins. "She went without taking leave of K., as if she knew he would stay for a long time yet." Unnoticed she slips away and reappears, loses herself again in the darkness of the hut, and yet she seems to dominate it with her personality even when she sleeps. Almost superhuman powers are noticeable in her who dared defy the Castle.

This, then, is Amalia's story. Three years ago, on the third of July, the village celebrated the dedication of an engine which the Castle had presented to the local Fire Brigade. The gift was accompanied by a number of trumpets, "extraordinary instruments on which with the smallest effort . . . one could produce the wildest blasts; to hear them was enough to make one think the Turks had come already." These trumpets produce angelic and satanic sounds, as do the brass instruments used in the Oklahoma theatre in *Der Verschollene*; they indicate that a moment of great importance is at hand and prepare the reader for a meeting between the human and more-than-human.

At this point, a point remote and vague in Olga's memory, the Castle and the village are united for the first and only time in the novel. Accordingly the season is summer, and on the scene the customary snow and fog are replaced by a green meadow and a murmuring brook. The whole gathering is devoted to a wholesome human purpose, the control of the demonic force of fire. On the other hand, the wild blasts of the trumpets evoke the image of polygamous Turks and these, in turn, the hordes of philandering Castle servants, who, one can surmise, are converging also on this lawn. Nor can one overlook the suggestively ambiguous central image, the fire engine, which is really a big water squirter (*Feuerspritze*).

Even a Castle representative is present, Sortini, who "is supposed to be partly occupied with fire problems." But the joyful occasion has not succeeded in breaking down the barriers traditionally existing between officials and villagers. Keeping close to the Castle's gift, the phallic fire engine, Sortini refuses to mingle with the crowd. Only when Barnabas' father, the third in command of the Fire Brigade, offers apologies to him (for what?), does Sortini react. He lets his eyes rest on Amalia, "to whom he had to look up, for she was much taller than he. At the sight of her he started and leaped over the shaft to get nearer to her; we misunderstood him at first and began to approach him . . . but he held us off with uplifted hand and then waved us away. That was all." It is not all, alas. For the one glance he exchanged with the girl seems to have impressed Amalia unduly. Her stunned silence ever after almost seems to justify a remark made by Brunswick, the cobbler, that "she had fallen head over ears in love." The following morning she receives a letter, couched in most vulgar terms, ordering her to visit Sortini at once at the Herrenhof. The girl tears the letter to pieces and throws the shreds in the face of the messenger who has waited outside the window. This constitutes Amalia's sin.

The Castle, in its majestic impassivity, refrains from punishing Amalia in any overt way. But the villagers begin to withdraw from the girl as well as from her relatives. As if the daughter's guilt were by association also the father's, he loses first his honorary post with the Fire Brigade, then his customers. The family becomes anonymous; it is now named after Barnabas, the "least guilty." Amid a community of primitive serfs, the Barnabas family lives in a ghetto assigned to pariahs by the slaves who are their neighbors. The only indication of the Castle's participation in the general ostracism of this family is the fact that it waited for the appearance of so lowly a creature as K. before it allowed Barnabas to go on his semiofficial errands on his behalf. The view of the pariah serving the outcast would indeed be a prime specimen of the double-edged irony indulged in so brilliantly by Klamm and his colleagues.

Now we understand why Barnabas felt called upon to serve the Castle as a messenger; he wanted to atone for the insult inflicted upon Sortini's errand boy. By the same token Olga attempted to expiate Amalia's refusal of Sortini's embrace by becoming the prostitute of the Castle's subordinates. Her sacrifice fails. There is no indication of the official's reconciliation; but then neither he nor the Castle has ever given any indication of having taken offense. Olga comments bitterly, "We had no sign of favor from the Castle in the past, so how could we notice the reverse now?"

A further complication in the story is that it is impossible to establish with certainty the identity of the woman whom Sortini had summoned to the Herrenhof. The latter is addressed to "the girl with the garnet necklace." This disastrous piece of jewelry had passed hands twice before it landed around Amalia's neck. The Bridge Inn landlady, the owner of the Bohemian garnets, had lent them to Olga, and Olga had decorated her sister with them, she did not know why. Sortini's summons, then, is directed at each of the three women who had been seen with the jewels at one time or another during this day: at Gardena, who had been Klamm's mistress but being no longer a "girl" was the least probable choice; at Olga, who certainly would have responded to the official's crude beckoning, since she is willing to surrender to the still cruder calls of the servants; and at Amalia, who actually wears the garnets when she is introduced to Sortini. She is the most unlikely to be singled out by Sortini, and this is the very reason why his letter descends upon her as one of those fatal lightning flashes which, bursting forth from indistinct heights, hit the target least expected to be their aim.

Sortini is as elusive as the Castle he represents. His function at the celebration is dubious; "perhaps he was only deputizing for someone else." He is described as "very retiring," and yet he is capable of savage aggression, as his letter shows. He is "small, frail, reflective looking," but backed up by the huge and loudly colored fire engine, he seems to fill the festive scene with his portentous presence. Although he is smaller than Amalia, even his upward look is condescending. Moreover, "one thing about him struck all the people who noticed him at all, his forehead was furrowed; all the furrows . . . were spread fanwise over his forehead, running to the root of his nose." Imitating the ground plan of a labyrinth, these furrows attract the onlooker and lead him inevitably down to the level of Sortini's eyes, the eyes that have proved so fateful to Amalia.

A rather hectic discussion has developed as to the meaning of this official ever since Brod compared Sortini's letter to Kierkegaard's vision of Mount Moriah, where God asked Abraham to sacrifice his child. For Brod, Sortini's epistle represents "literally a parallel" to Kierkegaard's *Fear and Trembling*, "which starts from the fact that God required of Abraham what was really a crime . . . ; and which uses this paradox to establish triumphantly the conclusion that the categories of morality and religion are by no means identical." Brod's attempt at coordinating God's claim on Isaac and Sortini's design on Amalia has prompted Heller to observe that it means,

without any polemical exaggeration, to ascribe to the God of Abraham a personal interest in the boy Isaac, worthy rather of a

Greek demi-god. Moreover, He, having tested Abraham's absolute obedience, did not accept the sacrifice. Yet Sortini . . .
can, to judge by the example of his colleagues, be relied upon not
to have summoned Amalia to his bedroom merely to tell her that
one does not do such a thing.

Emrich, on the other hand, sees in Sortini an allegory of the spirit per se:
"Where spirit is nothing but spirit any more and appears as an isolated and
abstract region, it is the very perversion of the human spirit." In the final
analysis Emrich is merely translating Brod's theological position into
philosophical terms: what is good for the God of Abraham is also good for
the spirit of pure abstraction. Heller's rebuttal is strong and sharp enough to
puncture Emrich's thesis as well as Brod's. To visualize this Sortini as an
absolute of any sort amounts to positing a paradox too paradoxical even for
Kafka's wildest imagination. To answer the question raised by Sortini's
letter, Kafka would have had to finish the novel and reveal the meaning of
the Castle, the secret of which is shared by its officials. Hence we are not
surprised to find the image of Sortini veiled by the same insoluble mystery
which distinguished the Count Westwest, his master.

There is, however, an element of surprise in the Amalia episode. It
offers us at least the hint of a turn to the better, which Kafka may have had
in mind for his hero at one point or another. To grasp this hint we have to
turn to the heroine rather than to her would-be seducer, Sortini. Amalia
astonishes us indeed, and not only because of the space Kafka has devoted to
her story. (The scene in her house covers approximately one-sixth of the
book.) He granted his heroine what he denied his heroes: the ability to
survive, and even transcend, despair.

Amalia is the only female in Kafka's gallery of women who does not
conform with the observation he made in a letter to Brod, early in May 1921:
"It is strange how little sharp-sightedness women possess; they only notice
whether they please, then whether they arouse pity, and finally, whether one
is hankering for their compassion; this is all; come to think of it, it may even
be enough, generally speaking." Amalia is sharp-sighted, although in a very
peculiar way. Like Olga she is a "great strapping wench"; and yet she is
distinguished from her by her "cold, hard eye," which, K. remembers,
frightened him when he saw her for the first time. To be sure, this does not
indicate much more than K.'s inability to view himself in her as he is wont
to do in the eyes of Frieda, Gardena, and even Olga. The narrator, more
perceptive than his hero, confirms the hardness of Amalia's glance but also
mentions its clarity. It was, he adds, "never leveled exactly on the object she

was looking at, but in some disturbing way always a little past it, not from weakness, apparently, not from embarrassment, nor from duplicity, but from a persistent and dominating desire for solitude." Even K. is both startled and spellbound by this look, "which in itself was not ugly but proud and sincere in its taciturnity." Thus he is moved to tell her, "I have never seen a country girl like you." Here the narrator allows K. to articulate an insight more profound than he can consciously grasp. It seems that Kafka himself is subtly playing with his language here, demonstrating once more the inner unity of his imagery. Amalia is no country girl, no feminine version of the man from the country. She is no *Am-ha'aretz* like Joseph K. and K., the Land-Surveyor. She knows, for she has seen.

We shall have to assume that Amalia learned whatever she knows about the Castle from looking at Sortini. We are told precious little about her history before this meeting. She is the youngest member of the family and may have enjoyed the advantages which a family concedes to its youngest child. This is probably the reason why her mother has lent her every bit of her lace for the blouse she is to wear at the celebration, an injustice which induces Olga, the older one, to cry half the night. Both sisters have been looking forward to the occasion, but Amalia seems to be in a state of special expectation. Her father, with the one-track mind of a man, predicts, "To-day, mark my words, Amalia will find a husband." Olga, on the other hand, notices her somber glance; "It has kept the same quality since that day, it was high over our heads and involuntarily one had almost literally to bow before her." About the meeting with Sortini we have likewise only negative evidence: although we are told that the official looks up to her, the fact that she returns his glance is not mentioned. (As can be seen from the silence with which Kafka enveloped K.'s transition from the bridge to the village, he refrains from spelling out decisive moments involving the total existence of his figures.) That Amalia's life has been changed here and now we can only guess from her behavior later on in the day: she is even more silent than usual and remains sober among the crowd which has partaken freely of the sweet Castle wine. She preserves this attitude of extreme composure even after she has read Sortini's letter; her gestures reveal no hint of surprise, disgust, or horror; indeed, it is Olga who notices her tiredness—"how I always loved her when she was tired like this"—the deep exhaustion of one who has in a short moment understood and accepted his fate. Tearing the letter to pieces, Amalia appears to perform a ritual. Yet Olga is not quite correct when she concludes the report of this scene by saying: "This was the morning which decided our fate. I say 'decided,' but every minute of the previous afternoon was just as decisive." The decisive moment was the one when Amalia read in

Sortini's eyes a secret, the secret of the Castle.

Whatever this secret may be, it forces her to reject Sortini's summons. To defend her on the ground that she is simply trying to maintain her self-respect is to reduce her to the proportions of a sentimental heroine in a tragedy of middle-class manners. After all, there is no greatness in falling in love with a man of higher social rank, and, being disappointed in the most offensive way, she could be expected to react emotionally to the insult. But Amalia's attitude is informed with heroism. "She stood," says Olga, "face to face with the truth and went on living and endured her life then and now." Her experiences afterward only translate the view that opened itself before her into tangible fact: "We saw only the effects, but she looked down into the bottom" ("Sie sah in den Grund"; *Grund* connoting "ground," "reason," and "cause.")

Since it is the Castle's secret she saw there at the bottom of Sortini's eyes, it must remain hidden from K. as well as from the reader. When K. tries to obtain information about Barnabas and the Castle from her, Amalia recoils with unusual violence: "I am not initiated, nothing could induce me to become initiated, nothing at all, not even my consideration for you." This is the voice of a burnt child who has been asked to discuss the nature of fire, and it sounds so convincing that K. ceases plying her with questions. Even he understands that she keeps "her motives locked in her bosom and no one will ever tear them away from her." Yet she is not prevented from talking by shame or fright—her sharp-sighted eyes have penetrated to regions deeper than her words could ever reach. Its very ineffability identifies Amalia's secret with the mystery of Kafka's Castle.

But whatever horror she saw, it did not destroy her; nor did her defiance of the dreadful prove fatal to her and her house. She goes on living in the village and enduring her life outside the jurisdiction of the Castle. She has scorned authority and has paid her price; K. observes that she has "the ageless look of women who seem not to grow any older, but seem never to have been young either." She stands apart, outside any community, even the most intimate communion of sex; exposed to despair, she faces despair upright and cold, for her eyes have seen beyond it. In the lone figure of this woman Kafka accepted what came to be known after him and partly through him as existential solitude. (Had he been able to divulge the content of Amalia's vision, he could actually be said to have been an existentialist.)

Yet Kafka remained silent. Amalia alone knows what she has seen, and she is only one episode along the path of the Land-Surveyor. She is not even a decisive one by his standards, since he can hardly make use of her. Yet precisely because she refuses to function as his mirror, she is set opposite him to serve him as an example. She demonstrates the possibility of living in this village, neither by right nor by sufferance, but independent of the Castle. Sick and exhausted, she goes on scorning her fate amidst her family, which, while still trying to curry favor with the authorities, is lost in its own labyrinths. She has dragged them down along with herself, and they have become strangers to her. Still, Olga has to admit that "hers is the decisive voice in the family for better or worse." Each emergency is met by her whose very name means "labor"; she needs "hardly any sleep, is never alarmed, never afraid, never impatient, she did everything for the parents; while we were fluttering around uneasily without being able to help, she remained cool and quiet whatever happened." Having resigned from all her claims to humanity, she has become a holy sister of despair.

In the image of her sister, Olga inadvertently has shown K. a way to survive the Castle, if not to conquer it. This way would also have lead him out of the labyrinth. But he remains blind to the door which opens before him. Having been told Amalia's story, he assures Olga that he prefers her and her ways. "If he had to choose between Olga and Amalia it would not cost him much reflection." With these words he takes his leave of Barnabas' hut and gropes his way back into the darkness. It is, presumably, the darkness of his last night.

MARK SPILKA

Amerika: *Sinful Innocence*

In his introduction to *Amerika*, Klaus Mann speaks of its resemblance to Dickens as "only accidental and superficial":

> The adolescent heroes of the English master-novelist have to endure suffering and adventures because the world is wicked. But Karl Rossmann . . . is harassed by more profound and complicated dangers: the problem of guilt *as such*, the mystic curse of Original Sin follows him over the ocean. . . . He seems almost happy, in spite of the hardships ahead—happy, at least, as compared with his tragic relatives, the doomed heroes of Kafka's two other novels, *The Castle* and *The Trial.* . . . He is a younger, more fortunate brother of that nameless being, K., for whom there will be no America.
>
> It may be, however, that Karl is guilty. He is not responsible—according to human judgment. But our judgment is, of course, subject to error and is easily refuted by the sentence of the higher authorities.

Mann seems to treat each artist in blanket fashion here, as if Dickens had never developed beyond the world of *Oliver Twist*, or as if Kafka were forever writing *The Castle* and *The Trial*. Rossmann is viewed as another K. or Joseph K., a bit younger and more fortunate, but apparently just as guilty of Original Sin. Yet in comparing *Amerika* with *The Trial*, Kafka himself speaks of "Rossmann and K., the innocent and the guilty." The distinction could scarcely be clearer, but there is little provision for it in Mann's

From *Dickens and Kafka: A Mutual Interpretation.* Copyright © 1963 by Indiana University Press. Originally entitled "Sinful Innocence."

thought, and few other writers have followed up the lead. Parker Tyler has argued that Karl is "essentially *innocent*" because of his real moral action, "whereas the symbolic action of K.'s subjectively ambiguous world establishes his guilt." This is a good description of the movement of each novel, yet it fails to explain the sense of Kafka's terms. A more careful appraisal is needed, one which begins with the premise which (as William Madden observes) is central for Kafka: namely, that sinfulness is a state of being "quite independent of guilt."

For guilt, in Kafka's world, implies responsibility, choice, freedom, awareness; while sinfulness is an imposed condition, a necessity, a state of being which, in the early stories especially, is aggravated and inflamed by social and familial pressures. In *The Metamorphosis*, for instance, Gregor suffers from the exhausting rigors of commercial travel. He would like to quit his job, but is forced to support his parents and to clear their debt to his office "father." Their dominance thus extends to the system which deprives him of creative life and married love, and exposes him to his own suppressed desires. It is *their* world, *their* stake in the commercial scheme to which he is committed. Here, as in "The Judgment," Kafka caught deeply and accurately the connection between home and office, the thwarting of independence in both realms, the depletion of the spirit, and, in consequence, the reduction of urban man to bestial immaturity. Such immaturity is "sinful" in its aggressive or regressive aspects—its psychological vileness; but Georg and Gregor, since neither *chooses* that vileness, are truly "innocent" of sinfulness. Once their condition is exposed, however, they must accept it as their private burden, and either remove it or efface themselves. Since there is no question of removal, they exonerate themselves in choosing (or accepting) death. In each case their last thoughts of the family are loving; yet their deaths ironically promote commercial values. In "The Judgment" an unending stream of traffic flows across the bridge, as if released by Georg's suicide. In *The Metamorphosis* the family returns to bourgeois normalcy: their economic prospects brighten, and, as if to confirm their dreams, the daughter flaunts her marriageable body. Thus her animal health is sharply qualified. Like the panther in "The Hunger Artist," who supplants the dying artist, she is simply more adaptable than Gregor, more suited for survival in a voracious world. "In the family," writes Kafka, "only certain clearly specified people have their place, people who come up to clearly specified requirements, and, more than this, to terms dictated by the parents." Plainly the daughter meets these terms. As the parents agree blandly to find her "a good husband," they seem more inhuman than their ill-adapted son.

Thus Kafka's view of sin is hedged with qualifications. His characters are never guilty of sinfulness, *per se.* Their guilt depends on what they *do* about what they *are*, once their sins have been exposed; and even then, they often seem less culpable than the system which engulfs them. Such issues bear importantly on *Amerika*, where the hold of the family has been broken, and where commercial fathers can only check (they cannot thwart) the hero's progress. For Kafka, America is a land where the outcast child can move toward independent growth, toward *removal* of his sinful burden. In the meantime, his very youth redeems him. As an adolescent boy, Karl Rossmann is sinful but innocent, beyond any question of guilt. He has not yet reached that "certain point in self-knowledge" when he will either have to admit and accept his limitations, or transcend them, or take on guilt by denying them. He is not a young adult, like Gregor Samsa or Georg Bendemann or Joseph K. He is sixteen years old, and he has never been confronted by the fact of his sinfulness, in concrete form, as Gregor is confronted by the abominable state of his own being, or as Georg is confronted by his father's judgment, or Joseph K. by the Inspector, on his thirtieth birthday. In *The Trial*, for example, the priest explains the legend of the doorkeeper, who stands before the Law and guards it from the man "for whom alone the entrance is intended":

> One must assume that for many years, for as long as it takes a man to grow up to the prime of life, his service was in a sense an empty formality, since he had to wait for a man to come, that is to say someone in the prime of life, and so had to wait a long time before the purpose of his service could be fulfilled, and, moreover, had to wait on the man's pleasure, for the man came of his own free will.

This is the important principle: at the "prime" of life, a man is able to grasp the facts of his own creation. In the meantime he is simply sinful without being quite responsible for it, or even aware of it. But what does Kafka mean by sinfulness, *per se?* Is it a "mystic curse," as Mann vaguely implies? Or is the answer sharply Freudian? In his diaries, Kafka cites the nethermost and uppermost levels of the mind, and the filth and dissimulation which exist at each level. By dissimulation he seems to mean something like the Freudian concept of ambivalent motivation; and by filth, the incestuous longings, the aberrant sexuality, the deep-seated hatreds of the young child, who comes "dripping into the world with this burden." In the early fiction this burden is seldom given much metaphysical depth: one is sinful (and later guilty) before the human rather than the divine tribunal. But in

The Trial and *The Castle* and the later parables, both sinfulness and guilt are clearly metaphysical in depth. So there is a development in Kafka's thought which critics often overlook; and there are stages and progressions, as well, in his concept of guilt, whether social or metaphysical.

If this is true, then the attraction to Dickens becomes more comprehensible. For in Dickens there is also a progression from adolescence to young manhood, or from "sinful innocence" to acknowledged guilt. Franklin's concept, that he was never willfully evil as a boy, but evil only out of *necessity*, because of "youth, inexperience, and the knavery of others," seems helpful here. For it describes the sort of crimes which Dickens' heroes often commit, in the course of growing up. And the point is, they do commit crimes, they do make appalling mistakes, out of necessity rather than willfulness; for on the one hand, the child is inexperienced and impulsive, while on the other, the world is full of wicked Murdstones, charming Steerforths, and doll-like Dora Spenlows, and involvement with such people is as inevitable as it is fortuitous. The process is inescapable, that is, in one form or another, and every child inherits it as part of the human condition. Still, until he can comprehend this for himself, he is not responsible for his inheritance; and the adults who would make him so are doing him an injustice. Wenn David flunks his spelling lessons, under Murdstone's baleful eye, he needs help more than he needs a beating; and when he bites Murdstone's hand, he commits the act not deliberately but impulsively, and needs love more than he needs confinement. In later life, however, David comes to see his own culpability. When his blind affection for Steerforth leads to the seduction of young Em'ly, he admits his own "unconscious part" in the calamity; and when his love for Dora Spenlow ends in a disastrous marriage, he admits his own dissimulation. "The first mistaken impulse of an undisciplined heart," he calls it, and these words recur to him whether he is awake or asleep. So Dickens' hero suffers from the errors of his own "undisciplined heart," and not merely because "the world is wicked," as Klaus Mann suggests. Most of these errors work grievous harm upon others; all of them bring pain and disquiet upon himself; and all of them are connected with his youth and inexperience.

In a more complicated way, the same holds true for Kafka's hero in *Amerika*. While Rossmann works at the Hotel Occidental, he is visited and exploited by the drunken Robinson. When the drunkard crumples in a corner, Karl foolishly tries to hide him in the employee's dormitory. But he fails to cover his absence from the lift completely, and the Head Waiter discovers it. Karl is fired in short order, and even his erstwhile protector, the Manageress, seems convinced of his guilt. In the meantime, Robinson has been knocked out by the other lift-boys and thrown out of the hotel. As Karl attempts to leave, he is manhandled by the Head Porter. To complete the farce, Robinson then blames him for his damaged state. Karl is to blame, of course, both for leaving the lift untended and for Robinson's misfortune. Yet his sins were committed out of necessity, and there is simply no one in the hotel who is willing to recognize the fact, and to offer counsel and forgiveness. "It's impossible to defend oneself," Karl thinks, "where there is no good will."

Or where there is no parental indulgence. For with Kafka as with Dickens, the necessary crime should be forgiven, and the child's sinfulness balanced by his youth, his inexperience, and the knavery of others. This was the attitude which he found articulated in Franklin, and which made him recommend the *Autobiography* to his father; this was the principle which he also found in Dickens, and which made him turn to Dickens, rather than Dostoevsky and other novelists, during the composition of *Amerika*. In each case, it was the image of an outcast child, sinful but innocent, who deserves the indulgence of his elders and who travels along strange roads, which caught and held his attention.

Yet his attraction to Dickens runs still deeper, in this regard, since the above examples involve only the "uppermost" forms of sinfulness. There is also a nethermost depth in Dickens which Kafka might have adapted to his purpose. We have already seen the oedipal nature of David's hatred for Murdstone, and of his love for his mother, Nurse Peggotty, and the childish Dora Spenlow. Kafka was sensitive to such matters, and might have deliberately reshaped them in his early fiction. In writing about *Amerika* he speaks of "sharper lights . . . from the times" which he used to enhance his Dickens novel. I believe these lights were largely Freudian, and are reflected in the many parent-child relations which recur throughout both novels. Consider Uncle Jacob and Mr. Peggotty, in this respect, in their attitudes toward Karl and little Em'ly. When Em'ly runs off with her seducer, her uncle dedicates his life to tracking down the lovers. His decision seems peculiar, since Ham, the jilted suitor, is the more natural pursuer. But Ham remains at home, in stolid silence, while Peggotty roams the world in search of Em'ly. As their reconciliation suggests, his avuncular love conceals erotic feeling. Thus, when David and Martha eavesdrop in the tenement where Em'ly is reviled by Rosa, they witness an unusual rescue:

> The foot upon the stairs came nearer—nearer . . . [and] rushed into the room!
> "Uncle!"

A fearful cry followed the word. I paused a moment, and, looking in, saw him supporting her insensible figure in his arms. He gazed for a few seconds in the face; then stooped to kiss it—oh, how tenderly!—and drew a handkerchief before it.

"Mas'r Davy," he said, in a low, tremulous voice, when it was covered, "I thank my Heav'nly Father as my dream's come true! I thank Him hearty for having guided of me, in His own ways, to my darling!"

With those words he took her up in his arms: and, with the veiled face lying on his bosom, and addressed towards his own, carried her, motionless and unconscious, down the stairs.

To Kafka, Peggotty's dream might well have seemed incestuous, and his kiss unconsciously erotic. The scene which follows would support him:

"All night long," said Mr. Peggotty, "we have been together, Em'ly and me. 'Tis little (considering the time) as she has said, in wureds, through them broken-hearted tears; 'tis less as I have seen of her dear face, as grow'd into a woman's at my hearth. But all night long her arms has been about my neck, and her head has laid heer; and we knows full well, as we can put our trust in one another ever more."

These are lovers' vows, but they are mutely exchanged by Peggotty and his niece, not Ham and Em'ly. When uncle and niece set off for Australia, to live together in sexless harmony, the oedipal drama is complete. In *Amerika*, Kafka's weak, passive, innocent hero plays out a similar drama. He too sets off for a distant land, where he lives for a time with an uncle, after his shameful seduction in Europe. When he arrives in New York, moreover, his uncle meets him on the ship, from which the two descend in virtual union:

The Senator was just warning Karl to be careful how he came down, when Karl, as he stood on the top rung, burst into violent sobs. The Senator put his right hand under Karl's chin, drew him close to him and caressed him with his left hand. In this posture they slowly descended step by step and, still clinging together, entered the boat, where the Senator found a comfortable place for Karl, immediately facing him. . . . Karl took a more careful look at his uncle, whose knees were almost touching his own . . . [but] his uncle evaded his eye and stared at the waves on which their boat was tossing.

Karl's tears seem like an especially Dickensian touch, and the descent down the ladder, with such careful posturing, resembles Peggotty's descent with Em'ly. Later on, the sexual implications of the scene are reinforced by Mr. Green's remark, that Jacob's affection for Karl "was too great to be called the mere affection of an uncle"; and they are further buttressed by Karl's immoderate desire to return to his uncle, while staying in the country:

> He pictured to himself . . . how in the morning . . . he would surprise his uncle. True, he had never yet been in his uncle's bedroom, nor did he even know where it was, but he would soon find that out. Then he would knock at the door and at the formal "come in" rush into the room and surprise his dear uncle, whom until now he had known only fully dressed and buttoned to the chin, sitting up in bed in his nightshirt, his astonished eyes fixed on the door. In itself that might not perhaps be very much, but one had only to consider what consequences it might lead to. Perhaps he might breakfast with his uncle for the first time, his uncle in bed, he himself sitting on a chair, the breakfast on a little table between them; perhaps that breakfast together would become a standing arrangement; perhaps as a result of such informal breakfasting, as was almost inevitable, they would meet oftener than simply once a day and so of course be able to speak more frankly to each other . . . perhaps his uncle was lying in bed and thinking the very same thing at that moment.

This is like one of Florence Dombey's obsessive dreams about reconciliation with her father; then too, in its hints of intimacy it suggests the night which Em'ly spends in her uncle's arms. Of course, the sexual roles are reversed to accommodate Karl's inverted nature (already apparent in his passive seduction, his adolescent crush on Mack, and his humiliation by Clara, which resembles Em'ly's abuse by Rosa Dartle); but if such comparisons hold weight, they suggest how deliberately Kafka might have transformed maudlin or melodramatic scenes in Dickens into sharp depictions of perverse (yet truly innocent) sexuality. We see again, at the least, how an aesthetic fault in Dickens becomes a solid virtue in Kafka, for his revelations of the unconscious are superbly controlled, thanks to the "sharper lights . . . from the times" he was able to apply to Dickensian situations.

Karl meets other lecherous elders in his early days in America. In his uncle's rooms he is introduced to Green and Pollunder, two business friends of amazing girth with odd designs on Karl. When Pollunder takes him off to his country house, they sit close together in the car, and Pollunder holds Karl's hand while they talk, or puts his arm around him. At the house itself he again encircles Karl and draws him between his knees; and at one point he leads him away from Green and blows his nose for him. Karl himself compares Pollunder's lips with his daughter's, and seems anxious to lure him away, in turn, from the massive Green. But Green continually intrudes: he dominates the conversation, insults Karl openly, sends him off for a "pleasant time" with Clara, and withholds the uncle's note until there is no time left for reconciliation; then he provides Karl with emblems of filial dependence (his lost cap, and the missing box and umbrella from the ship), and pushes him roughly out of the house, when Karl discovers his ruse with the letter.

In their ambiguous kindness and hostility, Pollunder and Green present conflicting aspects of authority. For Karl they even "blur together," at several points, as one gigantic father. His attraction to the affectionate Pollunder, and his repulsion from the seductive Clara, suggest the latent homosexuality which results from Green's hostility—or from harsh paternal rule. Always the surface mixup is rooted in such deeper "filth," so that Karl resembles an innocent victim of a sexual free-for-all, or better still, a sexual charade, though he also contributes to that charade without his conscious knowledge. Later on, in his relations with parental figures like the Manageress, he will again be the victim of absurd sexual conflict, played out in conjunction with surface ambiguities. In all such cases youth and inexperience will exonerate him from guilt; yet by the very nature of his being he will participate in sinfulness.

According to some observers, Freud has presented the modern world with a new interpretation of sin, as a normal stage in the development from childhood to maturity. Kafka seems to accept this interpretation, though he refuses to accept it on merely psychological grounds. Instead he considers the oedipal situation, and the ambivalent sexuality of the growing child, as forms of spiritual disorder, or as conditions of being which the child inherits in all innocence, and for which he must take responsibility at a later stage in self-development. At that stage he will recognize the duplicities of conscious motivation, and will accept and perhaps transcend the degrading urges which originate at deeper levels. Or he will refuse to accept such knowledge, and will take on guilt by asserting innocence, though (as we shall see later on) even that assertion will acquire validity at his death.

As this summary indicates, Kafka is preoccupied with sin rather than guilt, and with the possibilities of guilt and innocence which sinfulness involves. The widely-accepted image of a despairing, self-flagellating Kafka is largely valid; but a comparison with Dickens brings out his stubborn, unremitting hold on innocence. In the early fiction especially, where sinfulness is the result of social and familial pressures on unconscious urges, the possibility of grace, of independent growth, of spiritual as well as psychological maturity, is never wholly absent. *Amerika* is unique, however, in its exploration of that possibility in hopeful terms. After the example of Dickens and Franklin, it postulates a world where the family hold is broken, and where society itself is open-ended, so that the struggle toward maturity may eventually succeed. In America as in Europe, the child seems thwarted by familial and social pressures; he sins out of necessity, errs from youth and inexperience, and obeys degrading urges; yet his very "independence"—his peculiarly American heritage—brings him finally to the Oklahoma Theatre. In that socialist-anarchist Eden, which accepts and employs all comers, he presumably acquires the strength to master sinfulness. In the meantime, he follows the road which Dickens' hero travels in his search for maturity and belonging; and the psychological texture of his travels, their intensely projective quality, derives from Dickens' novel.

MARTIN GREENBERG

Art and Dreams

"The Judgment" marks a decisive turning point in Kafka's work and he immediately recognized it as such. The same day that he finished the story, he described its composition in a diary entry which exults at having discovered, in the nighttime hours, the way to write "with such coherence, with such a complete opening out of the body and the soul":

> This story, "The Judgment," I wrote at one stretch on the night of the 22nd–23rd from ten o'clock in the evening to six o'clock in the morning. I could hardly draw my legs from under the desk, they had got so stiff from sitting. The terrible strain and joy, how the story unfolded before me as if I were advancing over water. At times during this night I was carrying my own weight on my back. How everything can be said, how for everything, for the strangest ideas, a great fire is prepared in which they perish and rise up again. How it turned blue outside the window. A wagon went by. Two men walked across the bridge. At two I looked at the clock for the last time. As the maid walked through the anteroom for the first time, I wrote the last sentence. Putting out the lamp and the light of day. The faint heart pains. The tiredness that disappeared in the middle of the night. Going in trembling to my sisters' room. Reading aloud. Before that, stretching in front of the maid and saying: "I've been writing till now." The way the undisturbed bed looked, as though it had just been brought in. The conviction confirmed that with my novel

From *The Terror of Art: Kafka and Modern Literature*. Copyright © 1968 by Martin Greenberg. Basic Books, Inc., 1968.

writing I am in the shameful lowlands of writing. This way is the *only* way to write, only with such coherence, with such a complete opening out of the body and the soul. Morning in bed. Eyes clear still. All sorts of feelings during the writing, for example delight at having something fine for Max's *Arkadia*, thoughts about Freud, of course . . . of course too about my "Urban World."

The entry shows that Kafka wrote "The Judgment" in a kind of seizure in which his ordinary constraints and inhibitions fell away so that the story seemed to write itself. Some months later, when he was correcting the proof sheets of the story, he said that it had come out of him "like an actual birth." Although Kafka cultivated his style with painstaking effort, most of his manuscripts show very few corrections—his hand moved as if possessed across the page, the sentences flowing with uncanny smoothness. (Characteristically, he tended to delete whole sentences, paragraphs and pages and to substitute new writing for them; he wrote anew, rather than correcting.) His mode of creativity was inspiration rather than making. He was the inspired poet rather than the poet as maker. He did not make or construct so much as he transmitted, even though what he transmitted was shaped at every point by the pressure of his conscious art. Through him "another" voice makes itself heard.

Only so could Kafka write. What he abominated was "constructions," the deliberate contrivances of the calculating consciousness. When his confidence deserts him, then he cries out that *Alles erscheint mir als Konstruktion*— that everything looks like an artificial construction to him, false and dead, as opposed to the "power of life" that he feels. Inspiration meant the spontaneous expression of his more intuitive, more unconscious side, with its truer grasp of reality, with its grasp of the hidden living rather than the mentally constructed reality:

> For us there are two kinds of truth, as they are represented by the Tree of Knowledge and the Tree of Life. The truth of [purposeful] striving and the truth of [purposeless] being at rest [*Die Wahrheit des Tätigen und die Wahrheit des Ruhenden*]. In the first, good separates itself from evil, the second is nothing but good itself, knowing neither of good nor of evil. The first truth is given to us actually, the second only intuitively. That is the sad side of it. The happy side is that the first truth is of the moment, the second of eternity, which is also why the first truth fades away in the light of the second.

The soul is sick because it is divided against itself, knowledge against life. Our ignorance is wiser than our knowledge because our knowledge has become separated from our life. Like Kleist, who influenced him so strongly, he believed that "every first inclination, whatever is involuntary, is beautiful; but everything is distorted and displaced as soon as it understands itself." Thought, the deliberating consciousness of man, has lost its creative power, civilization its creative life. Kafka has the head of the castle village say to K. about the oppressive castle bureaucracy, that tremendous representation of the rationalizing consciousness: "Nothing here is done without taking thought." Reason, consciousness, conscience no longer serve the self to find its true way, but are the means by which an oppressive world rules it for ends not its own.

Yet Kafka is the opposite of an irrationalist or an antinomian who preaches liberation from law and reason in a post-ethical paradise of pure instinctual truth, even though he sometimes seems to talk that way in his aphorisms. His aphorisms are often rhetorically one-sided, whereas his stories are always imaginatively complex. And the note in his stories is not only one of protest against the unjust law, but of striving for the true law that is absent from the world. "Where was the Judge whom he had never seen?" Joseph K. asks as he is being executed. "Where was the High Court, to which he had never penetrated?" Although our thinking has become the enemy of our life, only through our thinking can we recover our life. Only when life and reason, life and conscience, life and law are reunited, shall we be reborn. As Kleist puts it in his essay "On the Puppet Theater," we must "eat of the Tree of Knowledge a second time in order to fall back into a state of innocence"—we must rediscover our innocence through *increased* consciousness. (But that is "the last chapter of the history of the world.") Kafka said to Gustav Janouch, the very young friend with whom he used to walk and talk in the early 1920's: "The poet has the task of leading the isolated and mortal into eternal life; the accidental into conformity to law."

But if Kafka is an inspired poet rather than a maker-poet, why did he have to wait until the writing of "The Judgment" for the channels of his inspiration to become unstopped? We have works of his that go back to 1904 and we know that his pen was busy even earlier than that—why should he have had to wait till 1912, till he was twenty-nine, to produce a story of some fifteen pages which, suddenly bursting out with powerful effect, starts him on his course as a major writer? Because in writing that story he discovered the narrative form which made it possible for him to "free" the "gigantic world" that he had "in his head," because with "The Judgment" he discovered "the only way to write." He had been shaping a style that was capable of everything and had been making tentative, laborious efforts (one judges by the very few writings of his early period which escaped destruction at his own hands) in the direction of a composition which leaned now toward poetic fantasticality and now toward prosaic realism, when the discordant elements of composition, poetic and prosaic, sprang together in "The Judgment" into a narrative form modeled on the dream. Kafka became a major writer when he discovered his dream narrative. "The Judgment" was the beginning of a development that advanced through "The Metamorphosis," fell back in *Amerika*, still faltered in "In the Penal Colony," and then succeeded on a large scale in *The Trial* and *The Castle*.

The dream-narrative form made it possible for his imagination to plumb depths of the self which were otherwise out of reach. The inward, introspective, visionary character of a main tendency of modern literature is carried by Kafka to a very far point indeed. With him, literature gropes its way to the very bottom of the mind, seeking the unconscious self in its very condition of hiddenness, in all its turbidity and strickenness.

His writing was a struggle with himself. He speaks in his diary of his "hatred" of introspection, but it is an "inescapable duty" which he must carry out even though it "tears him apart" and threatens him with "madness." Kafka's writing is a brave effort to penetrate the depths of his life-fear and his life-failure. Though there is a morbid admixture of self-abasement and self-abnegation in it, his dominant effort is to affirm himself in spite of fear and failure, *through* his fear and failure. Georg Bendemann in "The Judgment" executes his father's verdict on himself and drops into the river; but the story is as much an outcry as a surrender, and ultimately K. sets out to conquer the castle of fear of the world-as-given by taking its measure with his exact surveyor's instruments.

The theme of Kafka's work is the theme of his life: the struggle of the self with itself to be itself. The struggle starts out as a psychological one (although ontological overtones are never absent), but then becomes more and more ultimate. One of the reflections that he jotted down in the years 1917–1918 is almost a curse: *Zum letztenmal Psychologie!*—which may be freely translated as, "From now on, to hell with psychology!" Kafka's struggle with himself to be himself in spite of the adverse influences of father, family, education, and milieu became more and more the universal struggle of the self to be in spite of all the forces of nonbeing. It took courage to stare into the Gorgon's face of universal senselessness and despair without flinching away cynically or idealistically or religiously or in any of the innumerable ways there are of flinching; and in fact he was always on the point of turning to stone. Milena Jesenská, the courageous, vivid-spirited Czech woman who burst into his dead man's life (as he called it) in

1920, says about him in one of her vehement letters to Max Brod:

> . . . [H]e . . . never escaped to any such sheltering refuge. . . .
> He is absolutely incapable of lying, just as he is incapable of
> getting drunk. He possesses not the slightest refuge. For that
> reason he is exposed to all those things against which we are
> protected. He is like a naked man among the clothed.

Kafka represents the struggle of the self with itself to be, in the form of a dream. The truth revealed in the dream is the real truth and asserts itself against the official truth of the waking self which is an official lie. The dream is an intuitive avenue to the truth; it is a part of what in one of his notebooks he terms "man's intuitive capacity," which, "though it often misleads, does lead, does not ever abandon one." His stories exercise a magical effect, but his magic is not the magic of illusion but of revelation. His gift is only superficially a gift for the fantastic and unreal. In fact his art is devoted to reality. We see this in his style, which is sober to the point of plainness, and in his humble realistic detail. Yet at the same time it is modern in its profound feeling for the mystery of reality, which is felt as a mystery of hidden depths. " 'The Metamorphosis' is a terrible dream, a terrible conception," young Janouch said to him. "Kafka stood still. 'The dream reveals the reality, which conception lags behind. That is the horror of life—the terror of art.' " The conceiving consciousness lags behind—fails to grasp, indeed seeks to stifle knowledge of—the reality that is known unconsciously and revealed in dreams. The horror of life lies in the fact that the self is split in this way rather than being whole, so that we do not know who we are or what we do. The terror of art lies in the representation of the hidden reality, with its shattering effect.

One reason for the starkness of Kafka's style is his renunciation of metaphors. For Kafka, metaphors were embellishments that obscured rather than revealed the clear lines of things; they were not "true." In rigorously excluding figures of speech from his prose, he was reacting against the turgid, rhetorical style cultivated by his Prague contemporaries, among whom were Franz Werfel and even Rainer Maria Rilke. The German dialect spoken in Prague by a narrow official and bourgeois class at the beginning of the twentieth century, when Bohemia made part of the Austro-Hungarian Empire, formed a little island in the Slavonic sea and was not a truly living language; the Prague writers, in straining to surmount its linguistic poverty, jumped over into extravagance and artificiality. Kafka went the other way, *with* rather than against the limitedness of Prague German. By building on the very poverty of the language, which he purified and strengthened, Kafka was able to arrive at his classically plain style. Of course, his "classicism" has a more than local explanation. He was not only reacting against the Prague *littérateurs*, he was reacting against "literature" in general. Everywhere in Europe (and America) around the end of the nineteenth century, literature had become literary—affected and unreal, conventional and false, working a worn-out machinery of words and ever more words. It was not the first time European literature had been overtaken by debility. But now the revitalization that followed this decline was to an unusual extent the work of provincials and outsiders: the Irishmen Joyce and Yeats, the American Eliot, the French half-Jew Proust, the coalminer's son Lawrence, and Kafka, both a provincial and an outsider. All these men were able to see from their vantage point on the periphery how literature was caught in the lying surface of things and tried in their different ways to strike through to the truth. Kafka's way was antiliterary—through the renunciation of literary effects.

And yet at the same time that Kafka turned away from metaphor as a stylistic element because it derogated from the strict truthfulness he aimed at in his prose, metaphor became the very basis of his narrative art. Most of his stories are founded squarely on a single metaphor; they are the literal enactment of an abstraction, the embodiment in a concrete image of an idea. The death sentence literally passed on Georg Bendemann in "The Judgment" is a metaphor for the father's condemnatory opinion of his son. Gregor Samsa's metamorphosis into vermin is a metaphor for his banishment from "the human circle." Joseph K.'s literal trial metaphorically expresses his spiritual trial. The wound the country doctor is helpless to heal is the spiritual sickness of "this most unhappy of ages"—the whole story rests on the medical image. In German the word for castle (*Schloss*) also means lock—the castle of the novel is locked against all K.'s efforts to fight his way into it, a fortress of impersonal mediate authority which expresses the tyranny of automatic social, biological, and psychological processes, barring the way to the ultimate self-authority of the individual person freely choosing himself and choosing to be free.

Kafka's stories are essentially metaphors, images. He said to Janouch (about Karl Rossmann and the stoker in *Amerika*): "I was not describing [actual] people. I was telling a story. They are images, only images." His narrative art lies in the elaboration, the unfolding of a basic image, rather than in the traditional representation of an action. The Kafka story is not dramatic but visionary; it does not move from the beginning through the middle to the end of an action, it progresses through intensities of seeing toward an ever deeper vision. Nothing really happens in the typical Kafka story, not even death. Death is already there, implicit in the situation of the story. The protagonist sees more and more clearly till he sees his own death.

K. says to Olga in *The Castle*: "If a man has his eyes bound, you can encourage him as much as you like to stare through the blindfold, but he'll never see anything. He'll be able to see only when the blindfold is removed." The Kafka story is a removing of blindfolds.

Kafka's kind of metaphor—the literal expression in a concrete image of an abstraction—works essentially like dream metaphors. Embarrassment, in a dream, is not a long word with two *r*'s and two *s*'s; it is being naked in public. In a dream about someone who "makes you sick" you literally throw up. The literal dream image supplies the basic structure of Kafka's dream narrative. The breakthrough that he made in writing "The Judgment" was a breakthrough to a narrative form based on dream literalism.

Literalism is at the heart of his art. It is responsible for the elemental quality of his stories, which in *The Castle* reaches an epical level. That novel is a great conception of the imagination because of its elemental simplicity: there are K., the village, and the castle, and over everything the snow, nothing more. And yet the simple, concrete image of the castle world is able to embrace the entire modern world, expressed as an unfree bureaucratic automatism—Kafka is able to imagine the modern world in its entirety through the literal image of his novel. Only the literal expresses the truth; the abstract weaves a web of mortal confusion. Kafka's classicism of style and modernism of feeling are one in his literalism; the prosaic literalness of his style and the poetic literalness of his narrative are one.

Kafka's work of course consists of more than dream narratives, but they represent the major part. Stories like *The Great Wall of China*, "The Hunter Gracchus," "Investigations of a Dog" are not dream narratives; they have virtually ceased to be narratives at all and have become a kind of thinking in images, imaginative reasonings in which an image is not represented or delineated in the usual way, or unfolded through a process of enactment as in his own dream stories, but, as it were, excogitated—a good name for these peculiar compositions is "thought-stories." When the thought-story becomes highly condensed and succinct—as for instance in "An Imperial Message" and "Before the Law," both of which are excerpts from larger works which they sum up—it resembles the traditional parable. But the old parable illustrated a meaning already established in some other realm of discourse, whereas the thought-story elaborates a meaning which exists only through the image it excogitates.

A number of Kafka's works fall somewhere in between the dream narrative and the thought-story, straddling the two forms. "A Country Doctor," for example, shares characteristics of both forms. But in spite of the brilliance of its writing there is something unsatisfactory about it; it challenges one to read it as a narrative and yet it is most successful as a thought-story. At the end of his life, in his last novel, Kafka was able to unite his two story forms: *The Castle* is a dream narrative in that the castle image is unfolded by a process of enactment, yet at the same time it is a thought-story in that the process of enactment is an excogitation of the castle image by K. and his interlocutors in the lengthy colloquies which make up most of the novel.

Kafka found his way to the dream narrative through his own experience. He was acquainted with Freud's work, but he did not acquire his knowledge of dreams and depths of the mind by getting up the psychoanalytic literature. He "was not an academic student of the mind. He was however a meticulous observer of his own mental activity"—his notebooks and diary, with their intensely introspective contents and wealth of recorded dreams, make that very plain. His conception of the dream indeed is in a narrow sense opposed to Freud's. Freud stressed the hallucinatory nature of dreams, the illusory fulfillment they give to wishes. Like art, Freud thought, they deal in illusion. With characteristic moral rigor he saw dream distortion as a "dishonest" attempt to conceal the very wish the dream is trying to satisfy. Dreaming is an underhanded enterprise, a sort of truancy which the schoolboy unconscious tries to hide from the schoolmaster consciousness. With equally characteristic moral rigor Kafka saw in the fantastic incoherence of dreams the stammering efforts of the humble client unconscious to make its true petition heard against the angry shouts and denunciations of the bureaucrat consciousness. For him, as we have seen, the dream is the opposite of hallucinatory, it is truth-telling and creative—"the dream reveals the reality."

Kafka inherits directly from the same tendency of European thought and feeling that Freud inherited from: the tendency that sees man at odds with himself and his own works; the tendency that, with Rousseau, sees civilization as a question to be weighed rather than as given, that weighs the cost exacted by "the progress of the sciences and the arts." In the background of the influences that shaped Kafka's thought looms the figure of Goethe, dim but grand, as it looms behind Freud; that he was an adherent of Nietzsche in his youth we know; and in the foreground of the influences is the well-loved Kleist (and also Flaubert)—all representatives of the tendency to question the traditional consciousness and conscience of European civilization.

But Kafka also inherits from Freud. Freudian ideas undoubtedly influenced Kafka and may indeed have helped him to find himself as a writer in 1912. Kafka's subjective world of apparent irrationality hiding a heart of meaning is Freudian through and through. His literal and mythopoeic quality is Freudian. His conception of the dream is in the larger sense the same as Freud's; both understood it as an expression of unconscious experience. Kafka was preternaturally self-absorbed and, Freud or no Freud, would have lived in his own subjectivity and dreams. But one may suppose that Freud's ideas encouraged him to take his dreams more seriously than he might otherwise have done. And Freud's impress, one guesses, rests on Kafka's concern with "the opposition between fathers and sons," as he puts it in his diary in 1911. In his diary entry (really an essay on the character of the literature of small nations—he has in mind Czech and Yiddish literature) he lists the "dignifying of the opposition between fathers and sons, with the possibility of discussing it," as one of the benefits of literary activity. Perhaps Freud's influence, direct or indirect, helped to give him the courage to understand his quarrel with his father as a worthy contest rather than a puerile one, which he could "discuss" in his stories rather than turn away from ashamed. The three works that he achieved in such a sudden outburst in the fall of 1912, "The Judgment," "The Metamorphosis," and a substantial part of *Amerika*, are all concerned with the opposition between fathers and sons. Later Kafka expands and deepens that opposition beyond the psychological sphere into an antithesis established in the very ground of modern existence, which he expresses in the opposition between the individual and the huge bureaucracies of *The Trial* and *The Castle*. But at first he remains within a sphere that one may broadly term Freudian. The fathers whom he portrays in his early stories, and notably in "The Judgment," are Freudian cartoons. Bendemann Sr. in the latter story thunders like a little Jehovah, but the effect of the story is to expose his pretensions to almightiness. The story does more than that; but it is thoroughly "Freudian" in its exposure of the arbitrary, purely personal nature of the father's authority over the son. It reduces the father to a human "comedian" (as his son calls him) rather than elevating him into a god, just by letting his poor flesh exercise the powers of a god.

Kafka defends the human by exposing the all-too-human basis of inhuman authority; he "reduces" the bigger than human to the human in characteristic psychoanalytical fashion. But he is also concerned, as he moves from his early to his middle and last years, with defending the human against being itself reduced psychoanalytically to "nothing but" this or that illness or "neurosis," and here he becomes positively anti-Freudian—"From now on, to hell with psychology!" If in his first important works he wishes (among other things) to show that the all-too-human father possesses godlike power over the son only because of the latter's spiritual captivity ("neurosis"), and if later in *The Trial* Joseph K. submits to the arbitrary godlike authority of the world-as-given because of his spiritual impotence, and if in *The Castle* the land-surveyor K. tries to bring the power of critical intelligence to bear on the arbitrary godlike authority of the world-as-given in his struggle for spiritual freedom—if in all this Kafka struggles to "reduce" the bigger-than-human to the human according to the finest ethos of psychoanalysis, he is always steadfast on the other hand in his search for a faith in "something indestructible," something eternal which does not lie beyond man but within him. He hates the presumption that would reduce all hunger for belief in something permanent, all "matters of faith," to "nothing but" psychological matters. Insofar as religious faith is such a hunger, Kafka respects it. But Kafka does not affirm God, however negatively or paradoxically, in his work. He does not care about God, he does not care about theism or atheism, he leaves all that behind; his world is entirely the human world. But he does care about the "indestructible" in the human world. "Man cannot live without a permanent trust in something indestructible in himself," he says in one of his "Reflections on Sin, Pain, Hope and the True Way,"

> and at the same time that indestructible something as well as his trust in it may remain permanently concealed from him. One of the ways in which this concealment can express itself is as faith in a personal God.

One of the ways in which the indestructibly human is concealed from us is through faith in a personal God. But another, opposite way of concealing it is to call the longing for such trust in something indestructible a neurotic illness. A letter that he wrote to Milena Jesenská in 1921 or 1922 runs as follows:

> You say, Milena, you don't understand it. Try to understand it by calling it illness. It's one of the many manifestations of illness that psychoanalysis believes it has uncovered. I don't call it illness and I consider the therapeutic part of psychoanalysis a hopeless error. All these so-called illnesses, sad as they may appear, are matters of faith [*Glaubenstatsachen*], efforts of human beings in distress to find an anchorage in some maternal ground or other. . . . Such anchorages, which have a hold in real ground, are not a private possession of individuals which they can surrender, but are established from before in man's nature and go on

forming his nature (as well as his body) in the direction already laid down. And they think they are going to cure that?

Religious faith—which, as we have seen, Kafka distinguishes from belief in God—the hunger for a lasting meaning, is not an illusion of mankind but a true spiritual striving implanted in man's nature from before, an anchorage in real ground; trust in something indestructible is man's hope, not man's illness. When Joseph K. dies seeking the judge whom he has never seen, the High Court to which he has never penetrated—seeking the indestructible something in himself in which he may trust—he dies in true spiritual anguish and not in neurotic illusion. When K. crosses the wooden bridge into the castle village he stands "gazing into the apparent emptiness above him"—the emptiness is only apparent, the castle is really there, his goal is a real goal and not a neurotic obsession. Kafka called his "fear," which is the subject of the following letter, "perhaps the best part" of him:

> The most beautiful of your letters (and that means a lot, for as a whole they are, almost in every line, the most beautiful thing that ever happened to me in my life) are those in which you agree with my "fear" and at the same time try to explain that I don't need to have it. For I too, even though I may sometimes look like the bribed defender of my "fear," probably agree with it deep down in myself, indeed it is part of me and perhaps the best part. And as it is my best, it is also perhaps this alone that you love. For what else worthy of love could be found in me? But this is worthy of love.

In an earlier letter he had written that "this fear is after all not my private fear—it is simply that, too, and terribly so—but it is as much the fear of all faith since the beginning of time."

And yet there is a deep defensiveness in his calling the whole "therapeutic part" of psychoanalysis a hopeless error. He himself is guilty of a reckless "nothing but" when he writes, in a letter to Brod, that "there is only one sickness, no more, and this one sickness medicine hunts blindly like an animal through endless forests." By tracing every illness, mental and bodily, to a universal spiritual one, to a question of faith, he justified his doing nothing about himself here and now. In the end he chose to stay the way he was. Which is only to say that he chose to be the writer he was. To accomplish his literary destiny he needed to fail in his life. Or in the words of Sartre: "The genuine poet chooses to lose, even if he has to go so far as to die, in order to win. I repeat that I am talking of contemporary poetry. . . . This is the deeper meaning of that tough luck, of that malediction with which he always claims kinship and which he always attributes to an intervention from without; whereas it is his deepest choice, the source and not the consequence of his poetry. He is certain of the total defeat of the human enterprise and arranges to fail in his own life in order to bear witness, by his individual defeat, to human defeat in general."

Kafka called medicine blind and psychoanalytic medicine hopeless, but he took a lively interest in every kind of half-cracked nature cure. He was looking for salvation, though only half-seriously, not for anything as mediate as "medical assistance." Max Brod writes:

> Franz's attitude to nature cure methods and similar reform move-
> ments was one of very intense interest, tempered by the good-
> natured irony he felt toward the follies and eccentricities which
> accompany these movements. Fundamentally he saw in efforts to
> create a new, healthy man by utilizing the mysterious curative
> powers freely offered us by nature, something extremely positive
> which agreed with many of his own instincts and convictions.

Vegetarianism, fruit-and-nut diets, fresh air regimens, anthroposophy, sun-bathing, nudism—Kafka dabbled in them all, always to be sure with a certain irony. When Rudolf Steiner lectured at the Fanta house in 1911, he was an attentive listener to the theosophist's mystagogic utterances ("Downfall of the Atlantic world, the Lemurian downfall," "Ahrimanian powers") and recipes ("two liters of emulsion of almonds and fruits that grow above ground level"), which he duly noted in his diary. He describes his visit to Dr. Steiner irreverently, and yet he visited him; the account he gives the doctor of the "confusion" of his life—because of the irreconcilability of his two professions of insurance company official and writer—is in dead earnest. He does not ask Steiner seriously how to clear up the confusion, he only asks him, half-seriously, if his taking up theosophy would not constitute a third endeavor which would only add to the confusion. Kafka does not record what Steiner said to him. He does record what Steiner said to Frau Fanta when she complained to him about her bad memory: "Don't eat eggs." Thus he consulted a doctor to whom he was able to give a serious account of a fundamental impasse in his life, but whose own words he did not have to take seriously. He was ready to talk seriously about himself to somebody to whom he did not have to listen seriously.

Anything that promised a salvation which he could regard half-jokingly drew him like a magnet. But he did not believe in the possibility of real salvation. Or rather he believed in it as a possibility, but *only* as a possibility. "The Messiah will come," he said, "only when there is no longer any need for him, he will come only the day after he comes, he won't come on the last day, but on the last day of all."

That is, the Messiah will come only when it is too late, when everything is over and done with; that is, the Messiah will never come; that is, there is no Messiah. Salvation is an illusion.

But at the same time he is saying that the Messiah will come only when it is too late because the world will already have been saved; and so the Messiah will never come, and there is no Messiah, but for the very opposite reason—because salvation is already present in human existence. (The Messiah will not come because there is no miraculous agency but only human life; the Messiah will have come already because human life is the miracle.)

In this glittering paradox, in which the apes of feeling mimic the rationality of discourse in order to mock it, all Kafka's hopelessness as well as all his hope is expressed. The Messiah will not come in any case—without hesitation Kafka brushes aside all supernaturalism and religious irrationality. But his not coming is the source of hope as well as despair. It is not that hopelessness was strong in him and hope weak even if never quite dead. Hope, too, was strong in him. The given world, his own given self were so hopeless, so immovable, but the world as it might be within itself, himself as he might be within himself, promised paradise. Another of his aphorisms runs:

> The expulsion from Paradise is in the main eternal: So it is indeed
> true that the expulsion from Paradise is final and life in the world
> unavoidable, yet the eternalness of the event (or, expressed in
> temporal terms, the eternal repetition of the event) makes it
> possible nevertheless that not only might we live in Paradise
> permanently, but that we are actually permanently there, no
> matter whether we know it here or not.

If the expulsion from paradise is eternal, then we dwell eternally in it; for we have to keep on being in it in order to keep on being driven out of it.

Kafka, with his sense of unlimited human possibility, is in the line of Rousseau. He goes back still further to the Jewish messianic tradition. But he also goes back, at the very same time, to a Jewish rationalist tradition which sardonically postpones the coming of the Messiah to "the day after he comes." He reflects the essential hopelessness of his own father, and so many of the fathers of Jewry, on whose sense of the possibilities of life the gates of the ghetto still remained shut. "In us," Kafka said to Janouch, the ghetto "still lives—the dark corners, the secret alleys, shuttered windows, squalid courtyards. . . ." But he also reflects the essential strength of his own father and so many of the fathers of Jewry: the strength to endure, to endure in spite of everything, feeling despair but not yielding to it finally, defeated but not ever giving in. In him one feels a hope of life that somehow outlasts life itself, a hope after all hope is gone, the Messiah who will come the day after he comes.

On one side stood the possibility of marriage, of children, of human connection and contentment—everything he understood by life in the world (what he called Canaan)—but also defection from his own spirituality; writing and the freezing solitude of his own subjectivity and spirituality stood on the other (what he called the wilderness). He had to die as a human being to live as a writer, to lose in order to win. It was an old (by now it is a conventional) attitude of the modern age, but with him it was not an attitude, it was his life, the antithesis that he lived and died from. . . .

His estrangement from the world and from himself of course had sociological as well as personal reasons. In its sociological aspect it showed itself in a sense of unreality which he shared with his contemporaries in Prague (most of whom were Jews) and which found expression in a literary genre of nightmares peculiar to the Bohemian capital at the turn of the century. The sense of unreality reflected the situation of Austria-Hungary, an ancient empire whose outward panoply concealed an advanced stage of inner decay. The traditional external forms, political, social and moral, hid the truth within; under the placid surface of things breakdown threatened. Something of this situation went into the making of a Freud, who saw with the clear judgment of a physician and an outsider the toll in illness and debility that the split took and extended his observations of the symptoms he noted in Vienna into a universal diagnosis. But most of Kafka's contemporaries exploited the sense of unreality and alienation for its sensational interest, producing second-rate works that specialized in the extravagant and outré. They exploited the dream for its bizarre effects. He used it for its truth.

Kafka also used the Prague German dialect for its truth. In Prague, Wagenbach writes, German was, actually, a foreign tongue, "a kind of officially subsidized language employed on holiday occasions . . . dry and artificial, a foreign element." Kafka's contemporaries tried to deny the lifelessness and alien character of *Prager Deutsch* by a forced vivacity and colorfulness of style. But Kafka accepted its essential foreignness, as he accepted his own foreignness in all things, building his style on the actual character of Prague German (as mentioned earlier) rather than trying to invent another character for it—building his style, that is, on the truth of Prague German.

PETER HELLER

"Up In the Gallery":
Incongruity and Alienation

THE CROWS AND THE METAPHYSICAL HEAVENS

Kafka's works engage us in questions in order to frustrate the hope that questions can be answered. They compel us to formulate theses if only to prove to ourselves that the results are illusory. In a seemingly dispassionate manner Kafka dramatizes the confrontation between entities which prove to be mutually exclusive. Typically, he suggests that these relationships are nonetheless inevitable, at least if seen from the vantage point of *one* of the participating parties.

This generalization concerning Kafka's writings might serve as the thread of a thesis, were it not a paraphrase and circumlocution of the fact of labyrinthine paradox. The imaginary maze cannot be disentangled. There is no exit. But since with Kafka all roads may be trusted to lead to a central dead end, at least the question of where to begin the journey should not be troublesome.

> The crows [he writes, for instance] claim that a single crow could destroy heaven. That is undoubtedly so but proves nothing against heaven, since heavens mean precisely: impossibility of crows.

> Die Krähen behaupten, eine einzige Krähe könnte den Himmel zerstören. Das ist zweifellos beweist aber nicht gegen den Himmel, denn Himmel bedeuten eben: Unmöglichkeit von Krähen.

From *Dialectics and Nihilism.* Copyright © 1966 by University of Massachusetts Press. Originally entitled "Franz Kafka: Incongruity and Alienation."

Like all of Kafka's writing, this aphorism, which is one of a series of "Reflections," seems to demand the effort of exegesis. In a hypersensitive mood, whether induced by a somewhat hysterical sense of aesthetic refinement or by melancholy, exhaustion, anxiety, one might feel that the flight of a black bird destroys the perfection of the sky. However, the German *Himmel* obviously refers to both the physical firmament and the spiritual heaven, and only in a metaphorical sense can the heavens and the crows be said to exclude one another. Are then the black birds to be associated with a state of doom or misery as, say, Poe's raven, or closer to German readers, the crow that joins a melancholy wanderer in Müller-Schubert's *Winterjourney*? And are Kafka's crows drawn to the heavens? Are they doomed to yearn for heaven even in their vain attempt at rebellious denial?

Once questions of this sort have been raised—and all of Kafka's works are sufficiently enigmatic to raise similar questions—the labyrinth will freely receive the reader and compel him to seek out further and further interpretations even though he may be convinced by previous experience that his venture will terminate in the despairing conviction that Kafka's texts are conclusively inconclusive, that the very labor of interpretation merely serves to reduplicate the experience of indissoluble paradox, of irreducible incongruity, of final incompatibility which is the prime source of Kafka's inspiration and the epitome of his art.

The final experience of frustration does not preclude some illusory progress. On the contrary, it requires the momentum gained by partial advance, enlightenment, coherence, and hope of meaning in order to dramatize the check, the darkness, the loss of coherence, the movement of despair. This consideration applies not only to the *objective* features of Kafka's works, his protagonists, and his plots, but equally to the subjective movement of emotional and intellectual quest which Kafka's writings induce in the mind and heart of the reader.

What, then, is the significance of the black birds? In Kafka's fragments an ancient raven of misfortune (*Unglücksrabe*) appears as an embarrassed if persistent travelling companion. Another raven (or perhaps the same one) makes bold at a tea party; a crowlike specimen attracted to "dark unbounded fields" is sought out by a fellow bird, and a host of opinionated birds argue as judges on questions of good and evil, and particularly on the transition from evil to good. In a finished sketch entitled "An Ancient Page," ravenous and barbaric nomads, attracted to the Emperor's palace, communicate in unintelligible sounds reminiscent of the "scream" of "jackdaws." Again, in the most comprehensive of Kafka's fragmentary novels, the crows, whether defiant or yearning or both or neither, encircle the tower of the castle, chief symbol of the inaccessible and ultimate authority which dominates the village and the world of K. Moreover, throughout Kafka's strangely discolored and desiccated work, black dress—the anticolor and the garb of death, sin, guilt, but also of ascetic denial and judgment—would seem to be of paramount significance. The black birds, then, are a complex and problematic crowd while the heavens of the aphorism appear to be associated unambiguously with purity, happiness, beauty, in short, with bliss.

There is further evidence to be considered. By way of Czech *kavka* for German *Dohle* (jackdaw), the black birds, crows, ravens, the family of the *corvidae*, not excluding ashgrey varieties, appear to occur in Kafka's works as synonyms for the voices of the author's self or selves. The *kavka* was the emblem of the store of Kafka's father, a Jewish businessman in Prague, dealer in fancy goods, imitation jewelry and trinkets, shiny objects which are said to stimulate the greed of the thievish bird. The *kavka* is thus associated with the mythical paternal power which dwarfed, frustrated, and inspired Kafka's entire life. For on the authority of his own tortured and self-lacerating confession and accusation—as recorded in the autobiographical "Letter to his Father"—all of Kafka, every line he wrote and every step he took or failed to take, was related to the agonizing conflict of rebellion and dependence, the relationship of admiration and contempt, the romance of love and hatred which forever bound him to his father.

Emrich quotes Kafka's characteristic estimate of himself as an "impossible bird" ("eine Dohle—eine kavka"), lost among men ("verwirrt hüpfe ich zwischen den Menschen herum") who regarded him suspiciously as a dangerous person, a thief, a jackdaw. And yet, Kafka added, this was mere appearance. For he lacked the "sense of shiny things." He was grey as ashes, a jackdaw longing to vanish among the stones, to disappear, to die. According to Emrich, this bird is nonetheless a dangerous thief since, in keeping with Kafka's ruminations, e.g., in the "Investigations of a Dog," the individual who denies the accustomed frameworks and orders of existence or who is exiled from them will also seem to deprive his fellow men of the way of life that is dear to them. Matured to awareness of the "universal," he does not, it is true, attain transcendent reality, but he will demand nonetheless the rejection of the sensory terrestrial sphere. Consequently, according to Emrich, Kafka distinguishes between the common thefts attributed to the jackdaw's delight in shiny objects and his—the *kavka's*—spiritual thievery.

However, this interpretation will hardly fit the crows of the aphorism, which seem to defy the spiritual heavens, though it may fit the author who points out that their attempt is in vain. But is not the author himself a crow, a jackdaw, a *kavka*? So he is, according to Rochefort, who claims that Kafka was both the most radical proponent of a nihilistic experiment and the recorder of his own failure to liquidate "hope," the "sun," the "indestruct-ible," the irreducible basis of life, the Law, Truth, Being, the absolute. To put the matter in Nietzschean terms: according to Rochefort, Kafka was the recorder of his own abortive attempt at total denial, at the murder of God, and at the consequent liberation of man. Man, rid of all burdens, would know that heaven is empty, that there is neither grace nor mercy nor justice. Thus released from the yoke of heaven, guilt, and responsibility, he would arise from his self-destruction to enjoy, in perfect freedom, paradise re-gained, a world and life which are nothing but "nothingness," a pure and weightless game, a hovering in eternal calm and infinite emptiness. Accord-ing to Rochefort, Kafka did not, in his own estimate, succeed in revealing that "everything . . . including his own work" was but a dream and "literal-ly mere smoke and ashes." He found himself deficient in his will to self-annihilation. He wanted to demonstrate the essential meaninglessness of life. However, he did not succeed in proving that the truth consists only in the nonexistence of truth. At the rock bottom of absolute despair he was forced to recognize the mysterious "fact of non-extinction" and "silent guidance." He could not, consequently, pursue the "way of denial" to its conclusive terminal point. He had to renounce his goal "to found life upon nothingness, to liberate himself from God." He was forced to record that the crow did not, after all, destroy heaven. The birds of the aphorism would thus be related negatively—rebelliously or in a mode of deprivation—to both the terrestrial and the heavenly sphere. For in Rochefort's view, the crows, as radical nihilists, desire in vain their freedom from the chain and collar of the world and heaven.

It seems certain that the author of the "Reflections," as distinct from the crows in the aphorism, rejects the sensory world of appearance. "There is nothing but a spiritual world. What we call the sensory world is the evil in the spiritual world, and what we call evil is only a necessity of a moment in our eternal development." He adds that "evil is a radiation of human consciousness in certain positions of transition." Actually, he claims, it is not the sensory world which is mere "appearance." Only the "evil" in this sensory world is said to be illusory. And yet, according to Kafka's circular reasoning, this "evil" constitutes "the sensory world in our eyes." Even so, the world as we know it is to be dissolved by eyes which can penetrate its seeming solidity. And this task requires man not to withdraw or escape from this world but to meet it, to accept its victory, to bear it, and suffer through it.

One might recall in this connection Kafka's perennial sense of guilt about his failure to involve himself in marriage and thus in life, as well as his ruminations about the fact that even if he had involved himself, he could have done so only with the mental reservation that he must not succumb to life, that he must engage in the world and meet its chief representative, woman, in order to be better equipped to fight life in this world. And one might also recall that K., the hero of *The Castle*, is accused of having his love affair with Frieda merely in order to promote his own scheme of rebellion and salvation. However, while this raises a question as to the way of overcoming the world, there is no question that in the "Reflections" the overcoming itself is the one and only goal. If, as Rochefort claimed, Kafka, the nihilist and rebellious crow, wanted to reveal the world as nothing, its illusory realities would have to be dissolved. However he would not hope that a spiritual authority, a heaven, would take their place. He desired to enjoy perfect, supreme, autonomous, and godlike freedom. His ideal was a state of free suspension in the awareness of the pure game-character and nothingness of the world. There would be neither ruler nor ruled. There would be freedom both from the constraints exercised by the illusions of the material world and from those imposed by ideal authority, metaphysical law, or heavenly illusions.

However, the author of the "Reflections" differed from the crows in the aphorism; in the light of this difference the condition of the crows, heaven, and possibly even the world might assume an altogether different aspect. If the crows' defiance of heaven is vain, the desperate birds might appear not as emancipated revellers in the freedom of nothingness but as abject outcasts excluded not only from the perfect being of heaven but equally alienated from the terrestrial condition and thus condemned to hover in limbo.

Even in the series of aphorisms entitled "He" which contains the decisive passage for Rochefort's thesis, namely Kafka's confession of his long-standing wish to reveal life as "nothingness, as a dream, as a hovering" (*als ein Traum, als ein Schweben, als ein Nichts*), the author observed that he had failed to wish this wish aright. For his desire had been merely "eine Verbürgerlichung des Nichts," the rationalization of his own sense of belonging to nothingness. It should have been—this would seem to be the implication—the expression of his sense of belonging to "another world," the world of the indestructible and true being, and of his acceptance of this terrestrial world of illusion as a mere transition, a momentary, if necessary, state of insubstantial illusion. Under the altered aspect the sensory world of appearance is still nothing. But if heaven is everything (i.e., the "indestructible," the only true condition of being), and if "heaven" means "impossibility of crows," the consequence for the crow matured to insight into its own condition could not be to persist in the futile attempt to gain the hovering freedom of nothingness. Rather, the crow would have to realize that it must do away with itself in order to vanish and/or to become one with indestructible being. And consequently Kafka notes that the "first sign of dawning realization is the wish to die" and that the true death is our redemption.

Given the knowledge that this world is an evil zero and that heaven cannot be destroyed, the crow, temporal man, must destroy himself. In eating of the tree of knowledge and in failing to eat from the tree of life, man entered a condition in which he has knowledge of good and evil but lacks the power to live according to this knowledge. Though his world may be nothing but the expression of his attempt to conceal from himself the inadequacy and the inherent sinfulness of his state, man knows that he cannot live according to his knowledge of the good and he must therefore destroy himself in the hope of gaining true being. But he is afraid, and his life in this world is, so to speak, the postponement of his duty to will the negation of himself as finite being. In short, man's life in this world is the hesitant hovering of the crow that clings to its defiance of heaven.

However, if this is now to be accepted as Kafka's doctrine, would it not seem that he holds out no hope whatever to man? For if the term self-destruction is not metaphorical, if it means that crow or man must annihilate himself in order to gain being, one might question whether this radical recipe for salvation is more than a restatement of a desperate paradox. Where individuated man exists, being is not; where true being is, man's illusory existence is not. But surely to state the matter thus is to paraphrase once more a condition of radical incongruity between the illusory self of individuality and the universal being which, however absolute, remains inaccessible.

Even so, the preceding speculations may represent some further advance into the labyrinth. Emrich's interpretation of Kafka's "Hunter Gracchus," a name derivable from the Latin stem *gracc* which imitates the crawing and croaking of jackdaws, crows, and ravens, confirms that the symbol of the black birds applies in particular to those who are suspended between the illusory realities of this world and the indestructible, essential reality which is beyond the sensory sphere of individuation. It applies to the hunter who has lost life and yet missed death, as well as to the crows of the "Reflections" which hover between earth and firmament.

With its economy of metaphor, the aphorism condenses a variation on the perennial story or predicament which is Kafka's main theme. The crows, Gracchus, the *kavka*, the ravens, Raban, the K.'s of *The Trial* and of *The Castle*, who, in their very effort and futile striving, must fail to come to grips with their ultimate *other* (whether it be heaven, death, the core of their own being or indestructible life, the Law, or marriage, or community, guilt, justice, grace, or redemption), are intended to be more than representatives of their author, or even of those who are beyond the pale of common illusions and yet barred from essential truth. They are prototypes of man and of his radically inadequate condition, or, in theological terms, of his fallen state. From the vantage point of the "Reflections" it appears that everywhere and at all times, the human illusion of an evil sensory world and of man's illusory and evil existence as a temporal individual constitutes the same paradoxical condition. Man or the crow, that is, man as he sees himself, man as a fictitious and illusory creature, retains his knowledge of the indestructible (heaven) and his relationship of dependence on true being, even if only by way of denial. Yet fallen or temporal humanity and the supreme and only reality of true being prove mutually exclusive, so that wherever man takes his universe of lies and illusions, the truth is "destroyed." This proves nothing against the truth but proves that truth is the "impossibility" of temporal or fallen humanity with its individuation, ratiocination, quest and impurity. The typical protagonists of Kafka who are bound to temporality yet cursed and blessed with an inkling of truth serve best to dramatize the author's general view of a fallen humanity. At every instance mankind is ineffably close to, and barred from redemption so that the "decisive moment of human development is always," and there is always "a goal but no way," since "what we call way is hesitation."

The black birds are a traditional symbol for this interesting condition of self-conscious sin, of the sinner brought to unwilling, defiant, despairing or abject awareness. To begin *ab ovo*, there is the raven sent out by Noah. His alleged failure to return to the ark has long been subject to varied interpretation. According to the Jewish tradition, the family of the *corvidae* is unclean; their croaking an ill omen. According to the Fathers, the raven signifies the blackness of sinners or demons (Eucherius) or, according to Augustine, "peccatores nondum dealbati remissione peccatorum" [sinners have never yet been cleansed by the remission of sins]. For the sinner given to the pleasures of the world, ever hesitant, ever putting off his conversion, would have been whitened or purified, had he not been obstinate, crying incessantly "cras, cras" (tomorrow), when penitence was proposed (cf. "what we call way is hesitation"). The raven did not return to the saving ark but perished in the waters of the flood like the heretics who received a false baptism; but no, he survived by feeding on floating carcasses, and he is thus the shameless sensualist gloating on wordly sham-gratifications.

And yet, a purely negative interpretation would not seem to be in keeping with the Judaic-Christian tradition, for the ravens fed Elijah by divine command and they are mentioned expressly, even as the lilies, as instances of God's protecting love and goodness (Job xxxviii; Luke xii, 24:

"they neither sow nor reap . . . and God feedeth them"; Psalms, cxlvii), and the "locks of the beloved" are compared to the glossy blackness of the raven's plumage (Cant., v, 11). In some measure, the ambiguity of the taboo governing creatures both shunned and venerated appears to be applicable at least to some of the *corvidae*, even apart from the fact that in some classical and Germanic traditions the raven (e.g., of Odin) is exalted to a position of eminence, and similarly, the *kavkas*, Raban, Gracchus, *Krähen* are not merely bearers of a curse but at the same time set apart and even exalted above and beyond the sphere of seemingly less problematic creatures.

Finally, it should be recognized that the relationship of radical incongruity is to be found once more in the verbal structure of the aphorism of the crows. For by designating the crows (*Krähen*) as K (plural) and k (singular), and their opposite (*Himmel*) and H (plural) and h (singular), the pattern of the aphorism can be represented as K, k, not h; h, H, not K. This chiastic arrangement corresponds to the vicious circle of man's predicament. For in being led from the crows to heaven and from heaven back to the crows, we are led from the crows' argument against heaven to the realization that the validity of their argument is a conclusive indication of their accursed condition. The only central certainty ("Das ist zweifellos") which occupies the center of the meditation proves "nothing" with respect to essential being and yet everything with respect to the "unquestionable" reality of a state of evil and delusion. Nor is it surprising that this figure of speech which might be termed the chiasmus of mutual exclusion (if A, then not B, if B, then not A) should be approximated in varied degrees in other sentences of Kafka. For it dramatizes on a small scale the same condition which dominates Kafka's mind and heart, and consequently also shapes the macrostructures of his writings.

In the "Letter to his Father," for example, Kafka sets out to prove the law of mutual exclusion by arguing that he is barred from all that he takes to be his father's mansion and that his father is consequently barred even from the recognition of the essential character of his son. In a decisive chapter of *The Castle* the long-awaited promise of miraculous opportunity serves only as a lullaby to put the exhausted protagonist to sleep, so that the representative of the universal power who appears ready to fulfill the boundless aspiration of his visitor and the migrant and unredeemed soul of K. will irretrievably miss one another. Moreover, the entire novel is based on the proposition that wherever K. appears, the *other*—the Castle—will not reveal itself (the mere presence of K. in a passageway prevents the emergence of the officials), and that the supreme activity of the Castle excludes the awareness of K. And similarly, Kafka bases both the central parable "Before the Law" and the entire novel of *The Trial* on an analogous relationship of desperate exclusion obtaining between the individual and the Law.

However, a further aspect remains to be considered. For while the crows and their like are desperately involved with the object which they are destined to miss, Kafka's works are generally characterized by the contrast between the calm, the quiet, or even the quietism of the author's style and manner, and the desperation which prevails in the content of his communication. This relation of contrast is describable in terms of an inversion of proportions occurring within a framework of analogies. For at least in the context of the "Reflections," the quiet lucidity of Kafka's manner corresponds to the immutable, indestructible essence or light which is the only truth offered to the artist by the ever receding grimace of a transient world. Kafka's impassive voice seeks to suggest, on the verbal plane and within a linguistic framework essentially alien to the one and only spiritual truth, the immutable calm of timeless perfection.

Conversely, the *tangible* objects of representation, the concrete images, characters, events, must reflect predominantly the temporal grimace, though even on this plane there are intimations of the indestructible essence apprehended by way of negation. It is suggested by the crow's denial of the heavens or by the futility of the striving and the quest of Kafka's K.'s. It is represented by the ray of light which, only upon the approach of death, is seen to emanate inextinguishably through the gates of the Law, by the positive, if minimal, inkling of the essential X that has been missed irretrievably by temporal man, who remains suspended between his dim apprehension of the very perfection of his and all being and his inability to attain this essence.

The aphorism of the crows thus involves three distinct entities: heaven, the crows, and the author who both confirms and contradicts the crows' assertion. However, a triad of this sort is rarely as explicit and as demonstrable in Kafka's other writings. Particularly in his novels, the narrator usually recedes—not quite but almost—to a vanishing point by identifying or by seeming to identify his own perspective with the perspective of his main protagonist, although the style of delivery always suggests distance and comment. For Kafka is three in one: a lost and desperate soul, a voice that hints at the promise of perfect being and a hovering, dispassionate and disembodied observer who reports on the incompatibility between crows and heaven.

SOCIAL ASPECTS

The metaphysical approach to Kafka illustrated by the preceding discussion is perhaps the most comprehensive. It is also the most abstract. Kafka's texts have been subject to a variety of widely divergent approaches. And since this high degree of interpretability appears to be a distinctive feature of Kafka's work, it may be well to illustrate some of the major modes of Kafka exegesis with reference to another brief and complete composition of his, the poem in prose entitled "Up in the Gallery" (*Auf der Galerie*) which runs as follows:

> If some frail consumptive equestrienne in the circus ring were driven around in circles on a reeling horse for months on end without respite by a whip-swinging pitiless ringmaster before an unrelenting audience, whizzing along on her horse, throwing kisses, swaying to and fro from her waist, and if this game went on and on into a gray and ever yielding future amid the incessant roar of the orchestra and the ventilators, accompanied by the receding and the renewed applause of hands which are actually steamhammers,—then, perhaps, a young visitor from up in the gallery would run down the long stairs past all the rows, rush into the ring and shout his "Stop!" through the fanfares of the ever accommodating orchestra.
>
> But since this is not so, a beautiful lady, white and red, flies in through curtains opened before her by proud men in liveries; the director, devoutly seeking her eye, breathes toward her in humble animal-posture; lifts her on the dapple-gray horse as if she were his most beloved granddaughter about to set out on a dangerous journey; cannot make up his mind to give the signal with his whip; finally masters himself and gives it with a loud crack; runs alongside the horse, open-mouthed; follows the leaps of the rider with a sharp eye; can scarcely comprehend her skill; tries to warn her with English exclamations; angrily admonishes the grooms who hold the loops, to painstaking attention; implores with raised hands the orchestra to be silent before the great *salto mortale*; finally lifts the little one down from the trembling horse, kisses her on both cheeks and deems no ovation from the audience sufficient; while she herself, supported by him, high on tip-toes, in a cloud of dust, her arms wide open, her little head tilted back, would share her happiness with the entire circus—since this is so, the visitor up in the gallery puts his face on the railing and submerging in the final march as in a heavy dream, he weeps without knowing it.

Again the text consists of two sentences. Each of these is a circus act, a virtuoso feat of German style. In the first sentence the hectic rhythm and diction dramatize the hopelessness of an endless effort. In the second even vocabulary and cadence assume the bland and somewhat fraudulent splendor of a *de luxe* performance. Again relationships of mutual exclusion and incompatibility dominate the two sentences. The two aspects of the circus appear to be contradictory, and both exclude the spectator although his consciousness contains them. He cannot relate himself to the circus either by negating the negation (by attempting to call a halt to the evil and misery of the show)—or by accepting it as positive bliss. He appears as an impotent and frustrated outsider suspended in limbo, yet compelled to attempt the establishment of a meaningful relationship to the circus. And again the enigmatic piece solicits the effort of exegesis though it promises to frustrate this attempt in a manner similar to the way in which the circus frustrates the spectator.

In order to start this process one might summarize the parable as follows: 1) If the circus were recognized for what it is, a perpetual lie, the spectator might stop it, and consequently the perpetual lie might cease to be. 2) Since, however, the perpetual lie of the circus is not recognizable, the spectator dimly realizes that he cannot stop it, and consequently the circus will continue to be what it is, namely a perpetual lie. The form of the passage would appear to be that of an ironical inversion. The reality of misery and evil—the consumptive equestrienne, her ruthless exploitation, the inhumanity of the crowd who function as steamhammers—is represented in the hypothetical subjunctive, while the lie—the radiant star, the solicitous director, the bliss shared by performer and spectators—appears as reality in the indicative. However, the irony of this irony is that because the fiction appears as reality and the reality as fiction, the triumph of fiction and the denial of underlying reality seem to constitute a permanent and unchangeable condition. In describing the circus-world from the vantage point of human reality (and what other perspective could be available to us?), it would seem just as true to say that the fiction *is* the reality and that the underlying truth is a mere fiction. This being so, Kafka's account of how matters appear to the spectator in the gallery should create in the reader's mind a doubt analogous to that of the young spectator, except that this doubt will stand in inverse proportion to the state of mind that is reached by the young man. For the reality of the circus would appear to envelop and finally to submerge the consciousness of the spectator: he will accept the sham-reality, at least to the point of becoming oblivious to his own sense of tragic farce. The spectator, to quote what is necessarily the author's own comment, finally "weeps without knowing it." But in the mind of author and reader, though they should be equally convinced that the circus will go on forever, the awareness of the *lacrimae rerum* [tears for things] will remain uppermost.

So far so good. Yet this interpretation is neither complete nor conclusive. For most of Kafka's readers feel compelled to question what the circus stands for, and quite a few have produced interpretations which differ radically from our reading without being necessarily less compatible with the text. Richter, for example, treats with impressive consistency all of Kafka's fiction either (disapprovingly) as a symptom or (with qualified approval) as critique and description of the late, imperialistic and decadent phase of western capitalism. He too finds that "Up in the Gallery" deals with a single event, not only in order to reveal the contradiction between essence (first sentence) and appearance (second sentence) but to dramatize the attitude of the man who is confronted with this contradiction. For each of the sentences culminates in the reaction of the spectator whose consciousness mirrors the discrepancy between the underlying reality of the "circus" of capitalist society and the generally accepted pretense. The spectator has seen behind the scene. However, the simultaneity of essential inhumanity and pretty illusion incapacitate even the man who has recognized the pernicious dialectic which obtains between a ruthless system and the semblance designed to conceal it. Where all applaud the splendid exterior, the knowing individual is reduced to resignation and silent tears, for on the surface all seems so well that nothing could justify the protest, let alone the hope of successful, incisive, revolutionary action. If only the inhumanity of exploitation were sufficiently apparent! As it is, the masses see only the veneer of order and propriety which safeguards the continuity of an insufferable condition destined, according to Richter's Kafka, to prevail inevitably and forever. The underlying truth remains invisible, hence the conditional, the subjunctive, the hypothetical form. The reality of apearance determines everybody's reaction, including even the attitude of the spectator insofar as it prevents him from active interference, hence the indicative of sham reality. And yet the protest of conscience remains unappeased, and the inner conflict isolates the knowing spectator from the mass of his fellow men. Aware of the crime against humanity perpetrated by capitalist exploitation, he is doomed by his very awareness to remain a helpless and hopeless outsider.

Richter's reading is based on something more than biographical evidence of Kafka's social consciousness, e.g., his early sympathy with the Socialists, his subsequent attendance at Anarchist meetings, his experience as a trusted employee of a Worker's Insurance Company where, in close touch with cases of social injustice, he expressed his sense of society's obligation toward its victims in unambiguous and aggressive terms (see

Wagenbach). It was not Richter, the East-German Marxist, but Emrich who interpreted the fragmentary novel, which Brod entitled *Amerika*, as a critique of the frantic, ruthlessly competitive world of work, as a denunciation of that mechanized, enslaved and enslaving industrial society which grinds us all to dust in its inexorable economic and psychological mechanisms. And while Richter objects to this interpretation as being too sweeping and too pat in its agreement with a cliché of America in particular and of industrial mass society in general, it is obvious that Kafka did reject a society where people think that they grasp in order to get at themselves when actually they merely grasp in order to grasp more, merely get in order to get on with getting, and ever miss themselves.

As for capitalism as a socio-economic system, Kafka, though he remained politically inactive even in his later leanings toward Zionism, was evidently opposed to it. Concerning a drawing by George Grosz showing a fat man with a top hat as capitalism incarnate sitting on the neck of the poor, Kafka said that this was correct insofar as the fat man did rule over the poor man within the framework of a certain system. Only the fat man was not the system itself. He too carried chains. For capitalism was a system of dependencies, of mutual enslavements from top to bottom and from bottom to top. Everyone and everything was dependent, everyone in chains. Capitalism, he observed, was a state of the world and of the mind.

At the same time this comment betrays Kafka's tendency to look upon capitalism as a symptom rather than as a cause of human depravation. It is hardly surprising if Richter objects that the author and the spectator in the gallery will both reject capitalism and accept it as an inevitable and unchangeable evil. According to Richter, the early Kafka had placed the burden of guilt on the outsider's failure to fulfill the human norm and on his incapacity to come to terms with a world which he could not but experience as alien, inhuman and devoid of meaning. Now, however, in "Up in the Gallery" and in the entire series of *A Country Doctor* which characterized Kafka's development between 1914 and 1917, he shifted the burden in order to present conflicts and contradictions inherent in a guilty (capitalist) society. However, since he did not reveal their underlying causes and since he neither suggested nor believed that these conditions could be overcome, he could not transcend a mood of desperate irony. Like the captured ape in "A Report to the Academy," the author is still the outsider forced to the wall, conscious of both his own weakness and the problematic nature of the so-called human universe. He has come to accept a compromise with the way things are in order that he may survive. His awareness of the inhumanity of the world may relieve him from the need to identify himself with this world and mitigate his sense of responsibility for its condition. But he cannot ignore the futility of his utterly isolated position.

According to Richter, the early Kafka, with his insistence on the tragedy and guilt of the maladjusted outsider, was an "apologist of the petty bourgeoisie." The later Kafka merely accepts the impossibility of changing an evil social world. However, insofar as ideologies of impotence characterize the social strata who have learned only to hover and to compromise between the exploiters and the exploited, the author of *A Country Doctor* still represents the vantage point of the powerless petty-bourgeois or of his relative and variant, the powerless intellectual who is altogether in limbo. The intellectual lacks a social basis. By virtue of his intellectual detachment he can see and diagnose social evil, but since he is isolated and believes himself to be without allies, he is reduced to resignation, to the mere capacity to endure. Oppressively, Kafka thus combines true social insight with the lack of all perspective on the future. He is now neither an apologist nor a fighter. He sees but does not combat an evil world and the irony with which he treats his own position suggests its ineffectuality. Kafka knows, Richter concludes, that the artist who reveals social perversion without engaging in active opposition plays a dubious role, but he conceives no other possibility. Only in his final works does he deal explicitly with the impossibility of maintaining the position of the artistic outsider. For ultimately Kafka comes to realize that art can be justified only insofar as it exercises a significant function in society, and that this is no longer the case in the western world.

Richter's conception of Kafka as representative of the critical and impotent petty-bourgeois intellectual contains at least a partial truth. Moreover, it is derived from a reading of Kafka's texts which is quite compatible with a metaphysical exegesis. For if, as Richter claims, Kafka does not discuss the underlying causes of the phenomena he describes, and if it is true that his descriptions are usually figurative rather than realistic, there is no compelling reason to assume that he deals specifically or exclusively with the evils of capitalism. Kafka may be presenting a generalized image of a dehumanized and materialistic modern society or, for that matter, depicting the evil inherent in a perennially fallen world which, from the beginning of time, has been alienated from the absolute. . . .

The conception of nihilism as a negative condition and of Kafka as an author irrevocably restricted to it, represents the majority opinion among the untutored readers. And while Kafka's negative attitude toward his own works will have to be considered in terms of his specific doctrine of positive self-destruction, it is not unreasonable to assume that this attitude at the same time expressed his own despair over the lack of positive substance.

Though writing was to Kafka occasionally a source of joy and even a "form of prayer," he frequently suspected it to be a confirmation of his alienation, a curse, another mode of damnation. He published only a fraction of his works and that reluctantly. While he himself did not destroy his literary remains, he requested that they be destroyed, and he stated quite unambiguously that he did not even wish his published works to survive him. He did not consider himself an ineffective writer, and since he did not believe in the fictitious autonomy of literary products but wanted literature to help men, he could hardly have ignored that it was, after all, not enough to represent the negative element of the age.

Admittedly, these considerations are tentative and provisional. But perhaps they are in keeping with the comments of a German critic who supplied still another interpretation of "Up in the Gallery." According to Glaser, the spectator portrayed in this "strangely confused and confusing piece of prose" represents an author who does not know what is true and what is false or how to distinguish the genuine show from the fraud, but who tarries ambivalently at the crossroads of doubt, hovering between nihilism and faith or between darkness and light. The *if*-clause, he claims, contains night thoughts, a dark notion of the world as if it were ruled entirely by evil. And yet this is denied. The assertion in the indicative, however, represents an all-too-bright picture, a surface aspect, almost a facade which, although accepted as reality by the man, is recognized as being deceptive—at least in part. Is the world a circus of evil in which true humanity is driven to death? If so, the final act of desperate rebellion against this world might promise release. But no, the world appears to be a bright and happy show, even though this show may be illusion. The world is too bright a place to justify desperate action, too dark a place to justify happiness and joy. And confronted with its ambiguous image, the perceptive spectator in the gallery is caught in the dilemma of doubt and must resign himself to frustration.

Glaser complicates matters by assuming that in the hypothetical clause the circus director represents a tyrannical father-god, and by claiming that the young spectator wanting to cry "halt" appears as the would-be conqueror of this god, as a Promethean rebel against an unjust deity. Somewhat in line with Rochefort, he suggests that Kafka's protagonist wishes to engage in a quasi-Nietzschean struggle against the embodiment of a presumably evil law or absolute that governs the world. However, while this daydream of rebellion is revealed as unjustified, the acceptance of the gloating circus director as a benevolent, worldly father-god, suggested by the second view, proves equally impossible. The "animal-posture" of the man, his gaping mouth, his attempts to catch the eyes of his beloved granddaughter, suggest a repulsive and blasphemous caricature of God as the solicitous manager of the human soul.

The implications of this interpretation are indeed strangely confusing. The dream of total negation, of a wholly evil world that can be destroyed, and of an evil God who can be abolished, proves not too desperate but rather too positive and too good to be true. For the nihilistic daydream is frustrated, the desire for a wholly negative release denied. And while Glaser's interpretation is as questionable as any, the complexities of despair which it suggests cannot be dismissed when considering an author who frequently expressed his sense of relief at the thought of final doom. As he puts it in his diary, Kafka felt "joy at the idea of a knife twisted in [his] heart"; his dream of bliss consisted in the phantasy that punishment came "and I welcomed it, so freely, with conviction, and happily."

If Kafka considered himself one of the damned, it was not apparently because he had certainty of any specific pain or failure but because he knew something worse, the almost inexpressible agony of being outside of everything, whether it be good or evil, pleasure or pain, joy or sadness, confidence or terror, life or death. The ultimate condition of being damned would deprive the victim and culprit even of an assured relationship to his curse. From the vantage point of this experience even the reality of evil or pain is a relative good. Thus some of Kafka's most horrible inventions, e.g., the execution machine of "In the Penal Colony" or the knifing of K. in *The Trial* are, in a sense, cause for optimism. They establish for a brief spell an intelligible texture, a fleeting if abysmal triumph over the threat of total loss of contact, cohesion, and intelligibility.

And yet it might be objected that all these readings are radically insufficient since the essential Kafka, though he knew of nihilism as a threat, evil, and affliction, had overcome the inferno of negation. It might be claimed that Kafka, though perhaps sympathetically affected by his age and subject to a sickness of mind and heart peculiarly his own, remained in essence superior to the lost world and self on which he wrote his symbolic commentary.

In his grandiloquent manner, Werfel asserted that Kafka was a messenger from above, one of the great elect sent down to this earth, who would never have expressed his otherworldly knowledge in poetic similes if "the epoch and the circumstances" had not induced him to do so. The austerities of his self-tortures, his mania for cleanliness, his essential purity of heart, his intellectual, ethical, or spiritual rigor and severity, the spectral sublimity which characterizes some of his visions, his quiet and lucid style, the distance from the recorded events maintained by the impassive voice of the recorder suggesting, even in the guise of irony or humor, that the common human concerns were ever somewhat alien at least to that superior being that resided within him—might all support this perspective. Interpreters who regard Kafka as an ascetic pronouncing a verdict against a fallen world or as a guide pointing the way through death to a mystical union with the indestructible essence beyond illusion, stress Kafka's own sense of being a messenger. He had suggested this, in a letter in which he claimed that he, or rather that "one," had been sent out as the "biblical dove."

But in Kafka's version of Genesis (8, 9), a shelter of life is turned into a symbol of death. On the outing in question, the dove, though not lost on the waters as the raven, did not return with glad tidings. As Kafka put it, one had not found "anything green" and so would slip back into the darkness of the ark. Thus the passage hardly supports those who make of Kafka a prophet of positive living in this world. Yet it implies a resignation to positive dying unto this world. And generally, the interpreters who stress Kafka's positive metaphysical mission in a nihilistic age have no difficulty in convincing themselves of Kafka's ability to rise above or beyond the fallen state which he surveyed in his work. Buber assumes a position in keeping with Judaism as does Brod who believes that Kafka's novels tell of men who missed the right way. A positive message in Christian terms is suggested by some of the French Neo-Thomists, by Kelly's interpretation of *The Trial* in terms of Barth, or by Gray's interpretation of *The Castle* in terms of K.'s quest for grace.

Again one might note that the choice between negative or positive evaluation frequently hinges on a decision as to whether Kafka's works are symptoms or symptomatologies, an expression or a critical record of a negative condition, and that the dividing line in question is exceedingly fine. Given the assumption that the poet is isolated from his fellow men by virtue of his superior insight into the rotten state of the human universe, the interpretation, for example, of "Up in the Gallery" would gain in simplicity. Suffering, as the one-eyed must among the blind, the visitor would see the truth of a disoriented and aimless world in its essential, if unadmitted, nihilism. However, all interpretations of this type are confronted with the difficulty that Kafka does not appear to offer a positive counter-image. The moralist in Kafka is constantly endangered by the ambiguity of a condition in which the radical absence of positive values argues the absurdity of the claim to such values.

THEODOR W. ADORNO

Notes on Kafka

Kafka's popularity, that comfort in the uncomfortable which has made of him an information bureau of the human condition, be it eternal or modern, and which knowingly dispenses with the very scandal on which his work is built, leaves one reluctant to join the fray, even if it is to add a dissenting opinion. Yet it is just this false renown, fatal variant of the oblivion which Kafka so bitterly desired for himself, that compels one to dwell on the enigma. Of that which has been written on him, little counts; most is existentialism. He is assimilated into an established trend of thought while little attention is paid to those aspects of his work which resist such assimilation and which, precisely for this reason, require interpretation. As though Kafka's Sisyphean labours would have been necessary, as though the maelstrom force of his work could be explained, if all he had to say was that man had lost the possibility of salvation or that the way to the absolute is barred, that man's life is dark, confused, or, in currently fashionable terminology, 'suspended in nothingness', and that the only alternative left is for him to do his duty, humbly and without great aspirations, and to integrate himself into a collective which expects just this and which Kafka would not have had to affront had he been of one mind with it. To qualify such an interpretation by arguing that Kafka of course did not say this in so many words but rather worked as an artist with realistic symbolism is to admit a dissatisfaction with formulas but not much more. For an artistic representation is either realistic or symbolic; no matter how densely organized the symbols may be, their own degree of reality cannot detract from the symbolic character. Goethe's play, *Pandora*, is no less rich in sensuous depiction than a novel by Kafka, and yet there can be no doubt concerning the symbolism of Goethe's frag-

From *Prisms*. Copyright ©1967 by Theodor W. Adorno. The MIT Press, 1981.

ment, even though the power of the symbols—as with Elpore, who embodies hope—may exceed what was originally intended. If the notion of the
symbol has any meaning whatsoever in aesthetics—and this is far from
certain—then it can only be that the individual moments of the work of art
point beyond themselves by virtue of their interrelations, that their totality
coalesces into meaning. Nothing could be less true of Kafka. Even in a work
such as Goethe's, which plays so profoundly with allegorical moments, these
still relinquish their significance, by virtue of their context, to the thrust of
the whole. In Kafka, however, everything is as hard, defined and distinct as
possible; in this his works resemble the novel of adventure, as described by
James Fenimore Cooper in his preface to *The Red Rover*: 'The true Augustan
age of literature can never exist until works shall be as accurate in their
typography as a "log-book", and as sententious in their matter as a "watch-
bill".' Nowhere in Kafka does there glimmer the aura of the infinite idea;
nowhere does the horizon open. Each sentence is literal and each signifies.
The two moments are not merged, as the symbol would have it, but yawn
apart and out of the abyss between them blinds the glaring ray of fascination.
Here too, in its striving not for symbol but for allegory, Kafka's prose sides
with the outcasts, the protest of his friend notwithstanding. Walter Benjamin rightly defined it as parable. It expresses itself not through expression
but by its repudiation, by breaking off. It is a parabolic system the key to
which has been stolen; yet any effort to make this fact itself the key is bound
to go astray by confounding the abstract thesis of Kafka's work, the obscurity
of the existent, with its substance. Each sentence says 'interpret me', and
none will permit it. Each compels the reaction, 'that's the way it is', and
with it the question, 'where have I seen that before?': the *déjà vu* is
declared permanent. Through the power with which Kafka commands interpretation, he collapses aesthetic distance. He demands a desperate effort of
the allegedly 'disinterested' observer of an earlier time, overwhelms him,
suggesting that far more than his intellectual equilibrium depends on
whether he truly understands; life and death are at stake. Among Kafka's
presuppositions, not the least is that the contemplative relation between text
and reader is shaken to its very roots. His texts are designed not to sustain a
constant distance between themselves and their victim but rather to agitate
his feelings to a point where he fears that the narrative will shoot towards
him like a locomotive in a three-dimensional film. Such aggressive physical
proximity undermines the reader's habit of identifying himself with the
figures in the novel. It is by reason of this principle that surrealism can
rightfully claim him. He is Turandot set down in writing. Anyone who sees
this and does not choose to run away must stick out his head, or rather try to

batter down the wall with it at the risk of faring no better than his predecessors. As in fairy-tales, their fate serves not to deter but to entice. As long as the word has not been found, the reader must be held accountable.

II

Far more than for most other writers, it may be said of Kafka that not *verum* [truth] but *falsum* [untruth] is *index sui* [index of himself]. He himself, however, contributed to the spread of the untruth. His two great novels, *The Castle* and *The Trial*, seem to bear the mark of philosophical theorems, if not in their details then in their general outlines, which despite all intellectual profundity, in no way belie the title given to a collection of Kafka's theoretical writings, 'Reflections on Sin, Pain, Hope and the True Way'. Still, the content of the title is not canonic for the literary work. The artist is not obliged to understand his own art, and there is particular reason to doubt whether Kafka was capable of such understanding. In any case, the aphorisms are hardly equal to his most enigmatic stories and episodes, such as 'Cares of a Family Man' or 'The Bucket Rider'. Kafka's works protected themselves against the deadly aesthetic error of equating the philosophy that an author pumps into a work with its metaphysical substance. Were this so, the work of art would be stillborn; it would exhaust itself in what it says and would not unfold itself in time. To guard against this short-circuit, which jumps directly to the significance intended by the work, the first rule is: take everything literally; cover up nothing with concepts invoked from above. Kafka's authority is textual. Only fidelity to the letter, not oriented understanding, can be of help. In an art that is constantly obscuring and revoking itself, every determinate statement counterbalances the general proviso of indeterminateness. Kafka sought to sabotage this rule when he let it be announced at one point that messages from the castle must not be taken 'literally'. All the same, if one is not to lose all ground on which to stand, one must cling to the fact that at the beginning of *The Trial*, it is said that someone must have been spreading rumours about Josef K., 'for without having done anything wrong, he was arrested one fine morning'. Nor can one throw to the winds the fact that at the beginning of *The Castle*, K. asks 'what village is this that I have wandered into? Is there a castle here?' and hence, cannot possibly have been summoned there. He also knows nothing of Count Westwest, whose name is mentioned only once and who is thought of less and less until he is entirely forgotten, like the Prometheus of one of Kafka's fables, who merges with the rock to which he is chained and is then forgotten. Nevertheless, the principle of literalness, probably a reminiscence

of the Torah exegesis of Jewish tradition, finds support in many of Kafka's
texts. At times, words, metaphors in particular, detach themselves and
achieve a certain autonomy. Josef K. dies 'like a dog', and Kafka reports
the 'Investigations of A Dog'. Upon occasion the literalness is driven to the
point of a pun. Thus, in the story of Barnabas' family in *The Castle*, the
official, Sortini, is described as having remained 'at the nozzle' during the
Fire Department party. The colloquial German expression for devotion to
duty is taken seriously, the respectable person stays at the nozzle of the
fire-hose, and simultaneously an allusion is made, as in parapraxes, to the
crude desire which drives the functionary to write the fateful letter to
Amalia—Kafka, disparager of psychology, is abundantly rich in psychological insights, such as that into the relation between instinctual and
obsessive personality. Without the principle of literalness as criterion, the
ambiguities of Kafka would dissolve into indifferent equivalence. This
principle, however, invalidates the most commonly held conception of the
author, one which seeks to unite in him the claim to profundity with
equivocation. Cocteau rightly pointed out that the introduction of anything startling in the form of a dream invariably removes its sting. It was
to prevent such misuse that Kafka himself interrupted *The Trial* at a decisive point with a dream—he published the truly horrifying piece in *A
Country Doctor*—and by contrast confirmed the reality of everything else,
even if it should be that dream-reality suggested periodically in *The Castle*
and *Amerika* by passages so agonizingly drawn out that they leave the
reader gasping for air. Among the moments of shock, not the least results
from the fact that Kafka takes dreams *à la lettre*. Because everything that
does not resemble the dream and its pre-logical logic is excluded, the
dream itself is excluded. It is not the horrible which shocks, but its self-
evidence. No sooner has the surveyor driven the bothersome assistants from
his room in the inn than they climb back through the window without the
novel stopping for one word more than required to communicate the event;
the hero is too tired to drive them away again. The attitude that Kafka
assumes towards dreams should be the reader's towards Kafka. He should
dwell on the incommensurable, opaque details, the blind spots. The fact
that Leni's fingers are connected by a web, or that the executioners resemble tenors, is more important than the Excursus on the law. It is true
both of the mode of representation and of the language. Gestures often
serve as counterpoints to words: the pre-linguistic that eludes all intention
upsets the ambiguity, which, like a disease, has eaten into all signification
in Kafka. "'The letter," began K., "I have read it. Do you know the
contents?" "No," said Barnabas, whose look seemed to imply more than his

words. Perhaps K. was as mistaken in Barnabas' goodness as in the malice of the peasants, but his presence remained a comfort.' Or: ' "Well," she said extenuatingly, "there was a reason for laughing. You asked if I knew Klamm, and you see I"—here she involuntarily straightened up a little, and her triumphant glance, which had no connection whatever with what she was saying, swept over K.—"I am his mistress." ' Or in the scene of Frieda's parting from the surveyor:

> Frieda had let her head fall on K's shoulder; their arms round each other, they walked silently up and down. "If we had only," said Frieda after a while, slowly, quietly, almost serenely, as if she knew that only a very short respite of peace on K's shoulder was reserved for her and she wanted to enjoy it to the utmost, "If we had only gone away somewhere at once that night, we might be in peace now, always together, your hand always near enough for mine to grasp; oh, how much I need your companionship, how lost I have felt without it ever since I've known you! To have your company, believe me, is the only dream I've had, that and nothing else."

Such gestures are the traces of experiences covered over by signification. The most recent state of a language that wells up in the mouths of those who speak it, the second Babylonian confusion, which Kafka's sober diction tirelessly opposes, compels him to invert the historical relation of concept and gesture. The gesture is the 'that's the way it is'; language, the configuration of which should be truth, is, as a broken one, untruth. ' "Also you should be far more reticent, nearly everything you have just said could have been implied in your behaviour with the help of a word here and there, and in any case does not redound particularly to your credit." ' The experiences sedimented in the gestures will eventually have to be followed by interpretation, one which recognizes in their mimesis a universal which has been repressed by sound common sense. In the scene of K's arrest at the beginning of *The Trial*, there is the following passage: 'Through the open window, he had another glimpse of the old woman who with genuine senile inquisitiveness had moved along to the window exactly opposite, in order to see all that could be seen.' Is there anyone who has lived in boarding-houses and has not felt himself observed by the neighbours in precisely the same manner; together with the repulsive, the familiar, the unintelligible and the inevitable, such a person has seen the image of fate suddenly light up. The reader who succeeds in solving such rebuses will understand more of Kafka than all those who find in him ontology illustrated.

III

Here one may object that an interpretation can no more rely on this than on anything else in Kafka's deranged cosmos, that such experiences are nothing but contingent and private psychological projections. Anyone who believes that the neighbours are watching him from their windows or that the telephone speaks to him with its own singing voice—and Kafka's writing teems with such statements—is suffering from delusions of persecution and of relation, and anyone who seeks to make a kind of system out of such things has been infected by the paranoia; for such a person Kafka's works serve solely to rationalize his own psychological injuries. This objection can be answered only through reflection on the relation of Kafka's work itself to the zone of psychology. His words, 'for the last time, psychology', are well known as is his remark that everything of his could be interpreted psycho-analytically except that this interpretation would in turn require further interpretation *ad indefinitum*; yet neither such verdicts, nor the venerable haughtiness which is the most recent ideological defence of materialism, should tempt one to accept the thesis that Kafka has nothing to do with Freud. It would be a bad sign for his much praised profundity if one refused to acknowledge what exists in those depths. In their conception of hierarchy, Kafka and Freud are hardly to be distinguished. In *Totem and Taboo*, Freud writes:

> A king's taboo is too strong for his subject because the social difference between them is too great. But a minister may serve as a harmless intermediary between them. Transposed from the language of taboo into that of normal psychology this means the following: the subject, who fears the great temptation involved in contact with the king, can still tolerate dealings with an official whom he does not need to envy so much and whose position may even appear within his grasp. The minister, however, can temper his envy of the king by considering the power which he has been allotted. Thus smaller differences in the magical power leading to temptation are less to be feared than particularly great ones.

In *The Trial*, a high official says: 'Not even I can bear the sight of even the third door-keeper', and there are analagous moments in *The Castle*. This also sheds light on a decisive complex in Proust, snobbism as the will to soothe the dread of the taboo by winning acceptance among the initiates: 'For it was not just Klamm's proximity as such that was worth striving for but rather the fact that it was he, K., only he, no one else with his wish or with any other, who approached Klamm, not in order to rest with him but rather to pass beyond him, farther, into the castle.' The expression, *délire de toucher* [temptation to touch], which Freud cites and which is equally germane to the sphere of the taboo, exactly describes the sexual magic that drives people together in Kafka, especially those of lower social station with those of a higher class. Even the 'temptation' suspected by Freud—that of murdering the father-figure—is alluded to in Kafka. At the conclusion of the chapter in *The Castle* in which the landlady explains to the surveyor that it is utterly impossible for him to speak with Herr Klamm in person, he has the last word: ' "Well, what are you afraid of? You're surely not afraid for Klamm, are you?" The landlady gazed silently after him as he ran down the stairs with the assistants following.' To come closest to understanding the relation between the explorer of the unconscious and the parabolist of impenetrability, one must remember that Freud conceived of an archetypal scene such as the murder of the primal father, a pre-historical narrative such as that of Moses, or the young child's observation of its parents having sexual relations, not as products of the imagination but in large measure as real events. In such eccentricities Kafka follows Freud with the devotion of a Till Eulenspiegel to the limits of absurdity. He snatches psychoanalysis from the grasp of psychology. Psychoanalysis itself is already in a certain sense opposed to' the specifically psychological inasmuch as it derives the individual from amorphous and diffuse drives, the Ego from the Id. Personality is transformed from something substantial into a mere organizational principle of somatic impulses. In Freud as in Kafka the validity of the soul is excluded; Kafka, indeed, took virtually no notice of it from the very beginning. He distinguishes himself from the far older, scientifically inclined Freud, not through a more delicate spirituality but rather through a scepticism towards the Ego which, if anything, exceeds that of Freud. This is the function of Kafka's literalness. As though conducting an experiment, he studies what would happen if the results of psychoanalysis were to prove true not merely metaphorically but in the flesh. He accepts psychoanalysis in so far as it convicts civilization and bourgeois individuation of their illusoriness; he explodes it by taking it more exactly at its word than it does itself. According to Freud, psychoanalysis devotes its attention to the 'dregs of the world of appearances'. He is thinking of psychic phenomena, parapraxes, dreams and neurotic symptoms. Kafka sins against an ancient rule of the game by constructing art out of nothing but the refuse of reality. He does not directly outline the image of the society to come—for in his as in all great art, asceticism towards the future prevails—but rather depicts it as a montage composed of waste-products which the new order, in the process of forming itself, extracts from the perishing present. Instead of curing neurosis, he seeks in it itself the healing force, that of knowledge: the wounds with which society brands the individual are seen by the latter as ciphers of the social untruth, as the negative of truth. His power is one of demolition. He tears down the soothing facade to which a repressive reason increasingly conforms. In the process of demolition—never was the word more popular than in the year of Kafka's death—he does not stop at the subject as does psychology, but drives through to the bare material existence that emerges in the subjective sphere through the total collapse of a submissive consciousness, divested of all self-assertion. The flight through man and beyond into the non-human—that is Kafka's epic course. The decline of genius, the spasmodic lack of resistance which so completely converges with Kafka's morality, is paradoxically rewarded by the compelling authority of its expression. Such a posture, relaxed virtually to the breaking point, is heir to what was formerly metaphor, significance, mind, and it inherits it as though it were a physical reality of its own, as 'spiritual body'. It is as though the philosophical doctrine of the 'categorical intuition', which was becoming well known at the time that Kafka wrote, were to be honoured in hell. The windowless monad preserves itself as the magic lantern, mother of all images as in Proust and Joyce. That above which individuation lifts itself, what it conceals and what it drove from itself, is common to all but can only be grasped in solitude and undistracted concentration. To fully participate in the process that produces the abnormal experiences which in Kafka define the norm, one must have experienced an accident in a large city; uncounted witnesses come forward, proclaiming themselves acquaintances, as though the entire community had gathered to observe the moment when the powerful bus smashed into the flimsy taxicab. The permanent *déjà vu* is the *déjà vu* of all. This is the source of Kafka's success, which becomes betrayal only when the universal is distilled from his writings and the labours of deadly seclusion avoided. Perhaps the hidden aim of his art as a whole is the manageability, technification, collectivization of the *déjà vu*. The best, which is forgotten, is remembered and imprisoned in a bottle like the Cumaean sibyll. Except that in the process it changes into the worst: 'I want to die', and that is denied it. Made eternal, the transient is overtaken by a curse.

IV

Eternalized gestures in Kafka are the momentaneous brought to a standstill. The shock is like a surrealistic arrangement of that which old photographs convey to the viewer. Such a snapshot, unclear, almost entirely faded, plays its rôle in *The Castle*. The landlady shows K. a photograph she has kept as a relic of her contact with Klamm and through him with the hierarchy. Only with difficulty can K. recognize anything on it. Yesterday's gaudy tableaux, drawn from the sphere of the circus—for which Kafka, with the avantgarde of his generation, felt an affinity—are frequently introduced into his work; perhaps everything was originally supposed to become a tableau and only an excess of intention prevented this, through long dialogues. Anything that balances on the pinnacle of the moment like a horse on its hindlegs is snapped, as though the pose ought to be preserved forever. The most gruesome example of this is probably to be found in *The Trial*: Josef K. opens the lumber-room, in which his warders had been beaten a day earlier, to find the scene faithfully repeated, including the appeal to himself. 'At once K. slammed the door shut and then beat on it with his fists, as if that would shut it still more securely.' This is the gesture of Kafka's own work, which—as Poe had already begun to do—turns away from the most extreme scenes as though no eye could survive the sight. In it what is perpetually the same and what is ephemeral merge. Over and over again, Titorelli paints that monotonous genre picture, the heath. The sameness or intriguing similarity of a variety of objects is one of Kafka's most persistent motifs; all possible demi-creatures step forward in pairs, often marked by the childish and the silly, oscillating between affability and cruelty like savages in children's books. Individuation has become such a burden for men and has remained so precarious, that they are mortally frightened whenever its veil is raised a little. Proust was familiar with the shiver of discomfort that comes over someone who has been made aware of his resemblance to an unknown relative. In Kafka, this becomes panic. The realm of the *déjà vu* is populated by doubles, *revenants*, buffoons, Hasidic dancers, boys who ape their teachers and then suddenly appear ancient, archaic; at one point, the surveyor wonders whether his assistants are fully alive. Yet there are also images of what is coming, men manufactured on the assembly-line, mechanically reproduced copies, Huxleyian Epsilons. The social origin of the individual ultimately reveals itself as the power to annihilate him. Kafka's work is an attempt to absorb this. There is nothing mad in his prose, unlike the writer from whom he learned decisively, Robert Walser; every sentence has been shaped by a mind in full control of itself; yet, at the same time, every sentence has been snatched from the zone of insanity into which all knowledge must venture if it is to become such in an age when sound common sense only reinforces universal blindness. The hermetic principle has, among others, the function of a protective measure: it keeps out the onrushing delusion, which would mean, however, its own collectivization. The work that shatters individuation will at no price want to be imitated; for this reason, surely, Kafka gave orders for it to be destroyed. No tourist trade was to blossom where it had gone; yet anyone who imitated its gestures without having been there would be guilty of pure effrontery in attempting to pocket the excitement and power of alienation without the risk. The result would be impotent affectation. Karl Kraus, and to a certain extent Schoenberg, reacted much like Kafka in this respect. Yet such inimitability also affects the situation of the critic. Confronted by Kafka his position is no more enviable than that of the disciple; it is, in advance, an apology for the world. Not that there is nothing to criticize in Kafka's work. Among the defects, which become obvious in the great novels, monotony is the most striking. The presentation of the ambiguous, uncertain, inaccessible, is repeated endlessly, often at the expense of the vividness that is always sought. The bad infinity of the matter represented spreads to the work of art. This fault may well reflect one in the content, a preponderance of the abstract idea, itself the myth that Kafka attacks. The portrayal seeks to make the uncertain still more uncertain but provokes the question, why the effort? If everything is questionable to begin with, then why not restrict oneself to the given minimum? Kafka would have replied that it was just this hopeless effort that he demanded, much as Kierkegaard sought to irritate the reader through his diffuseness and thus startle him out of aesthetic contemplation. Discussions concerning the virtues and deficiencies of such literary tactics are so fruitless because criticism can address itself only to that in a work wherein it seeks to be exemplary; where it says, 'as I am, so shall it be'. But precisely this claim is rejected by Kafka's disconsolate 'that's the way it is'. Nevertheless, at times the power of the images he conjures up cracks through their protective covering. Several subject the reader's selfawareness, to say nothing of the author, to a severe test: 'In the Penal Colony' and 'The Metamorphosis', reports which had to await those of Bettelheim, Kogon and Rousset for their equals, much as the bird's eye photos of bombed-out cities redeemed, as it were, Cubism, by realizing that through which the latter broke with reality. If there is hope in Kafka's work, it is in those extremes rather than in the milder phases: in the capacity to stand up to the worst by making it into language. Are these, then, the works which offer the key to an interpretation? There are grounds to think so. In 'The Metamorphosis', the path of the experience can be reconstructed from the literalness as an extension of the lines. 'These travelling salesmen are like bugs', is the German expression that Kafka must have picked up, speared up like an insect. Bugs—not *like* bugs. What becomes of a man who is a bug as big as a man? As big as adults must appear to the child, and as distorted, with gigantic, trampling legs and far-off, tiny heads, were one to catch and isolate the child's terrified vision; it could be photographed with an oblique camera. In Kafka, an entire lifetime is not enough to reach the next town, and the stoker's ship, the surveyor's inn, are of dimensions so enormous that one would have to return to a long-forgotten past to find a time when man saw his own products similarly. Anyone who desires such vision must transform himself into a child and forget many things. He recognizes his father as the ogre he has always feared in infinitesimal omens; his revulsion against cheese rinds reveals itself as the ignominious, pre-human craving for them. The 'boarders' are visibly shrouded in the horror—their emanation—which hitherto clung almost imperceptibly to the word. Kafka's literary technique fastens onto words as Proust's involuntary recollection does to sensuous objects, only with the opposite results: instead of reflection on the human, the trial run of a model of dehumanization. Its pressure forces the subject into a regression which is, so to speak, biological and which prepares the ground for Kafka's animal parables. The crucial moment, however, towards which everything in Kafka is directed, is that in which men become aware that they are not them-selves—that they themselves are things. The long and fatiguing imageless sections, beginning with the conversation with the father in 'The Judge-ment', serve the purpose of demonstrating to men what no image could, their unidentity, the complement of their copylike similarity. The lesser motives, conclusively demonstrated to the surveyor by the landlady and then also by Frieda, are alien to him—Kafka brilliantly anticipated the concept of the Ego-alien later developed by psychoanalysis. But the surveyor admits these motives. His individual and his social character are split as widely as in Chaplin's *Monsieur Verdoux*: Kafka's hermetic memoranda contain the social genesis of schizophrenia.

DORRIT COHN

Kafka's Eternal Present: Narrative Tense in "A Country Doctor"

One of the salient stylistic features in Kafka's first-person stories is his tendency to use the grammatical present as a narrative tense. The little sketch entitled "Home-Coming" will serve as an initial example. Its speaker is returning to his parental home after an unspecified absence: ["I have returned, I have passed under the arch and am looking around. It's my father's old yard. The puddle in the middle. Old, useless tools, jumbled together, block the way to the attic stairs. The cat lurks on the banister." (*Franz Kafka: The Complete Stories*, ed. Nahum N. Glatzer. New York: Schocken Books, 1971, story trans. Tania and James Stern. All further references will be to Stern.)] While the setting recalls the return of the biblical Prodigal, this son, arrested by silent questions, finds himself unable either to enter or depart; he remains on the doorstep, divided by the conflict within himself: ["Do you feel you belong, do you feel at home? I don't know, I feel most uncertain. My father's house it is, but each object stands cold beside the next. . . . What use can I be to them, what do I mean to them, even though I am the son of my father, the farmer. And I don't dare knock at the kitchen door." (Stern)] The unending argument with the self eternalizes the moment of failed return, shapes it into a motionless and poignant tableau. We leave the son as we have found him, immobilized in his threshold stance.

From *PMLA* 83, no. 1 (1968). Copyright © 1968 by the Modern Language Association of America. Originally entitled "Kafka's Eternal Present: Narrative Tense in 'Ein Landarzt' and Other First-Person Stories." Original quotations in German. The editor has substituted published translations, from several works, which are noted in the text. Where necessary for the author's point, the editor has provided literal translations, noted in the text.

This text gives the illusion of capturing the speaker's situation at the moment of experience, and it does so in the only way available to fiction written in the first person: by using the present tense. In contrast to a third-person narrative, a first-person narrative cannot eliminate the temporal distance between the moment of narration and the narrated moment while remaining within the past tense. The "Ich–Ich Schema" [I–I Scheme]—as Franz Stanzel has called the relationship between the recounting (present) and the experiencing (past) self—determines the structure of every *Icher-zählung* [first-person narrative]. Only if these two selves become fused, if the moment of narration coincides with the moment of experience, can a first-person narrative achieve absolute immediacy. By using the present tense, the act of narration is itself short-circuited and therefore becomes unreal; the result is an interior monologue.

However, "Home-Coming" is not a story in the usual acceptance of the term: nothing happens in it, there is no plot, no movement. In this it conforms to the rationale of the inner monologue, which does not readily lend itself to the narration either of outer actions or of the speaker's own activities, and the monologue therefore most successfully renders the consciousness within a body at rest. It is not fortuitous that the most famous interior monologue in literature, Molly Bloom's, takes place in bed. Kafka's bodies, never relaxed, are immobilized in suspension, while the mind is caught in an irresolvable and endlessly extended silent argument.

A number of Kafka's first-person fictions (some as brief as "Home-Coming," others considerably longer) are written entirely in the present tense: "A Little Woman," "My Neighbor," "The Burrow," "A Crossbreed [A Sport]," and others. Though they sometimes take on a communicative tone, they are essentially soliloquies describing their speakers trapped in a lasting, insoluble situation, or an unalterable impasse. They present static dilemmas or viciously circular altercations with the powers that be.

There is another group of Kafka's first-person stories ("The Bridge," "Jackals and Arabs," "The Vulture," and others) which are told entirely in the past tense. The incidents that they relate are marked by their total and at times fatal finality, they are *faits accomplis* that lie in the past. But more often, Kafka is drawn to unfinished dramas, which are essentially timeless and inconclusive. These texts contain surprising tense changes in midstream, and they are particularly interesting from the viewpoint of their narrative style. The mutations are invariably from past to present, and (with one notable exception in "A Country Doctor" which we will consider later) once the change to the present has been made, the new tense is maintained to the end.

One of the most instructive pieces for this stylistic process is entitled "Advocates." It tells of a man who searches for advocates in the corridors of an unknown building. The text begins in the preterite: ["I was not at all certain whether I had any advocates, I could not find out anything definite about it, every face was unfriendly, most people who came toward me and whom I kept meeting in the corridors looked like fat old women." (Stern)] It soon turns out that these absent advocates are not needed to plead a legal case in an ordinary court of laws, that this building, in fact, is not a courthouse at all. But the need and search for advocates therefore only becomes more urgent: ["Yet if it were not a law court, why was I searching for an advocate here? Because I was searching for an advocate everywhere; he is needed everywhere, if anything less in court than elsewhere, for a court, one assumes, passes judgment according to the law." (Stern)] We notice the shift to the present tense (["he is needed everywhere"]), as the narrator begins to reflect about his—apparently past—predicament. A page of general speculations (which continue to concern *man* [one] rather than *ich* [I]) follows; they establish the overwhelming necessity of advocates, not to defend one in a specific trial, but to protect one against perennial accusation in a world filled with foxy prosecutors. When the speaker returns from this generalization to his particular case, one would expect a return to the past tense of the beginning. Instead, Kafka continues in a present tense that now no longer conveys the reflections of the narrating self, but the inner discourse of the experiencing self: ["So look out! That's why I'm here, I'm collecting advocates. But I have not found any as yet, only those old women keep coming and going . . . I'm not in the right place—alas, I cannot rid myself of the feeling that I'm not in the right place." (Stern)] The past has, in a literal sense, *become present*: the speaker is no longer telling a story, but talking to himself. It seems as though he has been overcome by the force of his argumentation, has been convinced that his seemingly momentary (past) predicament is in reality a permanent (and still present) situation.

The subject of the inner debate that now follows is none other than the problem of human time. Since he is in the wrong place, the speaker reflects, why not reverse his course? This possibility meets with categorical resistance: to turn back is to admit defeat, to lose one's hold on time, and thereby on life itself: ["But back I cannot go, this waste of time, this admission of having been on the wrong track would be unbearable for me. What? Run downstairs in this brief, hurried life accompanied as it is by that impatient droning? Impossible. The time alloted to you is so short that if you lose one second you have already lost your whole life, for it is no longer, it is just as long as the time you lose." (Stern)] Life and time are irreversible: the continued pursuit of the false course, the persistence in the doomed search, is also the refusal to die. Therefore, as long as life continues, the past course of action continues into the present time. And the story ends in a crescendo of admonitions not to end the endless search: ["So if you find nothing in the corridors open the doors, if you find nothing behind these doors there are more floors, and if you find nothing up there, don't worry, just leap up another flight of steps. As long as you don't stop climbing, the stairs won't end, under your climbing feet they will go on growing upwards." (Stern)]

We must not mistake the present tense at the end of this story for a historical present (frequently used by writers for an intensification of the action): it does not refer to past time, but to the speaker's present moment, and it is a direct grammatical signal for the story's open ending. It signifies that the speaker's past experience is his present plight, that it ends in infinite regress. We may therefore take the change of tenses here as a stylistic corollary of a belief Kafka once expressed in the aphorism: ["The decisive moment in human evolution is perpetual." (*Dearest Father: Stories and Other Writings*, trans. Ernst Kaiser and Eithne Wilkins. New York: Schocken Books, 1954.)]

"A Country Doctor" displays an even more unusual tense structure. It starts like any traditional first-person story: ["I was in great perplexity; I had to start on an urgent journey; a seriously ill patient was waiting for me in a village ten miles off." (*Franz Kafka: the Complete Stories*, ed. Nahum N. Glatzer, story trans. Willa and Edwin Muir. All further references will be to Muir.)] Here a narrator relates a past experience by using the customary past tense. He tells of his horseless plight and of the inexplicable emergence of groom and horses from the pigsty, to his own and his servant Rosa's surprise and delight. But before long (at the beginning of the second page of the text), the tense changes to the present in mid-sentence: [" 'Give him a hand,' I said, and the willing girl hurried to help the groom with the harnessing. Yet hardly was she beside him when the groom *clipped hold of* (literally: *umfasst, clips hold of*) her and *pushed* (literally: *schlägt, pushes*) his face against hers. She screamed and fled back to me." (Muir)] (I italicize the shift to the present). For the next five pages, the present tense is used continuously; we hear about the country doctor's unwilling departure from home, about his instantaneous journey to the house of his patient, about the eventful and contradictory bedside visit, which ends with the conversation (quoted in direct discourse) between doctor and patient, and the former's word of honor concerning the distinction of the condemned boy's wound: ["It is really so, take the word of honor of an official doctor." (Muir)] In the next sentence, the text returns to the past tense of the beginning of the story: ["And he took it and lay still. But now it was time for me to think of escaping." (Muir)] The doctor's intended return-salvation, frustrated by the slow motion of the horses (["slowly, like old men, we crawled through the snowy wastes" (Muir)], continues into infinite time, and the story ends by returning to the present tense, now no longer narrating events, but describing a wretchedly stationary and eternal condition: ["Never shall I reach home at this rate . . . Naked, exposed to the frost of this most unhappy of ages, with an earthly vehicle, unearthly horses, old man that I am, I wander astray . . . Betrayed! Betrayed! A false alarm on the night bell once answered—it cannot be made good, not ever." (Muir)] In sum, a long present-tense passage, framed by two much briefer past-tense passages, forms the body of the story, a brief present tense forms the epilogue.

If, for a moment, we disregard the switch to the present within the body of the story, the past-present relationship of body to epilogue corresponds to a standard temporal structure of the first-person narrative: the present, narrating self looks back on the past, experiencing self. All traditional *Ichgeschichten* [first-person narratives], as we have seen above, imply these two temporal planes. The present-past relationship often becomes explicit in the image of the aged narrator who writes or tells the memoirs of his youth (see, for example the ending of *David Copperfield* or *Doktor Faustus*). In Kafka's own writings, such late stories as "A Report to an Academy" and "Investigations of a Dog," notwithstanding their irony, conform to this fictional archetype. The only difference in "A Country Doctor" is that his story is not recollected in tranquillity. The classic image of the old man sitting at his desk composing his memoirs has been radically modified: Kafka's hero is not an old man at peace; he will, most likely, not die in bed, it is indeed questionable whether he will die at all. Suspended in a hopeless and unbearable limbo, between life and death, his final situation is projected into an unending future: "*Niemals komme ich so nach Hause . . .*" ["Never shall I reach home at this rate . . ."] The polarity *einmal-jetzt* [once-now] has been replaced by *einmal-niemals* [once-never].

A number of Kafka's other first-person stories follow this *einmal-niemals* dialectic, in which faulty actions or responses lead to eternal punishment. We have already seen one version of this pattern in "Advocates." In "The Knock at the Manor Gate," his sister's possible tap on the gate results in the narrator's arrest by the powers of the village. The past narrative ends as the narrator is led into a room which ominously resembles torture chamber and prison cell. The final sentence through its shift to the present (and to the contrary-to-fact present conditional) simultaneously reveals the present situation of the narrator and the outcome of the proceedings against him: ["Could I still endure any other air than prison air? That is the great question, or rather it would be if I still had any prospect of release." (Muir)]

In "The Hunter Gracchus," as the mythical hunter tells his tale, we find the past-present, *einmal-niemals* pattern of "A Country Doctor" and "The Knock at the Manor Gate," revealed, this time, in its essential meaning:

> ["Many years ago, yes, it must be a great many years ago, I fell from a precipice in the Black Forest—that is in Germany—when I was hunting a chamois. Since then I have been dead."
>
> "But you are alive too," said the Burgomaster.
>
> "In a certain sense," said the Hunter, "in a certain sense I am alive too. My death ship lost its way; a wrong turn of the wheel, a moment's absence of mind on the pilot's part, the distraction of my lovely native country, I cannot tell what it was; I only know this, that I remained on earth and that ever since my ship has sailed (literally: *befährt*, is sailing) earthly waters." (Muir)]

The hunter Gracchus, it turns out, is the man who cannot die. Death, as the French critic Maurice Blanchot has shown, becomes an ambiguous factor in Kafka's world, and his heroes are often deprived of this final salvation. While "The Hunter Gracchus" is explicit about this deprivation, the country doctor's journey through the snow, as the brother's sojourn in the prison chamber of "The Knock at the Manor Gate" and the regressive ascent of the staircases in "Advocates," are parallel images for this state of life without death. The present tense used by these ghostly narrators is the grammatical signal for their unrelieved survival, a "caricature of immortality," to borrow a term Geoffrey Hartman applied to the Wandering Jew and his present-day progeny.

The grammatical present at the end of "A Country Doctor," then, signifies the present moment of narration from which the first-person narrator views his past experiences in retrospect. We would therefore expect him to describe these experiences in the past tense. And the fact is that he uses this tense in the beginning of his account, and again at its end, where it serves as a necessary reminder of the essential temporal relationship within the story. The long, intervening present-tense passage, however, seems to confound this logical arrangement. It is interesting to note that Willa and Edwin Muir, Kafka's English translators, have either not noticed this use of the present, or have found it too puzzling for literal translation; in any event, they have simply rendered the entire body of the story in the past—with the exception of three brief moments when the country doctor clearly engages in general observations—and have reserved the present tense for the epilogue. Many close readers of "A Country Doctor" (which is among the three or four most assiduously exegised Kafka texts) seem to be equally unaware of its unusual tense structure. I would suggest, however, that the incongruity and complexity that have generally been sensed in this story, and that have most usually been attributed to the multivalence of its meanings and to the contradictory quality of its images, are compounded by the difficulties arising from its tense structure.

It is obviously insufficient to see the use of the present tense in the major portion of "A Country Doctor" merely as a means of heightening the tension or of achieving greater vividness in the narration. To be sure, this is the effect most usually attributed to the narrative present, but its effectiveness quickly wears off when used too extensively. In this story the present-tense section is much too lengthy to allow for this interpretation; nor is it possible to find a correlation between tense and intensity of feeling, for the emotional pitch is unrelieved throughout. A careful examination of the text will show that the present was probably not preferred on account of its merits as a narrative tense, but because it is the tense of the interior monologue.

When the speaker begins—in mid-sentence at the beginning of the second page—to use the grammatical present, the altered tense, initially, merely serves to continue the narration. The speaker's thoughts are at first reported in the form of direct or indirect discourse, using *verba dicendi* to introduce them: *"besinne mich . . . dass er ein Fremder ist; dass ich nicht weiss woher er kommt"* [I remind myself that he is a stranger, that I do not know where he comes from (ed.)]; *" 'Ja,' denke ich lästernd, 'in solchen Fällen helfen die Götter' "* ["Yes," I think blasphemously, "in cases like this the gods are helpful" (ed.)]; *" 'Ich fahre gleich wieder zurück,' denke ich"* ["Better go back at once," I think (ed.)]. The outer events do not impinge directly on the speaker's consciousness, but are reported by such verbs as *"Ich höre . . . ich sehe"* [I hear . . . I see]. Adverbs of time (*jetzt, dann, gleich, noch, schon, kaum* [now, then, simultaneously, still, already, hardly]) indicate the narrative sequence, and they are particularly numerous on the first page that uses the present tense. But as the text proceeds, it becomes more and more frequently interlaced with interior monologue passages. Though a brief snatch of self-address already interrupts the past tense on the first page (["of course, who is going to lend a horse at this time for such a journey" (ed.)]), it is only on the third page that the first longer inner monologue appears: ["what do I do now, how do I rescue her, how do I pull her away from under that groom at ten miles' distance, with a team of uncontrollable horses" (ed.)].

From here on, narration and interior monologue alternate constantly, as, for example, in the passage where the doctor, having discovered the patient's wound, begins to scrutinize it closely:

> [But on a closer inspection there was another complication. *I could not help* (literally: *Wer kann das ansehen, ohne,* who can behold it without) *a low whistle of surprise.* Worms, as thick and long as my little finger, themselves rose-red and blood-spotted as well, were wriggling from their fastness in the interior of the wound toward the light, with small white heads and many little legs. *Poor boy, you were* (literally: *ist,* are) *past helping. I had discovered* (literally: *habe aufgefunden,* have discovered) *your great wound; this blossom in your side was destroying you* (literally: *gehst du zugrunde,* is destroying you). The family was pleased (literally: *ist glücklich,* is pleased); they saw (literally: *sie sieht,* it sees) me busying myself; the sister told (literally: *sagt's,* tells) the mother, the mother the father, the father told (no verb in the German) several guests who were coming in, through the moonlight at the open door, walking on tiptoe, keeping their balance with outstretched arms. "Will you save me?" whispered (literally: *flüstert,* whispers) the boy with a sob, quite blinded by the life within his wound. *That is what people are like in my district. Always expecting the impossible from the doctor. They have lost their ancient beliefs; the parson sits at home and unravels his vestments, one after another; but the doctor is supposed to be omnipotent with his merciful surgeon's hand. Well, as it pleases them; I have not thrust my services on them; if they misuse me for sacred ends, I let that happen to me too; what better do I want, old country doctor that I am, bereft of my servant girl!* And so they came (literally: *kommen,* come), the family and the village elders, and stripped (literally: *entkleiden,* strip) my clothes off me. . . .
>
>   (Muir)]

In the preceding quotation, I have italicized the passages that I take to be the doctor's soliloquy. But they cannot always be clearly distinguished from the narrative passages, since there are no syntactical distinctions: no change in grammatical person, no tense shift, no verbs of saying, no quotation marks. The only way to tell narration from inner monologue is by tone: the former is marked by meticulous quasi-objective description (of the wound and the gestures of the family), the latter by its emotional, exclamatory, argumentative rhetoric. The italicized passages also momentarily express general reflections of the kind a narrator might use to explain the happenings to an audience (["that is what people are like in my district," "but the doctor is supposed to be omnipotent"]), but these immediately give way again to the cantankerous silent argument (["Always expecting the impossible from the doctor," "Well, as it pleases them; I have not thrust my sevices on them"]). The inner discourse is connected with the next outer event by the simplest coordinating conjunction: ["And so they came (come)"].

The outer happenings are entangled with the speaker's thoughts to a point where they seem at times to be anticipated or determined by them; the village elders sacrifice the doctor to the patient only at the moment when he becomes plaintively resigned to his fate (["what better do I want"]). Walter Sokel has shown how this pattern is repeated throughout "A Country Doctor": ["The psychical attitude precedes the factual circumstances and primarily determines them." (ed.)] The story therefore demanded an effacing of the demarcation between outer events and inner reflections, in order to achieve a rapid, fluctuating interplay between the two realms. This interplay could not have been achieved nearly so well if the tense had changed between reflection and event. Only by adopting the tense of the interior monologue for the narration itself could this single flow of the language be achieved.

But the narration in the present tense achieves a second, no less important result: it seemingly eliminates the temporal distance between the narrating and the experiencing self, momentarily giving the illusion that the speaker recounts his tale as it unfolds, with no foreknowledge of the future. ["I will open the window" (ed.)], the doctor announces as he enters the stuffy sickroom; but actual events belie this statement of future action: not he, but the horses open the window, defying all natural laws, ["I don't know how, from outside" (ed.)]. No hindsight clarifies the obscure events; their unpredictable, incomprehensible succession negates every momentary insight. The immediacy of the interior monologue thus renders the baffling inconsequence of the events in a manner that would have been impossible in a retrospective view.

But in order to attain this dual purpose of immediacy and simultaneity, Kafka has had to pay a heavy price. For if we focus for a moment on this intermixture of reportage and inner thought, we find that it implies a hybrid, essentially illogical narrative situation, marked by two important contradictions: (1) When events are reported, the present is used as a narrative tense, assuming the telling of the story to potential or actual listeners. But when we get the doctor's interior discourse, the same tense is used for a non-narrative situation, in which words are used to communicate with no one but the self. These two mutually exclusive verbal gestures are fused into a continuous idiom in the text; (2) in the narrating passages, the present assumes past meaning, determined (as we have seen) by the use of the preterite in the beginning and at the end of the story's body. Like all narrative presents, it is merely a "metaphor" for the past tense, a "stylistic transposition" in which events known to be past are told *as if* they were present. In other words, it refers in the present to the speaker's past. In the interior monologue passages, on the other hand, the present tense refers to the speaker's present moment, it is (in this sense) a *true,* not a metaphorical *as if* present. And again, these two contradictory temporal references alternate within a unified current of language.

In his other first-person stories, Kafka avoided these difficulties, either by using the present tense throughout (as in "Home-Coming"), or by choosing to tell the story from an eternally present vantage point, and using the past tense for past events (as in "The Knock at the Manor Gate"). He chose the former when he wished to emphasize the psychic struggle within an everlasting predicament, the latter when he was more interested in telling of the calamity or mistaken action that led to this predicament. The basic tense structure (its *einmal-niemals* pattern) assigns "A Country Doctor" to the second of these two general types; but Kafka tried to inject it into the stylistic resources of the first type, to achieve within the past situation the spontaneity of the present-tense speaker and his interior monologue. It remained an isolated experiment.

We have no reason to suppose that Kafka was aware of the lack of logic in the narrative situation of "A Country Doctor," nor, for that matter, that he generally gave much thought to the differences between the uses of the first and the third person in fiction. But the fact remains that he wrote his three novels and most of his novellas in third-person form. What is more, the manuscript of *The Castle* bears witness that Kafka began to write his novel as an *Icherzählung* and, at a certain point of the composition, proceeded to change all the *Ich*s to *K*s. This fact has generally been used by Kafka's critics to prove the irrelevance of the distinction between third and first person in his writings. I would maintain that the opposite inference would be more logical: since Kafka bothered to make these changes, he must have sensed that the first-person form was not ideally suited for the particular purposes of his novel. Our analysis of his first-person stories provides a possible clue for this generic problem.

We have seen that Kafka has recourse to the present tense in first-person texts in order to convey the speaker's situation at the moment of experience, or else to show his psyche entrapped in an eternally present predicament. These designs are inhibited by the use of the past tense in an *Ichgeschichte,* because the related scene necessarily appears in its pastness, seen through the perspective of its reminiscing speaker. The same is not true for the past tense within the third-person form. If the author limits his angle of vision entirely to the perspective of one of his characters, the fictional world is seen through the latter's thoughts and sensations. This character's vantage point in time and space becomes the reader's own, and the past tense of narration loses its past meaning. Moreover, the impersonated viewpoint enables a novelist to weave in and out of a fictional consciousness by using the narrated monologue (or *erlebte Rede*) technique, without interrupting the flow of narration and without changing either tense or person. The internal angle of vision within a third-person idiom thus offered Kafka the advantages he seems to have sought by shifting to the present tense in "A Country Doctor," without the incongruities we pointed to in its narrative structure.

Kafka took full advantage of this mode of narration in *The Castle* and the other major narratives. This fact has been recognized and emphasized by such critics as Beissner, Walser, and Sokel, and linked, particularly by Walser, to the resultant "Gegenwärtigkeit [present situation]" of his novels. But it has not been clearly realized that the same illusion of present time could not have been attained if Kafka had told his novels in the *Ich*-form and the customary narrative preterite. I would suggest therefore that the radical change Kafka effected in the manuscript of *The Castle* was inspired by his desire to eliminate distance in time between narration and experience. Its mutation from the first to the third person would thus be analogous to Kafka's propensity for shifting to the present tense in his shorter first-person pieces.

HEINRICH HENEL

"The Burrow," or How to Escape from a Maze

Franz Kafka's "The Burrow" was written in the year before his death and is one of his last works. Like all his stories of any length, it deals with many subjects and touches upon many more, but two major subjects can be identified. The problem of securing one's life is the main concern of the first part of the story, while the question of how to live or to enjoy one's life forms the main concern of the second. The story is told by an animal who has built himself an elaborate burrow. In the first part he wonders just how safe the burrow is, in the second he worries about a noise which disturbs its peace. Both parts begin with contentment and end with perplexity and fear. In the opening sentence the animal, echoing the Lord in Genesis, declares that his creation is good, but he goes on to find one fault after another in his castle and to make—and reject—numerous plans for its improvement. Similarly at the beginning of the second part, when the animal returns from an excursion to the outside world, he greets his burrow with a joyous outburst of almost lyrical intensity, but soon is troubled by a mysterious hissing or whistling whose source he cannot establish. It should be noted, however, that the two parts (which are of almost equal length) are interdependent. The question of happiness is anticipated in several significant passages of the first, and the question of security is not forgotten in the second half. Thus, for example, only two pages from the beginning of the story the animal comes to realize that the real danger is an unseen foe under the earth and that all his preparations against outside attack are futile—although he continues to make them. Conversely, near the end of the story and long after the animal has decided that his burrow is not primarily a fortress but rather a home, he

119

reproaches himself for having lived in a fool's paradise, wishes he were young and strong enough to improve his defences radically, and even hits upon an entirely new device—provision for landslides to block his tunnels if an intruder appears. Thus, if the progress of the story at first seems to indicate that the animal makes a mistake in trying to be the master of his fate and should concentrate instead on being the captain of his soul, a more careful reading reveals that neither of these goals can be reached exclusive of the other. And since they are both unattainable, nothing is ever settled. The animal himself has flashes of insight in which he admits as much. But he keeps trying.

The disturbing element which undermines both the animal's reliance on his castle and his happiness in it is worry or *Sorge*. It is justified enough, for the world is full of danger. An animal's best weapon against danger is his mind, and Kafka's animal, being unusually intelligent, makes full use of it. An ounce of prevention is worth a pound of cure—that is the principle on which he acts. The trouble with the rational intelligence, however, is that it cannot cope with the contingent. 'Ah,' cries the animal in considering the many threats to his security, 'is there anything that may *not* happen?' And in the second part, when he tries to discover the cause of the hissing, he echoes his exclamation with the rueful sigh: 'The world is complex, and there is never a lack of unpleasant surprises.' Moreover, reasoning is a self-defeating activity because every argument produces a counter-argument. Kafka's sentences are peppered with 'if', 'but', 'yet', 'however', 'indeed', 'to be sure', 'nevertheless', 'on the other hand'. These particles do not negate the preceding observations, they merely qualify them; and since the qualifiers themselves are in turn qualified, the original statements are, at least in part, revalidated. Nothing is totally true or correct, but, on the other hand, nothing is totally false or wrong. What remains is possibilities which, on closer inspection, seem impossible, yet are possibilities after all, for the alternatives seem equally unpromising. This 'but' and 'all the same' style occasionally coagulates into aphorisms such as: 'Some ruses are so subtle that they defeat themselves', and: 'It is precisely caution which, unhappily all too often, demands the risk of one's life.' The grim humour of these comments is so persuasive that one is tempted to search for a similar formula to cover the whole story. Perhaps: 'An animal needs a burrow for his safety, but it is also a trap.' Or: 'A man's home is his castle, but what use is a castle if it is not a home?' Unwittingly almost, the reader who sums up the story in this fashion declares that all the animal does and thinks is paradoxical, and that his paradoxical existence is a parable for man's; and indeed *Parable and Paradox* is the sub-title of one of the best books on the works of Franz Kafka.

But is it really true that peace of mind depends on absolute security? Surely it is possible to withdraw within oneself, to find contentment in one's own company, and to await with equanimity whatever may befall. The Stoics thought so, and there are times when the animal thinks so, too. 'The most beautiful thing about my burrow', he says, 'is the silence.' Repeatedly and emphatically he describes it as quiet and empty. Here he finds peace, here he can play and sleep. The awareness of danger never leaves him, but he does not care; indeed he feels so completely identical with his burrow that he would be willing to be killed here, for his blood would be absorbed by his own soil and would not be lost. If this is so, however, why is he so dreadfully upset by the slight noise which rouses him from sleep and whose cause he tries to find, first in a frenzy of headlong digging, then by putting forth theory after fruitless theory? There are passages where he says that he actually worries more when he is inside the burrow than when he is outside; and there is a sentence—right in the middle of the long passage praising the burrow as a home rather than a mere protective hole—saying that the worries which plague him in his burrow are different, prouder, more weighty, often deeply repressed, but that their destructive effect is perhaps as great as that of the worries caused by life in the open. What these worries are is never said, but the reader is allowed to guess. They materialize in the mysterious hissing, and since it is heard equally clearly in every part of the burrow it must be in the animal himself. It may be his breath, panting from all the running around and digging, but in a deeper sense it is his fear of the void. If he had made the central cave of his burrow completely proof against attack, so the animal says in strange self-delusion, he could listen there with rapture to the murmur of silence. Well, he does hear it, and his reaction is not rapture, but terror. It has been remarked that he mistakes the inner enemy for an external enemy and that his searching and his theorizing are futile because of this mistake. What has not been noticed is the cause of his blindness and the nature of his enemy. He fails to draw the right conclusion not only from the fact that the noise is audible wherever he goes in his burrow, but also from the fact that it is inaudible when he lies at the entrance, just below the surface and under a thin cover of moss. When he is close to the outside world the hissing stops. Silence and emptiness are what frighten him. This is the worry which he has repressed, this is the knowledge which he must never admit to himself, because it would undermine his whole existence, the pride in his solitude. As a defensive structure, so he said earlier, the burrow simply is not worth the enormous labour that went into its construction. So he must believe, even at the cost of grossest self-deception, that it affords him the life he wants to live. But that life in silence, emptiness, and solitude ultimately drives him to desperation. This is the paradox around which the second part of the story revolves.

We have strayed from what is said in the story to what is not said but is merely implied. We have done so for good reason, but nevertheless prematurely because the emphasis in both parts is on the animal's tremendous effort to solve his problems and on the ironic fact that they become the more insoluble the harder he tries. Rationality is used to dispel fear, but actually makes it worse, for in devising defences against danger the mind constantly discovers new dangers. The impotence of the rational intelligence in the business of practical living is highlighted by a number of passages which refer expressly to scientific method. For example, towards the end of the first part the animal wants to return to his burrow but is mortally afraid of being caught from behind the moment he uncovers the entrance and descends. So he digs an experimental ditch (*Versuchsgraben*), hides in it, and gathers data about the volume and kind of traffic passing by. He classifies his observations with care, but cannot find 'a universal law or infallible method of descending'. Again in the second part he interrupts his theorizing about the possible cause of the hissing and decides to build a research tunnel (*Forschungsgraben*), listen to the noise every two or three hours, and patiently record his observations. In this way he will find the real cause irrespective of all theory. But he never builds the tunnel. His reasoning back and forth has left him so demoralized that he has no faith in the project. Building the tunnel would merely give him something to do, it would be playing at work—as if to fool a supervisor. The supervisor must be his conscience, his intellectual pride, his conviction that he ought to use his mind. It is a sensible project, he says a little later, which attracts him and attracts him not; but when he reflects how unlikely it is to yield results and how defenceless he will be while carrying it out, he declares that he cannot understand why he ever made the plan and that he cannot find the least bit of sense in what seemed sensible only a short while ago.

Abstract reasoning, experimentation, observation—all are discredited in turn. In searching for improvements of his burrow the animal loses himself in technical considerations and dreams the dream of an absolutely perfect structure. He knows this, and he knows also that while technical achievements are not to be despised, they cannot satisfy all the needs of life. Again, while searching for the cause of the noise, he acknowledges that it is mostly the technological problem which fascinates him. Indeed he goes so far as to say that the technocrat who concentrates on conquering his physical environment undermines his self-assurance and becomes restless and greedy. Yet he pursues his course until he is completely paralysed—not only unable to act, but also unwilling to think, to face reality, and to gain certainty about the noise.

When the animal watches his burrow from the outside he feels as if he were spying on himself in his sleep, as if he had the rare ability to see his dream images, not in the helpless state of the sleeper, but in full possession of consciousness and calm judgement. This is the only place in the story where Kafka goes beyond the form of the animal fable and offers an allegorical interpretation. What the animal is attempting is to psychoanalyse himself. He does not take long to realize that the enterprise is impossible. His experiment, he says, is a half-experiment, indeed a mere one-tenth-experiment: his observations outside the burrow cannot give him a valid impression of the dangers which threaten him inside, because when he is inside his scent attracts his enemies. Translated into the terms of Kafka's allegory, this means that the experiment is vitiated because the animal has split himself into an observing and an observed self. And since the passage forms the transition from the first part of the story to the second, it is clearly intended to explain the animal's inability to discover the source of the noise. To be conscious is to be separated from the unconscious, and this in turn means that the conscious mind can never grasp more than one-half, or perhaps only one-tenth, of one's unconscious knowledge. In the case of the animal, the hidden insight is that he himself is his own true enemy. It is entirely characteristic—and, I believe, psychologically true—that the animal can speak in the abstract of his 'prouder, weightier, often deeply repressed fears', but that he cannot admit their cause to himself when they have come to plague him.

Kafka's primary purpose is to have the reader share the animal's experience, to enmesh him in his dilemma, to make him feel the seriousness of his plight. This is why the story dwells so largely on the animal's anguished search for security and why it explores at such length, and in apparently superfluous repetition, the nine theories which the animal puts forth in trying to track down the troublesome hissing. But Kafka also wants the reader to transcend the dilemma and to resolve the paradoxes. With the cunning peculiar to him, he uses the same device to achieve both purposes. By letting the animal tell the story, not in interior monologue, but in a kind of speech which implies the presence of others, Kafka seems to subject the animal's statements of fact and his thoughts about them to objective verification. And the animal's credibility is enhanced by his ostentatious self-searching and his apparent eagerness to correct his observations and revise his views. But since in actual fact no interlocutors are present who might challenge him, the animal is allowed to indulge in a number of delusions and contradictions. These are not noticed (and perhaps are not meant to be noticed) on a first reading, but are certainly striking when the story is re-read. It is in them that the voice of the implied author is heard who, gently and almost imperceptibly at first, but then ever more clearly, adds a second perspective to that of the narrator-protagonist.

One such error occurs when the animal plans to build his famous research tunnel. He will build it, he says, in the direction from which the noise comes, but he forgets that he cannot make out the direction because the noise is heard equally clearly in all parts of the burrow. More telling is his confusion about the reason for his sensitivity. The noise was not audible when he first returned to the burrow, he reasons, because he had to feel at home again before he could hear it; perhaps practice in listening has made him quicker of hearing; possibly the years of solitary living have made him hypersensitive, although surely his hearing cannot have improved; it may be the excitement of coming home and the worries of the world which he has not shaken off yet; or is it that owning property has spoilt him and that the vulnerability of his property has rubbed off on the proprietor? These conflicting surmises are widely scattered (they appear over a stretch of thirteen pages, to be exact), their probability is not examined, and none is rejected before the next is made. In planning to strengthen his castle and again in theorizing about the noise the animal weighs the pros and cons and is stultified only because the world is too complex for the mind to figure out all possibilities. But when he turns inward to examine himself he makes wild stabs and neglects to reason.

Still closer to the core of the story is the contrast between the animal's obsessive occupation with his own safety and his naïve brutality towards others. Kafka, who never offends against realism unless he wishes to drop a hint to the reader (the best-known example is the Statue of Liberty holding a sword instead of a torch in *Amerika*), makes the animal store a huge supply of meat in his burrow—as if it could be kept without spoiling—revel in the smell of it, and on occasion gorge himself senselessly. Small creatures, insects or worms, which blunder into the burrow and disturb its silence 'are quickly put to rest between my teeth', the animal reports. On one occasion he falls asleep with a rat dangling from his teeth. There is a gruesome description of how he pushes his booty through the narrow passages of the maze between the entrance and the burrow proper: there is so much meat and blood that he has to eat and drink some of it and force the rest downward bit by bit. But the most striking illustration of the animal's naïveté is his reflection that the potential intruder might not be an actual enemy, but a person like himself, a connoisseur of fine architecture, a hermit—and a dissolute villain and dirty glutton. In the same passage he rails against innocent little things, loathsome little creatures who might follow him from sheer curiosity and thus betray him to the world. These snarls are hilariously funny because the animal shows an unexpected command of abusive language, but they are also tragic because he curses the harmless and denounces his own kind. They show what a writer of comedy Kafka could have been, had he allowed the ironically detached view of his implied author to prevail over the tragically involved view of his protagonist.

Anyone as wrapped up in himself as the animal must necessarily suffer from a persecution complex. This is suggested repeatedly, perhaps most clearly in the passage in which he wonders whether the hostility of the world against him might not have ceased. He does realize at times that people have their own business and might not even be aware of his existence, but his sense of being threatened by everybody and everything prevails. Finally, the animal's blindness is revealed by his frequent references to his advancing years. He built the burrow as a shelter for his old age, but does not understand that his constant fear is due in part to his failing strength. In a remarkable passage near the end of the story he recalls an experience of his youth when he had just begun to work on the burrow. He heard a noise similar to the noise made by his own digging, but the noise grew weaker and finally disappeared. The experience, he says, should have been a lesson to him, he should have heeded it in planning his burrow. What he does not see, but what the implied author points out by inserting the incident, is that the hissing is different from the noise heard years ago, that he is hearing it only now as he is growing old, and that no modification of his defences against external enemies would have prevented its appearance.

That maze just below the entrance to the burrow was built to trap an invader and to suffocate him. But it was built when the animal was a mere apprentice and not the master builder he has since become, it is the product of youthful playfulness rather than of mature planning, and—so the animal himself tells us—its walls are too thin to withstand serious attack. The metaphor of the maze has often been used to describe Kakfa's novels and stories; but should he not also be taken at his word when he says that the maze is a superficial part of the structure, that it is not the work of the master, that the real burrow is infinitely larger and located much farther down, and that escape is possible by breaking through the walls? As long as the reader is hypnotized by the voice of the narrator—and Kafka does much to so hypnotize him—he is aware only of the insoluble conflicts and problems described with such inescapable logic. It is the voice of the implied author which tells the reader to penetrate the wall and to realize that what the animal really fears is himself and the emptiness of his life. This resolution is suggested in the text by the examples of the animal's general blindness in matters of self-knowledge which have been cited, and it is suggested more specifically by his almost perverse obtuseness in failing to see the real fault of his castle and the real cause of the noise. The place of which he is proudest and which makes him happiest is a large central cave where he keeps his supplies—he calls it his castle yard or keep (*Burgplatz*). His dismay is correspondingly great when he discovers that the noise can be heard even in this supposedly inviolable precinct, and he reproaches himself for not having carried out an old and favourite plan. He should have dug a hollow sphere around the cave (not quite a complete sphere, unfortunately, for of course the wall between the cave and the sphere would have to rest on a pedestal or foundation), lived in the sphere, played there, enjoyed the cave and its treasures without actually seeing them, and above all never have let enemies get near it. A person who could choose between living in the cave and living in the surrounding sphere would certainly prefer the latter. What a most beautiful arrangement that would have been, cries the animal. But surely this is madness. To live all one's life in a hollow around a hollow is the *non plus ultra* of the animal's dreams; and different from all his other dreams of technical perfection, this dream is never questioned, much less revoked. The implied author could hardly have spoken more clearly.

Enough has been said, I think, to explain why the animal does not realize that his nine theories get increasingly implausible and why he does not draw the right conclusion from his observations. A person of his intelligence must know the answer, but he dare not admit it. He must repress the truth: he is living in a void and is his own enemy. In a significant climax he calls the world outside his burrow first 'the strange land' (*die Fremde*), then 'the open' (*das Freie*), and finally, on two occasions, 'the upper world' (*die Oberwelt*). *Das Freie* is one of Kafka's many puns; in everyday language it means 'the open', but it can also be taken literally and would then mean 'the land of freedom'. The implications are clear. When the animal decides to turn his back on 'senseless freedom', he chooses a state of self-imposed unfreedom and becomes the prisoner of his fears, trapped in his castle; and when he decides to leave the upper world, he enters the underworld and makes it his permanent abode. He dwells in a realm akin to the realm of death—silent, mute, empty, and hollow. He has neither wife nor child (in fact he never mentions the possibility of having them), and he takes it for granted that the hissing indicates the approach of an enemy rather than that of a friendly neighbour. He does indeed at one point consider the advantages of having a trusted person (*Vertrauensmann*—significantly, he does not use the word 'friend'), but decides that while it may be possible to trust a person whom one can watch, and perhaps even a person who is absent, it is impossible to trust someone outside while one lives inside the burrow, in 'a different world'. The animal's naïve brutality, his loneliness, his solipsism, are the psychological and social manifestations of his inner emptiness. Repeatedly he tries to regain his composure by telling himself that the noise is nothing, a mere nothing. This, too, is a pun of Kafka's or the implied author's: the noise is negligible, nothing to worry about, as a signal of external danger, but it is also the sound of nothingness. And when the animal calms his fear of never seeing his burrow again by saying that 'fortunately' this is impossible, he unwittingly makes a macabre joke. I do not have to force myself to climb down, he says, I can just lie here and do nothing, for the burrow and I belong so closely together that nothing can separate us in the long run: I shall most certainly get down there somehow in the end. The only place to which one comes without going there is the grave. So what the animal is saying is that his burrow is a metaphorical underworld, and that even if he does not get back to it, he will certainly get to the real underworld—death. But of course he does not know what he is saying.

The animal has hardly begun to tell his story when he interrupts himself to protest that he is not a coward and that the burrow was not built from cowardice. Who said so? Of course he is not a coward. When he imagines an enemy snooping around his entrance, and again much later, when he visualizes the emergence of the beast who makes the noise, he describes the fury with which he would fall upon him and fight him to the death. Then why the protestation? The point is that no enemy ever appears, and that the animal actually wishes he would appear. The negative, as always with Kafka, implies an unspoken positive. The animal is not afraid of the known, but he is afraid of the unknown—his fear is *Angst* rather than *Furcht*. He does not trust his fellow animals, but these fears can be dealt with, at least one can try to deal with them, by building a fortress, by tracking down enemies before they attack, by fighting when the worst comes to the worst. What cannot be dealt with is the unknown, the void, the repressed knowledge that getting old means approaching death and that the animal's death will make an end to a futile life, a life preoccupied with its own preservation and prolongation.

There is one more source of *Angst*. Although it is the most profound source, the story touches upon it only lightly. The animal's existence is deprived not only of the comfort of family, friends, and neighbours, but also of the comfort of faith. As is the case with all his anxieties, he knows it and he knows it not. Quite early in the story he says that there are inner enemies as well as external enemies, that the legends tell about them, but that even legend cannot describe them. These enemies are terrifying because they are not invaders whom one can fight in one's own house. Confronting them, we are not in our house, but in theirs. 'Legend' (*die Sage*) is Kafka's word for Scripture. The ultimate unknown, then, is God, and 'the enemies of the inner earth' are the animal's nagging fears of Him. Throughout the story he acts as if he were autonomous, but on this occasion at least he realizes that God's world is larger than his and that he cannot fight Him on his own ground. He needs the exit of his burrow as an escape-hatch, he says, but knows that it will not save him from the enemies of whom the legend speaks—and he believes firmly in the legend. That threat is easily forgotten, for everyday experience shows much more often that God's mill grinds slow than that it grinds sure. Nevertheless the animal harks back twice to the subject of religion. Admitting that he is too weak to make his fortress impregnable, he has a dim feeling that Providence may have a special interest in saving him, that it will make an exception in his case, and that by an act of grace it will let pass what does not normally pass. If he could trust this feeling, if he had faith, he would indeed be saved, but he mentions the feeling more in self-irony than in earnest and is quick to add that it soon dissipated. Lastly, towards the end of the story the animal wonders why things have gone so well for so long, who guided the paths of his enemies around his burrow all these years, and why he was protected so long only to be so terribly frightened now. He asks these questions when he is sobered by his inability to identify the source of the terrifying noise, but he still does not realize that they include their own answer. At this point the animal is once again quite close to solving the riddle, but the implied author blinds him and does not let him remember what he said earlier about the teaching of the legend. It is left to the reader to put the three passages together and to draw the conclusion.

The observations made so far allow the formulation of three critical principles: Kafka's works are parables, not allegories; their meaning resides in contrasting events and conflicting statements rather than single events or statements which would serve as key passages; and while their subject-matter is usually negative, their substance is positive. There is no common agreement on the distinction between parable and allegory. The distinction I have in mind is that allegories match objects and events from one sphere of experience point for point with those from another, whereas in parables the two spheres touch at only one point, that point being the import of the story as a whole rather than a specific character or incident. Allegories were popular in the Middle Ages. Among the best-known are those describing the battle between feminine virtue and masculine desire as a siege or a hunt, where walls, gates, weapons, or different kinds of game, dogs, and equipment, all have precise metaphorical equivalents. As Ralph Freedman has pointed out, metaphors and allegories do occur in Kafka, but none of his novels and stories may be read as a single, consistent allegory. Thus, for example, the allegory which we have noted in "The Burrow" must not be extended to cover the whole story: the thrust of the story is not simply the lesson that self-observation is impossible. Why it is impossible, or at least fruitless, for this particular animal is much more important. For this same reason I reject Heinz Politzer's assertions that 'in an almost allegorical way "The Burrow" is identical with Kafka's own work' and that it 'contains highly significant statements concerning Kafka's own creative paradox: the conflict which existed in his aims as a writer and a human being'. Politzer believes that the labyrinth in "The Burrow," being beginner's work, is a metaphor for Kafka's early story "The Judgement;" that the burrow or castle points to the late novel *The Castle*; that the animal's passing reference to his guilt invokes the theme of *The Trial*; that his playing and somersaulting recall Gregor Samsa's excursions across the walls in *The Metamorphosis;* and that his subterranean corridors 'indicate those parts of Kafka's work which were still unwritten . . . and would soon be buried with him'. These identifications (I have arranged them on a descending scale of probability) are so uncertain that Politzer himself wonders whether the labyrinth may not refer to *The Castle* rather than to "The Judgement." But even if all of them were accepted, we should have discovered nothing more than allusions, metaphorical overtones, that would enrich the passages in which they occur, but would not explain the story. After all, "The Burrow" progresses, it unfolds a situation. If it were the kind of allegory Politzer has in mind, its progress would have to resemble the process of literary production. Since this is not the case, his conception of 'the Burrow as the most appropriate cipher for his [Kafka's] work' turns the story into a mere catalogue of Kafka's output.

To give a final example of the insufficiency of allegorical interpretation, I myself thought upon first reading the story that the labyrinth might be a figure for the convolutions of the brain, and the much larger burrow beneath it a figure for the unconscious. Such a reading would go no further than Kafka himself goes in comparing the animal watching his entrance with the conscious mind's attempt to observe the unconscious. But again, if I said that the animal's reliance on the intellect is typical of youth and that experience should have taught him respect for the incommensurable, I should turn an incidental allegory into an all-embracing one and a complex story into a simplistic moral tale.

Concerning the second principle, it is true that Kafka often uses words or phrases which are more emphatic than the occasion demands, and since they are particularly noticeable in a narrative style which is normally level and even subdued, they act like snags on the reader's sensibility and persuade him that he has found the key to the story each time he hits one of them. One such word is 'the destroyer' (*der Verderber*). It occurs only once and in its immediate context is merely an alternative for 'pursuer', 'enemy', 'invader'—words which are used frequently to designate the animal's real or imagined foes. But because of its Biblical overtones it can be connected with the inner enemies known to The Legend and with the reference to Providence and may then lead to the view that The Destroyer is the Devil and that the animal's troubles are due to his godlessness. Now it is undoubtedly true that the Biblical overtones are evoked on purpose and that the animal's plight is remarkably akin to that of the wicked man (*der Gottlose*, says Luther) in the Book of Job 15:20–5. But to interpret "The Burrow" as an embroidery of the Biblical passage or, more generally, as a religious parable would be a simplification which disregards the multivalence both of Kafka's metaphors and symbols and of his stories as a whole. His mazes are equipped with many signposts, traffic lights, and alarm bells, and while each of them, when properly heeded, yields an important insight, none yields a wholly adequate insight and thus leads out of the maze. What the critic must realize is that there is not one key word or key sentence, but many. Every incident is qualified by a counter-incident, and every assertion by a counter-assertion. The critic must match them, and often he must gather together a whole sheaf of events or statements which are widely scattered in the text, but nevertheless belong together. Walter Sokel's reading of "The Burrow," for example, relies far too heavily on the passages where the animal describes how he cuddles up in the burrow, rolls over in childlike playfulness, or dozes, dreams, and sleeps. As a result, Sokel accuses the animal of narcissism, says he should have worked harder, and finds that his sense of guilt is due to his carelessness. Work still harder? Was he not actually glad when he bloodied his front pounding down the loose soil in building the central cave? It would be more justifiable to be sorry for the poor brute, for his periods of rest and relaxation are far outweighed by his tireless physical and intellectual toil. Besides, while he does occasionally accuse himself of self-indulgence (although never of self-admiration), his report makes it amply clear that still more work and still more thought would not have made his castle impregnable and would not have solved the riddle of the noise. What the story as a whole teaches is that the animal is incapable of self-examination, not that he is punished for culpable negligence.

Guilt and punishment—these are crucial concepts elsewhere in Kafka, and since the words occur in "The Burrow" they, too have been seized upon by some critics and treated as key words: 'Punishment' appears twice, and 'guilt' once. The animal finds that having to leave the burrow in order to replenish his supplies by hunting outside is unduly harsh punishment for his occasional binges of needless and immoderate eating. He does not know why he feels the punishment is excessive, and the implied author does not explain it until much later, near the end of the story. Overeating is the result of temporary despair in the earlier passage, and eating as much as he can while he still has the opportunity is the animal's last plan—the only feasible plan when all else has failed. In its second occurrence, the punishment is self-inflicted. The animal tries to force himself to re-enter the burrow, cannot bring himself to do it, and throws himself into a thorn-bush 'to punish myself for a guilt which I do not know'. The unknown guilt is his cowardice, his lack of self-confidence, and these in turn are caused by the repressed knowledge that his life in the burrow is meaningless and not worth the danger of descending. 'Guilt' and 'punishment', then, are indeed keys, but not master keys, not the pillars on which "The Burrow" is erected. Like 'the destroyer', they add a dimension to the story, although its meaning would not be vitally affected if they were absent. They connect it with some of Kafka's other works, but whereas Josef K. in *The Trial* does his best not to see what is wrong with himself and his life, the animal tries desperately to find out. The specific problem investigated in "The Burrow" is the impossibility of self-knowledge despite most strenuous effort, and since this failing is involuntary and unconscious, it is 'guilt' only in an extended sense of the word. Put as a general rule, the use of an author's other works for the elucidation of the work under consideration is as hazardous as the use of biographical facts, sources, letters, and diary entries. They may give valuable leads, but they can also lead astray.

That Kafka's negatives imply unspoken positives is, of course, the main contention of this essay, and some specific examples have already been given. The idea that the whole story, too, is a negative image of a positive thought is not new. It has been developed most resolutely by Wilhelm Emrich, but while I agree with his belief that the animal's intellectual failure points to a moral fault, I disagree with his definition of that fault. Emrich sees little if any difference between the animal and Josef K.: both deny their true selves and both shirk the duty to judge themselves. He quotes in support the passage from the end of *The Trial* which says that Josef K. knows not only that he should have judged himself, but also that he should execute the judgement—commit suicide. But in explaining "The Burrow" Emrich asserts that self-judgement, had the animal been able to perform it, would have brought about utopia: the knowledge of good and evil and its acceptance—applying its demands to oneself and only to oneself rather than to others—reconcile the individual with himself and with his fellow creatures. Now this assertion is at variance not only with the text of *Der Bau*, but with all of Kafka's works. No writer was more unwilling to indulge in utopian visions, and none insisted more firmly on the ineluctable problems of man's inner and outer existence. Specifically, the conflict in "The Burrow" is not between the animal's true self and his empirical self, but between his intellect and its objects, an outer world of contingencies which defies rational planning and an inner world so hidden that it eludes self-searching. What refutes Emrich most clearly are the totally different endings of the two stories. Whereas Josef K. realizes at last that he himself, and not the world, is at fault, the animal has no consciousness of guilt (except in the one fleeting moment mentioned), and hence does not feel the need to judge and punish himself. To accommodate the end of "The Burrow" to his interpretation, Emrich says that there is a pessimistic final turn and that the animal perishes of his hostility to himself. The fact is, however, that no enemy appears (not even an enemy who may be understood, as Emrich suggests earlier, as a metaphor for the animal's inner voice) and that the animal does not perish. He just sits there, perplexed and afraid. Thus, while it is true that both *The Trial* and "The Burrow" point to a moral fault which implies an unattained (and, for Kafka's protagonists, unattainable) virtue, Josef K.'s *Angst* is due to his repressed sense of guilt, but the animal's to his repressed sense of futility. Guilt must be punished, but a wasted life is its own punishment. Disagreeing with Emrich, I believe, then, that the two stories present different problems, expose different vices, and are negative images of different virtues. Josef K. lacks self-criticism, the animal lacks self-confidence.

ERICH HELLER

The Castle

The relationship of Kafka's heroes to that truth for which they so desperately search can best be seen in the image through which Plato, in a famous passage of his *Republic*, expresses man's pitiable ignornace about the true nature of the Ideas. Chained to the ground of his cave, with his back towards the light, all he perceives of the fundamental reality of the world is a play of shadows thrown on to the wall of his prison. But for Kafka there is a further complication: perfectly aware of his wretched imprisonment and obsessed with a monomaniac desire to know, the prisoner has, by his unruly behaviour and his incessant entreaties, provoked the government of his prison to an act of malicious generosity. In order to satisfy this passion for knowledge they have covered the walls with mirrors which, owing to the curved surface of the cave, distort what they reflect. Now the prisoner sees lucid pictures, definite shapes, clearly recognizable faces, an inexhaustible wealth of detail. His gaze is fixed no longer on empty shades, but on a full reflection of ideal reality. Face to face with the images of Truth, he is yet doubly agonized by their hopeless distortion. With an unparalleled fury of pedantry he observes the curve of every line, the ever-changing countenance of every figure, drawing schemes of every possible aberration from reality which his mirror may cause, making now this angle and now that the basis of his endless calculations which, he passionately hopes, will finally yield the geometry of truth or of that necessity which sometimes he opposed to the notion of truth.

In a letter (16 December 1911) Kafka says: 'I am separated from all things by a hollow space, and I do not even reach to its boundaries.' In another (19 November 1913): 'Everything appears to me construed . . . I am

From *Kafka*. Copyright ©1974 by Erich Heller. Fontana/Collins, 1974.

chasing after constructions. I enter a room, and I find them in a corner, a white tangle.' On 21 October 1921 he enters in his diary: 'All is imaginary—family, office, friends, the street, all imaginary, far away or close at hand, the woman; the truth that lies closest, however, is only this: that you are beating your head against the wall of a windowless and doorless cell.' And in one of his 'Reflections on Sin, Pain, Hope and the True Way' he writes: 'Our art is a dazzled blindness before the truth: The light on the grotesque recoiling mask is true, but nothing else.'

Kafka's novels take place in infinity. Yet their atmosphere is as oppressive as that of those unaired rooms in which so many of their scenes are enacted. For infinity is incompletely defined as the ideal point where two parallels meet. There is yet another place where they come together: the distorting mirror. Thus they carry into the prison of their violently distorted union the agony of infinite separation.

It is a Tantalus situation, and in Kafka's work the ancient curse has come to life once more. Kafka says of himself (in the sequence of the aphorisms 'He' contained in the volume *The Great Wall of China*): 'He is thirsty, and is cut off from a spring by a mere clump of bushes. But he is divided against himself: one part overlooks the whole, sees that he is standing here and that the spring is just beside him; but another part notices nothing, has at most a divination that the first part sees all. But as he notices nothing he cannot drink.' Indeed, it was a curse, and not a word of light, which called the universe of Kafka's novels into existence. The very clay from which it was made bore the imprint of a malediction before any creature had touched it. He builds to a splendid design, but the curse runs like a vein through every stone. In one of his most revealing parables, in the Fourth Octavo Note-Book (included in the volume *Dearest Father*), Kafka shows himself aware of this:

> Everything fell in with his intention and contributed to the building. Foreign workers brought the blocks of marble, already hewn and ready to be fitted together. In accordance with the indication, given by his moving finger, the blocks rose up and shifted into place. No building ever rose into being as easily as this temple did, or rather, this temple came into being in the true manner of temples. Only on every block—from what quarry did they come?—there were clumsy scribblings by senseless childish hands, or rather, entries made by barbaric mountain-dwellers in order to annoy or to deface or to destroy completely, scratched into the stone with instruments that were obviously

magnificently sharp, intended to endure for an eternity that would outlast the temple.

It is the reality of the curse that constitutes the ruthlessly compelling logic of Kafka's writings. If they defy all attempts to interpret them in a simple, straightforward manner, this is because he never thinks, or imagines, in disputable or refutable generalities. His thinking is a reflex movement of his being and shares the irrefutability of all that is. And it is at an infinite number of removes from the Cartesian *Cogito ergo sum* [I think, therefore I am]. Indeed, it sometimes seems that an unknown 'It' does all the thinking that matters, the radius of its thought touching the circumference of Kafka's existence here and there, causing him infinite pain, bringing his life into question and promising salvation on one condition only: that he should expand his being to bring it within the orbit of that strange intelligence. The formula has become: 'It thinks, and therefore I am not,' with only the agony of despair providing overpowering proof that he is alive.

There is, outside this agony, no reality about which he could entertain or communicate thoughts, nothing apart from the curse of his own separation from that intelligence. Yet it is a complete world that is to be found within that pain, the exact pattern of creation once more, but this time made of the stuff of which curses are made. Like sorrow in the Tenth of Rilke's *Duino Elegies,* despair is given a home of its own in Kafka's works, faithfully made in the image of customary life, but animated by the blast of the curse. Never before has absolute darkness been represented with so much clarity, and the very madness of desperation with so much composure and sobriety. In his work an intolerable spiritual pride is expressed with the legitimate and convincing gesture of humility, disintegration finds its own level of integrity, and impenetrable complexity an all but *sancta simplicitas*. Kafka strives to discover the moral law of a boundlessly deceitful world, and performs in a totally incalculable domain, ruled by evil demons, the most precise mathematical measurements.

It has been said that *The Castle* is a religious allegory, a kind of modern *Pilgrim's Progress*, indeed that the unattainable building is the abode of divine law and divine grace. This would seem to be not only a misapprehension reflecting a profound religious confusion, but an indication of the loss of all sureness of religious discrimination. Where there is a spiritual famine, *anything* that is of the spirit may taste like bread from Heaven, and minds imbued with psychology and 'comparative religion' may find the difference negligible between Prometheus clamped to the rock, and the martyrdom of a Christian saint; between an ancient curse and the grace that makes a new man.

The Castle is as much a religious allegory as a photographic likeness of the Devil in person could be said to be an allegory of Evil. Every allegory has an opening into the rarefied air of abstractions, and is furnished with signposts pointing to an ideal concept beyond. But *The Castle* is a terminus of soul and mind, a *non plus ultra* of existence. In an allegory the author plays a kind of guessing game with his reader, if he does not actually provide the answers himself; but there is no key to *The Castle*. It is true to say that its reality does not precisely correspond to what is commonly understood in the 'positive' world as real, namely, neutral sense-perceptions of objects and, neatly separated from them, feelings. (Hence our most authentic and realistic intellectual pursuits: natural sciences and psychology; and our besetting sins: the ruthlessness of acquisitive techniques and sentimentality). In Kafka's novels there is no such division between the external sphere and the domain of inwardness, and therefore no such reality. There is only the tragic mythology of the absolutely incongruous relationship between the two worlds.

Kafka's creations are at the opposite pole to the writings of that type of Romantic poet, the true poetical representative of the utilitarian age, who distils from a spiritually more and more sterile external reality those elements which are still of some use to the emotions, or else withdraws from its barren fields into the greenhouse vegetation of inwardness. The author of *The Castle* does not select for evocative purposes, nor does he project his inner experience into carefully chosen timeless settings. He does not, after the manner of Joyce, give away, in the melodious flow of intermittent articulation, the secret bedroom conversations which self conducts with self. There are no private symbols in his work, such as would be found in symbolist writing, no crystallized fragments of inner sensations charged with mysterious significance; nor is there, after the fashion of the Expressionists, any rehearsing of new gestures of the soul, meant to be more in harmony with the new rhythm of modern society. Instead of all this, the reader is faced with the shocking spectacle of a miraculously sensitive soul incapable of being either reasonable, or cynical, or resigned, or rebellious, about the prospect of eternal damnation. The world which this soul perceives is unmistakably like the reader's own: a castle that is a castle and 'symbolizes' merely what all castles symbolize: power and authority; a bureaucracy drowning in a deluge of forms and files; an obscure hierarchy of officialdom making it impossible ever to find the man authorized to deal with a particular case; officials who work overtime and yet get nowhere; numberless interviews which never are to the point; inns where the peasants meet, and barmaids who serve the officials. In fact, it is an excruciatingly familiar world, but reproduced by a creative intelligence which is endowed with the knowledge that it is a world damned for ever. Shakespeare once made one of his characters say: 'They say miracles are past, and we have our philosophical persons, to make modern and familiar things supernatural and causeless. Hence it is that we make trifles of terrors, ensconcing ourselves in seeming knowledge when we should submit ourselves to an unknown fear.' In Kafka we have the abdication of the philosophical persons.

In Kafka's work the terror recaptures the trifles, and the unknown fear invades all seeming knowledge—particularly that of psychology. Even the most mistaken religious interpretations of Kafka's writings show at least an awareness of its religious character, whereas the psychological analyses, in their devastating plausibility, tend to reduce them to symptoms of the Oedipus complex. Certainly, there cannot be the slightest doubt that Kafka's relationship to his father was exceedingly strained; but only one son, among the many unable to come to terms with their fathers, has written *The Castle*. To interpret this or any other novel of Kafka's in the perspective of the Oedipus complex is about as helpful to our understanding of his work as the statement that Kafka would have been a different person (and perhaps not a writer at all) if he had had another father: a thought, of which even psychologically less initiated ages might have been capable if they had deemed it worth thinking. This kind of psychology can contribute as much to the explanation of a work of art as ornithological anatomy to the comprehension of what the nightingale's song meant to Keats. But so deeply engrained is psychology in the epoch's sensibility that most readers, even when they are moved by the autonomous reality which the author has created, soon regain the balance of mind required for its 'reduction', its translation into what it 'really' means; and by that they mean precisely that meaningless experience which the artist has succeeded in transcending through his poetic creation. If, for instance, the writer believes he has discovered the meaning of his senselessly tormenting feud with his father—a discovery he has made in creating his work—; that he should find his place within a true spiritual order of divine authority, the psychological reader will insist that, by talking about God, the author 'really' means his father.

In Kafka we have before us the modern mind, seemingly self-sufficient, intelligent, sceptical, ironical, splendidly trained for the great game of pretending that the world it comprehends in sterilized sobriety is the only and ultimate reality there is—yet a mind living in sin with the soul of Abraham. Thus he knows two things at once, and both with equal assurance: that there is no God, and that there must be God. It is the perspective of the curse: the intellect dreaming its dream of absolute freedom, and the soul

knowing of its terrible bondage. The conviction of damnation is all that is
left of faith, standing out like a rock in a landscape the softer soil of which
has been eroded by the critical intellect. Kafka once said (in the Fourth
Octavo Note-Book): 'I should welcome eternity, and when I do find it I am
sad.'

This is merely an exhausted echo of the fanfares of despair with which
Nietzsche, who had some share in Kafka's intellectual education and is,
beyond any question of influence, in many respects one of his spiritual
ancestors, welcomed his vision of eternity. In one of the posthumously
published notes on *Zarathustra* he says about his idea of the Eternal Recurrence: 'We have produced the hardest possible thought—now let us create
the creature who will accept it lightheartedly and blissfully!': the *Übermensch*. He conceived the Eternal Recurrence as a kind of spiritualized
Darwinian test to select for survival the spiritually fittest. This he formulated
with the utmost precision: 'I perform the great experiment: who can bear the
idea of Eternal Recurrence?'. And an even deeper insight into the anatomy of
despair we gain from Nietzsche's posthumous aphorisms and epigrams which
were assembled by his editors in the two volumes of *The Will to Power,* many
of which refer to the idea of Eternal Recurrence: 'Let us consider this idea in
its most terrifying form: existence, as it is, without meaning or goal, but
inescapably recurrent, without a finale into nothingness. . .'. Nietzsche's
Übermensch is the creature strong enough to live for ever a cursed existence,
even to derive from it the Dionysian raptures of tragic acceptance. Nietzsche
feels certain that only the *Übermensch* could be equal to the horror of a
senseless eternity, and perform the great metamorphosis of turning this
'most terrifying' knowledge into the terror of superhuman delight. And
Kafka? On most of the few occasions when, in his diary, he speaks of
happiness he registers it as the result of a transformation of torture into bliss
as in those horrible diary entries such as (2 November 1911): 'This morning,
for the first time in a long time, the joy again of imagining a knife twisted in
my heart'. If Nietzsche's *Übermensch* is the visionary counterweight to the
weight of the curse, then Kafka is its chosen victim. What sometimes has
been interpreted as signs of a religious 'breakthrough' in his later writings is
merely the all-engulfing weariness of a Nietzschean Prometheus: in the
fourth of his Prometheus legends (Fourth Octavo Note-Book) Kafka writes:
'. . . everyone grew weary of the meaningless affair. The gods grew weary,
the eagles grew weary, the wound closed wearily.'

Thus Kafka's work, as much as Nietzsche's, must remain a stumbling-
block to the analysing interpreter to whom, in the enlightened atmosphere
of modernity, the word 'curse' comes only as a faint memory of Greek

tragedy, or as a figurative term for a combination of ill luck and psychological maladjustments. Yet the grey world of Kafka's novels is luminous with its fire. To be sure, Kafka's *Castle* is, as has been held, about life in the grip of a power 'which all religions have acknowledged'; but this power is not 'divine law and divine grace', but rather one which, having rebelled against the first and fallen from the second, has, in its own domain, successfully contrived the suspension of both. Undoubtedly, the Land Surveyor K., hero of *The Castle,* is religiously fascinated by its inscrutably horrid bureaucracy; but again it is a word from Nietzsche, and not from the Gospels, that sums up the situation: 'Wretched man, your god lies in the dust, broken to fragments, and serpents dwell around him. And now you love even the serpents for his sake'. . . .

There are allegorical elements to be found in *The Castle*: for instance, the names of many of the characters. The hero himself, who is introduced with the bare initial K. (undoubtedly once again an autobiographical hint—the novel was originally drafted in the first person—and at the same time, through its very incompleteness, suggesting an unrealized, almost anonymous personality) is a Land Surveyor. Kafka's choice of this profession for his hero has clearly a meaning. The German for it is *Landvermesser,* and its verbal associations are manifold. The first is, of course, the Land Surveyor's professional activity, consisting precisely in what K. desperately desires and never achieves: to produce a workable order within clearly defined boundaries and limits of earthly life, and to find an acceptable compromise between conflicting claims of possession. But *Vermesser* also alludes to *Vermessenheit,* hubris; to the adjective *vermessen,* audacious; to the verb *sich vermessen,* commit an act of spiritual pride, *and* also apply the wrong measure, make a mistake in measurement. The most powerful official of the Castle (for K. the highest representative of authority) is called *Klamm,* a sound producing a sense of anxiety amounting almost to claustrophobia, suggesting straits, pincers, chains, clamps, but also a person's oppressive silence. The messenger of the Castle (as it turns out later, self-appointed and officially never recognized) has the name of *Barnabas,* the same as that man of Cyprus who, though not one of the Twelve, came to rank as an apostle; 'Son of Consolation', or 'Son of Exhortation', is the biblical meaning of his name, and it is said of him that his exhortation was of the inspiring kind, and so built up faith. And the Barnabas of the novel is indeed a son of consolation, if only in the desperately ironical sense that his family, whom the curse of the Castle has cast into the lowest depths of misery and wretchedness, in vain expects deliverance through his voluntary service for the authority. To K., however, his messages, in all their obscurity and pointlessness, seem the only real link with the Castle, an elusive glimmer of hope, a will-o'-the-wisp of faith. Barnabas's counterpart is *Momus*, the village secretary of Klamm and namesake of that depressing creature, the son of Night, whom the Greek gods authorized to find fault with all things. In the novel it is he whose very existence seems the denial of any hope which Barnabas may have roused in K. *Frieda* (peace) is the girl through whose love K. seeks to reach the goal of his striving; *Bürgel* (diminutive of *Bürge*, guarantor) the name of the title official who offers the solution without K.'s even noticing the chance; and the secretary, through whom K. does expect to achieve something and achieves nothing, is called *Erlanger* (citizen of the town of Erlangen, but also suggestive of *erlangen*, attain, achieve).

This discussion of names provides an almost complete synopsis of the slender plot of *The Castle*. Someone, a man whose name begins with K., and of whom we know no more, neither whence he comes nor what his past life has been, arrives in a village which is ruled by a Castle. He believes that he has been appointed Land Surveyor by the authorities. The few indirect contacts that K. succeeds in establishing with the Castle—a letter he receives, a telephone conversation he overhears, yet another letter, and above all the fact that he is joined by two assistants whom the rulers have assigned to him—*seem* to confirm his appointment. Yet he himself is never quite convinced, and never relaxes in his efforts to make sure of it. He feels he must penetrate to the very centre of authority and wring from it a kind of ultra-final confirmation of his claim. Until then he yields, in paralyzed despair, broken by only momentary outbursts of rebellious pride, to the inarticulate, yet absolutely self-assured refusal of the village to acknowledge him as their Land Surveyor: 'You've been taken on as Land Surveyor, as you say, but, unfortunately, we have no need of a Land Surveyor. There wouldn't be the least use for one here. The frontiers of our little estates are marked out and all officially recorded. So what should we do with a Land Surveyor?' says the village representative to him.

K.'s belief appears, from the very outset, to be based both on truth and illusion. It is Kafka's all but unbelievable achievement to force, indeed to frighten, the reader into unquestioning acceptance of this paradox, presented with ruthless realism and irresistible logic. Truth and illusion are mingled in K.'s belief in such a way that he is deprived of all order of reality. Truth is permanently on the point of taking off its mask and revealing itself as illusion, illusion in constant danger of being verified as truth. It is the predicament of a man who, endowed with an insatiable appetite for the absolute certainty that transcends all half-truths, relativities and compromises of everyday life, finds himself in a world robbed of all spiritual possessions. Thus he cannot accept the world—the village—without first attaining to that certainty, and he cannot be certain without first accepting the world. Yet every contact with the world makes a mockery of his search, and the continuance of his search turns the world into a mere encumbrance. After studying the first letter from the Castle, K. contemplates his dilemma, 'whether he preferred to become a village worker with a distinctive but merely apparent connection with the Castle, or an ostensible village worker whose real occupation was determined through the medium of Barnabas'. From the angle of the village all K.'s contacts with the Castle are figments of his imagination: 'You haven't once up till now come into real contact with our authorities. All those contacts have been illusory, but owing to your ignorance of the circumstances you take them to be real.' The Castle, on the other hand, seems to take no notice whatever of the reality of K.'s miserable village existence. In the midst of his suffering the indignity of being employed as a kind of footman to the schoolmaster, and never having come anywhere near working as a Land Surveyor, he receives the following letter from Klamm: 'The surveying work which you have carried out thus far has been appreciated by me . . . Do not slacken in your efforts! Carry your work to a fortunate conclusion. Any interruption would displease me. . . . I shall not forget you.' From all this it would appear that it is, in fact, the village that disobeys the will of the Castle, while defeating K. with the powerful suggestion that he misunderstands the intentions of authority. And yet the authority seems to give its blessing to the defiance of the village, and to punish K. for his determination to act in accordance with the letter of its orders. In his fanatical obedience it is really he who rebels against the Castle, whereas the village, in its matter-of-fact refusal, lives the life of the Law.

Kafka represents the absolute reversal of German idealism. If it is Hegel's final belief that in the Absolute truth and existence are one, for Kafka it is precisely through the Absolute that they are forever divided. Truth and existence are mutually exclusive. From his early days onwards it was the keenest wish of Kafka the artist to convey this in works of art; to write in such a way that life, in all its deceptively convincing reality, would be seen as a dream and a nothing before the Absolute:

> . . . somewhat as if one were to hammer together a table with painful and methodical technical efficiency, and simultaneously do nothing at all, and not in such a way that people could say: 'Hammering a table together is nothing to him', but rather 'Hammering a table together is really hammering a table together to him, but at the same time it is nothing,' whereby

certainly the hammering would have become still bolder, still
surer, still more real and, if you will, still more senseless.

This is how Kafka, in the series of aphorisms 'He' (*The Great Wall of China*),
describes the vision of artistic accomplishment which hovered before his
mind's eye when, as a young man, he sat one day on the slopes of the
Laurenziberg in Prague. Has he, in his later works, achieved this artistic
justification of nonentity? Not quite; what was meant to become the lifting
of a curse through art, became the artistically perfect realization of it, and
what he dreamed of making into something as light as a dream, fell from his
hand with the heaviness of a nightmare. Instead of a vindication of nothingness, he achieved the portrayal of the most cunningly vindictive unreality.

It is hard to understand how *The Castle* could possibly be called a religious
allegory with a pilgrim of the type of Bunyan's as its hero. Pilgrimage? On the
contrary, the most oppressive quality of Kafka's work is the unshakable
stability of its central situation. It takes place in a world that knows of no
motion, no change, no metamorphosis—unless it be the transformation of a
human being into an insect. Its caterpillars never turn into butterflies, and
when the leaves of a tree tremble it is not due to the wind: it is the stirring of a
serpent coiled round its branches. Prilgrim or not, there is no progress to be
watched in *The Castle,* unless we agree to call progress what Kafka describes in
'A Little Fable' (*The Complete Stories*) as the 'progress' of the mouse:

> 'Alas,' said the mouse, 'the world is growing smaller every day. At
> the beginning it was so big that I was afraid, I kept running and
> running, and I was glad when at last I saw walls far away to the
> right and left, but these long walls have narrowed so quickly that I
> am in the last chamber already, and there in the corner stands the
> trap that I must run into.' 'You only need to change your
> direction,' said the cat, and ate it up.

It has been said that Kafka has this in common with Bunyan, 'that the goal and
the road indubitably exist, and that the necessity to find them is urgent'. Only
the second point is correct. Indeed, so urgent is it for Kafka to discover the
road and reach the goal that life seems impossible without this achievement.
But do road and goal exist? 'There is a goal, but no way; what we call the way is
only wavering,' is what Kafka says about it in 'Reflections on Sin, . . .'. And is
there really a goal for him? This is the answer that Kafka gives to himself in
'He':

> He feels imprisoned on this earth, he feels constricted: the mel-
> ancholy, the impotence, the sickness, the feverish fancies of the

captive afflict him; no comfort can comfort him, since it is merely comfort, gentle head-splitting comfort glozing the brutal fact of imprisonment. But if he is asked what he actually wants he cannot reply, for—that is one of his strongest proofs—he has no conception of freedom.

Kafka's hero is the man who *believes* in absolute freedom but cannot have any conception of it because he *exists* in a world of slavery. Therefore it is not grace and salvation that he seeks, but either his right or—a bargain with the powers. 'I don't want any act of favour from the Castle, but my rights', says K. in his interview with the village representative. But convinced of the futility of this expectation, his real hope is based on Frieda, his fiancée and Klamm's former mistress, whom he is obviously prepared to hand back to him 'for a price'.

In K.'s relationship to Frieda the European story of romantic love has found its epilogue. It is the solid residue left behind by the evaporated perfume of romance, revealing its darkest secret. In romantic love, as it has dominated a vast section of European literature ever since the later Middle Ages, individualism, emerging from the ruins of a common spiritual order, has found its most powerful means of transcendence. The spiritually more and more autonomous, and therefore more and more lonely, individual worships Eros, and his twin deity within the romantic imagination: Death, as the only gods capable of breaking down the barriers of his individualist isolation. Therefore love becomes tragedy: overcharged with unmanageable spiritual demands it must needs surge ahead of any human relationship. In its purest manifestations, romantic love is a glorious disaster of the soul, carrying frustration in its wake. For what the romantic lover seeks is not really the beloved. Intermixed with his erotic craving, inarticulate, diffuse, and yet dominating it, is the desire for spiritual salvation. Even a 'happy ending' spells profound disillusionment for the romantic expectation. Perhaps it is Strindberg, deeply admired by Kafka, who wrote the last chapter of its history. It is certainly Kafka who wrote its postscript.

For K. loves Frieda—if he loves her at all—entirely for Klamm's sake. This is not only implied in the whole story of K. and Frieda, but explicitly stated by Kafka in several passages which he later deleted, very probably because their directness seemed to him incompatible with the muted meaning of the book. As an indictment of K., it is contained in the protocol about his life in the village which Momus has drawn up, and in which K. is accused of having made up to Frieda out of a 'calculation of the lowest sort': because he believed that in her he would win a mistress of Klamm's and so possess 'a pledge for which he can demand the highest price'. On the margin of the protocol there was also 'a childishly scrawled drawing, a man with a girl in his arms. The girl's face was buried in the man's chest, but the man who was much the taller, was looking over the girl's shoulders at a sheet of paper he had in his hands and on which he was joyfully inscribing some figures.' But perhaps still more conclusive than Momus's clearly hostile interpretation is another deleted passage giving K.'s own reflections on his love for Frieda:

> And then immediately, before there was any time to think, Frieda had come, and with her the belief, which it was impossible to give up entirely even today, that through her mediation an almost physical relationship to Klamm, a relationship so close that it amounted almost to a whispering form of communication, had come about, of which for the present only K. knew, which however needed only a little intervention, a word, a glance, in order to reveal itself primarily to Klamm, but then too to every-one, as something admittedly incredible which was nevertheless, through the compulsion of life, the compulsion of the loving embrace, a matter of course . . . What was he without Frieda? A nonentity, staggering along after . . . will-o'-the-wisps . . .

The desperate desire for spiritual certainty is all that is left of romantic love. K. *wills* his love for Frieda because he *wills* his salvation. He is a kind of Pelagius believing that he 'can if he ought', yet living in a relentlessly predestined world. This situation produces a theology very much after the model of Gnostic and Manichaean beliefs. The incarnation is implicitly denied in an unmitigated loathing of 'determined' matter, and the powers which rule are perpetually suspected of an alliance with the Devil because they have consented to the creation of such a loathsome world. Heaven is at least at seven removes from the earth, and only begins where no more neighbourly relations are possible. There are no real points of contact be-tween divinity and the earth, which is not even touched by divine emana-tion. Reality is the sovereign domain of strangely unangelic angels, made up of evil and hostility. The tedious task of the soul is, with much wisdom of initiation and often with cunning diplomacy, gradually to by-pass the armies of angels and the strong-points of evil, and finally to slip into the remote kingdom of light.

The Castle of Kafka's novel is, as it were, the heavily fortified garrison of a company of Gnostic demons, successfully holding an advanced position against the manoeuvres of an impatient soul. There is no conceivable idea of divinity which could justify those interpreters who see in the Castle the residence of 'divine law and divine grace'. Its officers are totally indifferent to good if they are not positively wicked. Neither in their decrees nor in their activities is there any trace of love, mercy, charity or majesty. In their icy detachment they inspire certainly no awe, but fear and revulsion. Their servants are a plague to the village, 'a wild, unmanageable lot, ruled by their insatiable impulses . . . their scandalous behaviour knows no limits', an anticipation of the blackguards who were to become the footmen of European dictators rather than the office-boys of a divine ministry. Compared to the petty and apparently calculated torture of this tyranny, the gods of Shakespeare's indignation who 'kill us for their sport' are at least majestic in their wantonness.

From the very beginning there is an air of indecency, indeed of obscenity, about the inscrutable rule of the castle. A newcomer in the village, K. meets the teacher in the company of children. He asks him whether he knows the Count and is surprised at the negative answer: ' "What, you don't know the Count?" "Why should I?" replied the teacher in a low tone, and added aloud in French: "Please remember that there are innocent children present".' And, indeed, what an abhorrent rule it is! The souls of women seem to be allowed to enter the next realm if they surrender, as a sort of pass, their bodies to the officials. They are then married off to some nincompoop in the village, with their drab existence rewarded only by occasional flashes of voluptuously blissful memories of their sacrificial sins. Damnation is their lot if they refuse, as happens in the case of Amalia, Barnabas's sister, who brought degradation upon herself and her family by declining the invitation of the official Sortini.

No, the Castle does not represent, as some early interpreters believed, divine guidance or even Heaven itself. It is for K. something that is to be conquered, something that bars his way into a purer realm. K.'s antagonism to the Castle becomes clear from the very first pages of the book. This is how he responds to the first telephone conversation about his appointment which, in his presence, is conducted between the village and the authorities:

> K. pricked up his ears. So the Castle had recognized him as the Land Surveyor. That was unpropitious for him, on the one hand, for it meant that the Castle was well informed about him, had estimated all the probable chances and was taking up the challenge with a smile. On the other hand, however, it was quite propitious, for if his interpretation was right, they had underesti-

mated his strength, and he would have more freedom of action than he had dared to hope.

The correspondence between the spiritual structure of *The Castle* and the view of the world systematized into Gnostic and Manichaean dogma is indeed striking. There is, however, no reason to assume that Kafka had thoroughly studied those ancient heresies. In their radical dualism they are merely the model systems of a deep-rooted spiritual disposition, asserting itself over and over again in individuals and whole movements. Gnostic and Manichaean is, above all 'the face that is filled with loathing and hate' at the sight of physical reality. Kafka refrains from any dealings with nature, such as are found, for instance, in his earliest story 'The Description of a Struggle'. There is, apart from the mention of a starry sky, wind and snow, not one description of nature in *The Castle*. Within the human sphere everything that is of the flesh is treated with a sense of nausea and disgust. All the habitations of men are lightless, airless and dirty. The nuptial embrace between K. and Frieda takes place amidst puddles of beer on the floor of a public bar, the room still filled with the stale smells of an evening's business, while mass prostitution is carried on in the stable of the inn.

But Kafka has also found subtler means of conveying his revolt against 'matter'. One evening K. is waiting in the dark courtyard of the inn for Klamm to emerge from his village room and enter his sledge. The coachman, noticing K., encourages him to wait inside the sledge and have a drink from one of the bottles kept in the sidepockets. K. opens the bottle and smells:

> . . . involuntarily he smiled, the perfume was so sweet, so caressing, like praise and good words from someone whom one loves very much yet one does not know clearly what they are for and has no desire to know, and is simply happy in the knowledge that it is one's friend who is saying them. 'Can this be brandy?' K. asked himself doubtfully and took a taste out of curiosity. Yes, strangely enough it was brandy, and burned and warmed. How strangely it was transformed in drinking out of something which seemed hardly more than a sweet perfume into a drink fit for a coachman!

Whether intentional or not, this profanation of the aroma of a spirit in the process of its being 'realized' is a wonderfully subtle symbol of a Manichaean perspective on the world.

The Castle is, no doubt, the highest realm K. is capable of perceiving. This is what misled the critics, but not Kafka himself, into equating it with God. But it is certainly not quite irrelevant that in his personal confessions Kafka hardly ever utters the belief that the incessant striving of his spirit was directed towards God, or prompted by *amor Dei*. Almost all the time his soul is preoccupied with the power of Evil; a power so great that God had to retreat before it into purest transcendence, for ever out of reach of life. Thus the idea of final authority, merely by assuming the shape of physical reality in *The Castle,* falls, without the author's either willing it or being able to help it, under the spell of Evil. It is the paradox of spiritual absolutism that the slightest touch of concreteness will poison the purest substance of the spirit, and one ray of darkness blot out a world of light.

Although seemingly quantitative assessments of this kind are always problematical, it is true to say that *The Castle* is even more 'Manichaean ' than *The Trial.* Yet even here it sometimes, if rarely, seems that the sinister threat to the spirit, embodied in a senseless world, might suddenly reveal itself as a disguised promise of happiness, a happiness and even goodness born of the nonresistance to that world, indeed its resolute acceptance: '. . . you must take the side of the world.' Although the cursed rule of the castle is the furthest point of the world to which this wakeful mind can reach, there dawns, at its extreme boundaries, a light, half suspectingly perceived, half stubbornly ignored, that comes from things outside the scope of Klamm's authority. K. is possessed by only one thought: that he must come to grips with Klamm; yet at the same time he knows that his very obsession with this thought precludes him from reaching what he mistakenly believes only Klamm can give. He senses that, if only he could renounce his consuming desire, he would find what eludes him because of his very striving for it. In Pepi who, for a short time, was promoted to the rank of barmaid in the local inn, and thus enjoys the honour of serving beer to Klamm, K. meets the caricatured personification of his own ambition. In giving advice to her he shows a remarkable knowledge of his own malady:

> It is a job like any other, but for you it is heaven, consequently you set about everything with exaggerated eagerness, . . . tremble for the job, feel you are constantly being persecuted, try by means of being excessively pleasant to win over everyone who in your opinion might be a support to you, but in this way bother them and repel them, for what they want at the inn is peace and quiet and not the barmaid's worries on top of their own.

And later:

> . . . when I compare myself with you . . . , it is as if we had
> both striven too intensely, too noisily, too childishly, with too
> little experience, to get something that for instance with Frieda's
> calm and Frieda's matter-of-factness can be got easily and without
> much ado. We have tried to get it by crying, by scratching, by
> tugging—just as a child tugs at the tablecloth, gaining nothing,
> but only bringing all the splendid things down on the floor and
> putting them out of reach for ever.

But it is in K.'s adventure with the Castle official Bürgel that this insight
finds its most striking expression. K., summoned in the middle of the night
to an interview with the official Erlanger, has, in his weariness and exhaustion, forgotten the number of the door, and enters, more in the sleepy hope
of finding an empty bed there than an official of the Castle, another room.
There he encounters the official Bürgel. The ensuing dialogue, or monologue rather, is one of Kafka's greatest feats in the art of melting the solid
flesh of a grotesque reality and revealing behind it the anatomy of the
miraculous. Bürgel promises K. to settle once and for all his affairs in the
Castle. K. is not in the least impressed by this offer. He waves it aside as the
boast of a dilettante:

> Without knowing anything of the circumstances under which
> K.'s appointment had come about, the difficulties that it en-
> countered in the community and at the Castle, of the complica-
> tions that had already occurred during K.'s sojourn here or had
> been foreshadowed, without knowing anything of all this, indeed
> without even showing, what should have been expected of a
> secretary, that he had at least an inkling of it all, he offered to
> settle the whole *affaire* up there in no time at all with the aid of
> his little note-pad.

It is the unbelief of a labyrinthine mind in the very existence of simplicity.
And while K. grows ever more weary, Bürgel delivers, in a rapturous
crescendo, the message of the miracle: If a man takes a secretary of the Castle
by surprise; if, in the middle of the night, the applicant, almost unconscious
of what he does, slips, like a tiny grain through a perfect sieve, through the
network of difficulties that is spread over all approaches to the centre of
authority, then the Castle, in the person of this one secretary, must yield to
the intruder, indeed must almost force the utterly unexpected granting of his

request upon the supplicant: 'You think it cannot happen at all? You are right, it cannot happen at all. But some night—for who can vouch for everything?—it *does* happen.' It is an event so rare that it seems to occur merely by virtue of rumour, and even if it does occur, one can, as it were, render it innocuous 'by proving to it, which is very easy, that there is no room for it in this world'. And Bürgel goes on with his rhapsody, describing the shattering delight with which a secretary responds to this situation. But when he ends, K. is sound asleep, and, with the conditions of the miracle fulfilled before his eyes, as unaware of its possibility as he had been in his tortured wakeful pursuit of it.

Indeed, no comfort can be found *within* this world. Yet the power not only to experience but poetically to create this world must have its source outside. Only a mind keeping alive in at least one of its recesses the memory of a place where the soul is truly at home is able to contemplate with such creative vigour the struggles of a man lost in a hostile land; and only an immensity of goodness can be so helplessly overcome by the vision of the worst of all possible worlds. This is the reason why we are not merely terrified by the despair of this book, but also moved by its sadness, the melancholy of spiritual failure carrying with it a hardly perceptible faith, the very faith of which all but inexhaustible resources are needed, as Kafka believed, for merely carrying on the business of every day.

In one of his most Manichaean sayings—in 'Reflections on Sin, . . .' —Kafka speaks of the power of a single crow to destroy the heavens; but, he adds, this 'proves nothing against the heavens for the heavens signify simply: The impossibility of crows.' And although these birds swarm ceaselessly around The Castle, its builder built it from the impulse to render them impossible. Is it, one wonders, yet another phantom hope in a deluded world that prompts in the book a child, a simple girl and a wretched family to turn with a mysteriously messianic expectation to the Land Surveyor K.? And makes, in one version of Kafka's attempt to continue the unfinished manuscript, an old woman say of the homeless stranger: 'This man shouldn't be let go to the dogs.' Or is it perhaps the reflection of a faith, maintained even in the grip of damnation, a faith which Nietzsche once expressed: 'Whosoever has built a new Heaven, has found the strength for it only in his own Hell'?

ALWIN L. BAUM

Parable as Paradox in Kafka's Stories

One of Kafka's many parable fragments describes a remote mountain synagogue that has served through countless generations as a retreat for a small
animal occupying the narrow ledge surrounding the temple walls. Even its
descent into full view of the congregation, although initially disturbing,
finally may be taken for granted and forgotten. It is a situation familiar to
Kafka's narratives—a vast landscape brought into relief against a labyrinthine architecture which serves at once as burrow and ceremonial sanctuary.
The edifice is invariably occupied by an agent whose presence, or whose
absence, makes of the narrative Gestalt a paradox and forces the imagery to
assume iconographic connotations while the hero bares his throat on the altar
of hermeneutic sacrifice. For the congregation, however, the rupture throws
into question not so much the rationale of the intrusion, which in any event
would be recorded only in legend, but calls instead for the development of a
strategy of accommodation. The paradox in the synagogue is, in fact,
occasioned by the lack of attention drawn to the animal, even considering its
prolonged presence, its quiet habits, its color which is nearly indistinguish-
able from that of the masonry, its unusual shyness, and its apparent attach-
ment "only to the building." Like the leopards in another of Kafka's temples,
the intruder has broken into the sanctuary so often, and emptied the sacrificial pitchers so completely, that the violation may be calculated in advance
until it becomes part of the ceremony.

Yet it is the ceremonialization of the animal's existence that poses the
greatest threat to the congregation. As it fades from awareness into the walls
of the temple, like a fresco, it crosses the threshold of the subliminal, leaving

From *MLN* 91, no. 6 (December 1976). Copyright ©1976 by The Johns Hopkins University
Press. Originally entitled "Parable as Paradox in Kafka's *Erzählungen*."

behind only the symbolic trace of its presence. It becomes a catalyst of self-recognition, a "welcome pretext," particularly for the younger women in the congregation, to "attract attention to themselves" as it clings to the lattice which separates them from the older men. The movements of the animal thus serve to divide the interior space of the temple into zones of signification, and there are evident vestiges of Kafka's self-effacement, his ambivalence toward women, and his monumental father problem throughout this parable. But the lines of demarcation cross and recross each other, like the tracks of the animal on its narrow ledge, until they become obscure; and even the sounds of its quiet steps gather to reverberate through the sanctuary like the echoes of the litany until they are lost in a univocal babble. Yet in the center of this temple is that inevitable space reserved in Kafka's parables for the altar of *die Schrift*, the hermetic scripture which holds the key to the mysteries. It is the altar of the *Gesetzbuch*—a code of codes—such as the Ark of the Covenant around which the animal in the synagogue gravitates, fulfilling what might best be conceived literally as a marginal existence, *Randbemerkungen* on the text.

Similar codices may be discovered at the center of almost any of the labyrinths in which Kafka's heroes find themselves. "Late, and uncertain of the way," the protagonist reads every gesture as a sign with hidden significance upon whose interpretation his life depends; he clings to every scrap of conversation as if it were a shred of the map which would lead him out, while the sardonic echo of "Gib's auf!" [Give up!] rings through the empty streets. Or at the other extreme, he takes quite literally what is meant only in a figurative sense: as Georg Bendemann takes "the verdict" of his father condemning him to death by drowning; as the man from the country takes the word of the doorkeeper to the Law that he cannot be admitted at the moment, although "the door stands open as usual"; or, as K., in parallel credulity, accepts his arrest as a certain sign of some crime he has unwittingly committed, or as a sanction of the guilt he already feels. The seriousness with which Kafka's heroes pursue the quest for the *Gesetzbuch* threatens, however, to obscure the irony embedded in the parable of the quest itself. In *The Trial,* when the Washerwoman finally permits K. a glimpse of the official ledgers of the Examining Magistrate—old, dog-eared, *schmützig* volumes which are falling apart at the seams—he finds only an "indecent picture" of a man and woman sitting naked on a couch. The private intentions of the artist are clear enough, although the drawing is so clumsy and the perspective so false, that the couple turn toward each other only with great difficulty. Continuing his search through the ledgers, K. discovers merely a novel entitled: "The Plagues which Grete Suffered from Her Husband Hans." "These are the law books studied here," K. remarks with resignation, "by such men shall I be judged."

This would seem the cruellest of jokes if it could be taken seriously, but it is a transparent mockery of the poetic justice dispensed in the *Gesetzbuch* which condemns him "not only in innocence but also in ignorance." In other words, it is a parody of *The Trial* itself.

Max Brod recalls in his biography that in spite of the "fearful earnestness" of the first chapter of *The Trial,* the small number of friends to whom Kafka read the manuscript all "laughed immoderately," and he adds that Kafka laughed so hard he could scarcely continue. One might take any of Kafka's narratives as seriously as K. only at the risk of falling victim to the irony that discovers the "message of salvation" parading around in the rags of the burlesque. It is an irony witnessed in Maurice Blanchot's remark that Kafka's desire to have his posthumous work destroyed could be attributed to his foresight that it was "condemned to universal misunderstanding." For K. and for the rest of Kafka's heroes, nevertheless, *Missverständnis* [misunderstanding] assumes the function of a defensive strategy since it postpones self-recognition, the acceptance of guilt as a universal law. But there are ontological as well as psychological implications in the false perspective which suggest that truth may only lie in illusion: "For we are like tree trunks in the snow. In appearance they lie sleekly and a little push should be enough to set them rolling. No, it can't be done, for they are firmly wedded to the ground. But see, even that is only appearance."

In Kafka's narratives everything is a matter of appearance, *nur Schein,* in one sense because the world outside is mediated in perception, in another because the world inside is mediated in language. Thus, the implications of K.'s self-caricature are of neither more nor less consequence than the phenomenology of self-consciousness. In that respect, there is a paradox particularly appropriate to Kafka's work in a remark made by one of Borges' detectives (as he stands, like K., on the threshold of "divining the morphology" of his own murder) that unlike reality, "an hypothesis has no obligation to be true, but it does have an obligation to be interesting." Kafka's style is similarly hypothetical, characterized by an interminable *vielleicht* [perhaps], such as might be found in the parable "Passers-by" which finds the narrator arguing against catching hold of anyone who comes running down the street toward you in the moonlight, even if he is feeble and ragged, even if someone chases yelling at his heels:

> For it is night, and you can't help it if the street goes uphill before you in the moonlight, and besides, these two have maybe started that chase to amuse themselves, or perhaps they are both chasing a third, perhaps the first is an innocent man and the

second wants to murder him and you would become an accessory,
perhaps they don't know anything about each other and are
merely running separately home to bed, perhaps they are night
birds, perhaps the first man is armed.

And anyhow, haven't you a right to be tired, haven't you
been drinking a lot of wine? You're thankful that the second man
is now long out of sight.

There is a complex rationale indicated in this ambivalence. It reflects a
crossroads of the literal and the figurative characteristic of a rebus—*ein
Bilderrätsel*—or a "mystic writing pad" in the Freudian implications of
those psychological mechanisms which permit symbolic displacement and
metaphorical superimposition. At the same time, it is an obvious parable of
poetic ambiguity, the proliferation of narrative possibilities. But these two
functions are inseparable, at least in Kafka's fiction, because the entire
universe it represents is a *Zeichensprache,* the sign-language of consciousness
upon whose decodification the life of the hero depends, in both the literal
and the figurative sense. It is a quest perhaps best characterized as "the
adventure of a semiologist in spite of himself."

Many complain that the words of the wise are always merely
parables but of no use in daily life, and this is all we have. When
the sage says: "Go over," he does not mean that we should
actually go over to the other side, which we could still do if the
end of the journey warranted, but he means some mythical
yonder, something unknown to us, something too that he cannot
designate more precisely and consequently, something which can
scarcely help us here. All these parables really set out to say
merely that the incomprehensible is incomprehensible, and we
know that already. But that with which we have to struggle every
day is another thing.

Concerning this a man said: "Why are you so defensive? If
you only followed the parables you yourselves would become
parables and with that free of your daily cares."

Another said: "I bet that is also a parable."

The first said: "You have won."

The second said: "But unfortunately only in parable."

The first said: "No, in reality; in parable you have lost."

In this parable of parables the shadow of Kafka's everyday struggle with
language looms above the father-problem, the engagement-problem, the

existential question, *Judaïschefrage* [The Jewish Question], the bourgeois question that have dominated the hermeneutic *Prozess* [process—but *Das Prozess* is *The Trial*] to which Kafka's work has been subjected. Indeed, this parable is a parody of exegesis. It suggests that not only the idiom of the sage, but any discourse is comprehensible only metaphorically. The interpreter becomes Kafka's *Spielzeug* [plaything] and is forced along with the interlocutors into that paradoxical space between the actual and the fictive. It is the prototypic parable of a logocentric universe—that same wilderness which stretches forth endlessly from Kafka's "Great Wall of China" to "The Burrow." Language is the mythical yonder from which there is no return for the explorer because it does not exist in some actual space. The literal-mindedness characteristic of Kafka's heroes and the second speaker in this parable merely suggests the absurdity of taking any experience for granted, or unequivocally. The significance of each may depend solely upon its metaphorical interrelation with other possibilities. The court in which K. must write his own defense is the *Gerichtshof* [law court] of consciousness which adjudicates the process of figuration, and it is in this sense that Kafka's *Erzählungen* [tales] may be considered parables of themselves.

The term "parable," rooted in Greek *paraballein*, suggests analogical rather than analytical discourse. The German equivalent *das Gleichniss*, literally "likeness" or "simile," indicates more clearly the semiotic duplicity inherent in the narrative. Whether ancient or Kafkaesque, the parable assumes the form of extended metaphor, but it is an open-ended comparison in which the chain of signifiers automatically cancels its literal sense, in the process of articulation, to imply patterns of association which may be bonded to the actual signifier only by the slightest tether of semantic, or even phonemic paradigm. The semiotic unit essential to the parable is the symbol, particularly in its ancient form as *symbolus*, a token divided among members of secret fraternities, such as the Apostles, the fragments of which assume signification only in the absence of the referential set to which they belong, thereby assuring the hermetic nature of the order. Parable thus stands at the pole opposite allegory, although they resemble each other because of their common suppression of the signifier. Allegory secures an absolute bond between sign and referent while the parable derives its signification in the distance it sets between them. It is an intrinsically paradoxical narrative which, in essence, may mean anything except what it says.

This inherent ambiguity provides a rationale for the function of parable in the hermetic tradition generally. In the apostolic scriptures, for example, Matthew records that after delivering the "Parable of the Sower," Jesus responded to his disciples' impatience to know why he always addressed the masses in this occluded form of discourse by suggesting that it was the only language they could understand—the only tongue which would reveal to them the Mysteries—since, "They seeing see not, and hearing they hear not" (13:13). In Kafka's narratives as well as in the mythic and scriptural texts, the parable functions to illustrate the presence of symbolic ambiguity and secret codes at work in the most insignificant human gesture, the most trivial utterance. A young girl's playful knock at a manor gate is enough to warrant the arrest and imprisonment of her brother forever, while she runs home to change into clothes more suitable to the occasion. This ironic twist serves to demonstrate more than the absurd interrelation of power and justice. The entire narrative situation shifts to a metaphorical plane, from which (as is most graphically illustrated in Gregor Samsa's metamorphosis into a dung beetle) no return to a world of unambiguous events is possible. Any court which summons the accused to appear before a judge whose legal assistant carries the unlikely name of "Assman" must derive its authority from the bar of symbolic association.

Another parable relates that an ordinary child's top was sufficient to engage the lifelong attention of a certain philosopher. He would lie in wait until one was set spinning, then rush out in pursuit to try to catch it. "For he believed that the understanding of any detail . . . was sufficient for the understanding of all things. For this reason he did not busy himself with great problems, it seemed to him uneconomical". However, the providential order which this top sets in motion is not that of Blake, but that of Sartre. For "when he held the silly piece of wood in his hand, he felt nauseated. The screaming of the children, which hitherto he had not heard and which now suddenly pierced his ears, chased him away, and he tottered like a top under a clumsy whip." It is not so much the lack of a moral order that the philosopher discovers, but the lack of *Logos*. He sees in the top only an image of himself as Other, and the phenomenological dialectic sets him tottering because its rationale must remain subliminal. As the narrator observes in the parable, "Zur Frage der Gesetze" ["The Problem of Our Laws"]: "the essence of a secret code is that it should remain a mystery."

Kafka characterized his fiction as "a new occult doctrine, a kind of Cabala." It is to that esoteric tradition of hermeneutic that his narratives bear closest resemblance—interpretation, rather than the faith required of the penitent in the Gospels, is essential to decode the message of salvation. It has been observed that the gates to the Law encountered by the man from the country in "Vor dem Gesetz" ["Before the Law"] are reminiscent of the gnostic division into "gates of jurisprudence" of the *Babylonian Talmud*. And yet in each of these *Gezetzbücher,* the message is like that found in the

Persian parable of "Scheherazade"—the shortest route to the Law is through the endless proliferation of parables. Thus the message of salvation may be offered the suppliant only when he ceases to take literally the text, something the man from the country cannot do, of course, since the significance of his existence depends on "being-in-parable." But the message is also lost on K., for whom it is intended. Paradoxically, he fails to take the text literally enough because he is its counterpart.

"So the doorkeeper deluded the man," K. concludes after hearing the parable. "Don't be too hasty," the Priest counters, "don't take over an opinion without testing it. I have told you the story in the very words of the scriptures. There's no mention of delusion in it." He later continues to admonish K. for his peremptory exegesis: "You have not enough respect for the written word and you are altering the story." Among the implications of the Priest's catechism is a caution against any interpretive rationale which lies outside the actual text. At the same time, he suggests that nothing in the text may be overlooked, *die Schrift* admits no contradictions, it is not syllogistic, and nothing in it may be considered either extraneous or insignificant. Thus the parable not only admits paradox, but it depends on disjunction and contradiction to pry into its metaphorical associations. The Priest argues that the doorkeeper's mutually exclusive statements about the Law are not contradictory, but that one even implies the other; and in that regard, he invokes the commentator's opinion that "the right perception of any matter and a misunderstanding of the same matter do not wholly exclude each other," a conclusion which is reflected in his later insistence that it is really the doorkeeper who is deluded. He even argues against any distinction between subject and object in proposing that the Law and the doorkeeper are really one and the same. K. concludes that if no differentiation may be made between the Law and its agent, if to doubt one is to doubt the other, one must therefore accept as true everything the doorkeeper says. "No," the Priest counters, "it is not necessary to accept everything as true, one must only accept it as necessary." "A melancholy conclusion," K. admits, "it turns lying into a universal principle."

The problem for all of Kafka's heroes is to find a way to accept the necessity of delusion, or the authenticity of illusion, in a world where, as Heinz Politzer suggests, "language itself is the 'arch-liar.' " Noting the distrust of metaphor in some of Kafka's diary entries, Politzer argues that in the fiction there is a consistent concern to expose the "innate mendacity" of literary language by forcing it to reveal its self-contradiction. But the narrative can be no more mendacious nor contradictory than conciousness. In Kafka's parables, particularly, if truth may be approached at all, it will necessarily be through paradox and indirection, through pursuit of "the most senseless rumors," as Kafka's erstwhile "dog among dogs" reveals in "Investigations of a Dog." Remarking the set of events which has led to his obsessive preoccupation with investigations that have alienated him from the rest of dogdom, he continues, "and the most senseless seemed to me in this senseless world more probable than the sensible, and moreover particularly fertile for investigation." Although he has never seen the soaring dogs whose rumored existence he investigates, they nevertheless occupy an "important place" in his "picture of the world"—a place due less to the marvel of their flying technique than to the senselessness of their occupation. It is the stir caused by the stories, of course, and not the actual dogs, who only exist "in rumor," that makes the investigations worthwhile, as senseless as they are: "And though the truth will not be discovered by such means—never can that stage be reached—yet they throw light on some of the profounder ramifications of falsehood. For all the senseless phenomena of our existence, and the most senseless most of all, are susceptible to investigation. Not completely, of course—that is the diabolical jest—but sufficiently to spare one painful questions."

To be sure, the legends surrounding these flying dogs, who have "no relation to the general life of the community," are parables of self-reflection: "Someone now and then refers to art and artists," the dog adds, "but there it ends." Yet it is scarcely a dead end, for even the investigator's existence may be established only by pursuit of senseless rumors. Kafka observes elsewhere: "Confession and the lie are one and the same. In order to confess one tells lies. One cannot express what one is, for this is precisely what one is: one can communicate only what one is not, that is, the lie." If there is an avoidance of traditional figurative devices in Kafka's narratives, it is to acknowledge that existence itself is a fiction. One of Kafka's grandest illusions is Gregor Samsa's metamorphosis into a dung beetle, the absurdity of which lies not so much in the transformation itself, but in the lack of surprise it occasions among Gregor and his family. And yet such a protean existence could scarcely be more rational from the phenomenological perspective of consciousness "in itself." It is enough for Gregor to take literally, if only for a moment, a figure of speech. If he has been made to feel no better than "vermin" by his family—if his father has actually called him an *Ungeziefer*—what more appropriate defensive strategy for the son than to take actual shape in his metaphoric guise, to "become parable," and thus rid himself of his daily cares? This particular metamorphosis had been prefigured in Kafka's early "Wedding Preparations in the Country." Raban's ambivalence about his *Hochzeitsvorbereitungen* [wedding preparations] manifests itself in the schizophrenic alternative of sending his clothed body in his place, while he keeps to his bed and assumes "the shape of a large beetle," pretending it was a matter of hibernating. Yet the metamorphic principle is active throughout Kafka's narratives, not as a figurative device, but as an ontological structure. It is a strategy held in common by dreams, fantasies, and fetishism, but it is not especially neurotic. It forms the morphology of the symbolic function, as Freud observes, equally well in the ordinary observance of the reality principle. Or, in Jacques Derrida's critique of its implications in the semiology of consciousness, it constitutes the function played by *différance* in the dual sense of object deferment and displacement.

One could argue against an allegorical reading of Kafka on these categorical grounds—that there may be no assumption of substitution for an actual referent, since the signified concept, the *Ding-ansich,* has never been present in itself, as Derrida observes. Following Saussure's argument that the codification of any semiotic system depends upon the arbitrariness of the signifier and upon the maintenance of differences among the signifiers, Derrida concludes that *différance,* the "systematic play" of differing and deferring in the signifying chain, constitutes the very "possibility of conceptuality." This is the semiotic universe occupied by Kafka's protagonists, such as Gregor, whose struggle to rid himself of these illusions is impossible, since all existence is *nur Schein.* In any case it would be impractical for his illusions to drop away, since they provide the perfect *Scheingrund,* the pretext which allows him to exist in two places as the same time.

But if Kafka's protagonist is *eiron,* he is also condemned to play the inevitable role of *pharmakos.* It is almost too obvious that most of the characters in any given story of Kafka's are spectral refractions of a single, narrative consciousness that might as well be called "K." for the sake of convenience. In fact, the abbreviated name of the hero is most appropriate to the parable; it forces K. to hover in that space between the signifier and the signified. He exists as the unnameable *eidos,* the pattern of images bound together through his own self-effacement. The price paid for his metaphorical ubiquity is a loss of mnemonic coherence, particularly the sense of "being-in-time." He is submitted to a perpetual *sparagmos* in which he must play the role of executioner as well as the victim whose limbs are torn and scattered throughout the imagery of the text. He is subject and object of his quest at the same time, an ambivalence reflected in Kafka's indecision over choosing a narrative voice between the first and third persons. In "Wedding Preparations" the narrator finds himself "alone, a total stranger and only an object of curiosity. And so long as you say 'one' instead of 'I,' there's nothing in it and one can easily tell the story; but as soon as you admit to yourself that it is you yourself, you feel as though transfixed and are horrified." The narrative voice actually chosen vacillates between the first and third persons as does K. between the named and the unnameable. Of course K. may only appear as a reflection of the narrating consciousness, which remains subliminal, but even this is no guarantee that the narrator knows himself any better than K. or that he has any surer sense of the narrative's significance. The text is analogous to that of a dream in which nothing can be represented except through the agency of displacement; therefore nothing represented may be considered insignificant. Thus K. is condemned to question every detail, yet no land-surveyor could decipher the map of his own consciousness. His quest can neither complete itself in time, since the system under construction is also the process of its deconstruction, nor in space, since each sign may only find its reference in another displaced association.

All of the fragmentary architecture in Kafka's stories—the temples, cities, towers, walls, corridors, tunnels—stand as model ruins of the texts in which they appear. Although it appears that the construction has gone according to plan, that "Alles ging den Ordnung nach," as the narrators are fond of observing, yet each stone is deeply etched in the hieroglyphic idiom of "barbaric mountain dwellers," the "clumsy scribbling of senseless children's hands." "The Great Wall of China" similarly parabolizes the narrative process which proceeded in "piecemeal construction" throughout Kafka's life, despite his hopes that his writing would provide a coherence otherwise denied by ambivalent responsibilities, much as the Wall is distinguished by the irony of its unbridgeable gaps. "How can a wall protect if it is not a continuous structure?" the narrator wonders. Yet the wall of the text is designed to expose the lacunae in the morphology of consciousness. The Great Wall may only protect the peasants from those legendary northern barbarians if it is a discontinous structure, in part because they only feel safe in their continual preoccupation with the building process, but more importantly, it takes on a metaphorical connotation which would baffle the most persistent adversary. If the wall could be finished, if it were permitted to come together to enclose some actual space, however vast; or if it joined two points in time, no matter how remote, it would cease to signify anything other than the need to begin another wall. Such an edifice may be completed, as the scholar predicts, only when it is conjoined with the Tower of Babel. And since the Wall does not even form a circle, it could only serve as the foundation for such a tower—as the Scriptures make clear—"in parable."

This parable is thus representative of more than Kafka's attempt to mediate conflicting allegiances to his writing and to the world outside that wall. It reflects the paradox of the creation parables, a cosmology of the phenomenological dialectic. The Great Wall divides the universe into immanence and transcendence, time and space, being and becoming, self and other, conscious and unconscious, *noesis* and *noema,* the signifier and the signified. The Tower of Babel is the covenant of the text itself as phenomenal object around which no one could walk long enough to encompass its essence. It is built by the demiurge which inspires St. John to rewrite the Creation through explicit invocation of the Word as God. For Kafka's dogs, moles, and martens, for his explorers, builders, commercial travellers, land-surveyors, sons, fathers, and artists, the sign of authority is synonymous with the tetragrammaton of the alphabet that contains, like "Odradek" in "The Cares of A Family Man," all possible solutions in its meaningless.

The Wall marks the perimeters of language, a land "so vast . . . that no fable could do justice to its vastness." There is, nevertheless, a parable that, according to the narrator, "describes the situation very well." It tells of a message sent from the Emperor "to you alone," the humble subject, "cowering in the remotest distance before the imperial sun." Of course the messenger can never reach the subject. The multitudes are too vast, the chambers and courts which must be crossed are countless. As in Zeno's parable, the time it would take the messenger to reach the outermost gate of the palace squares in relation to the distance he must travel. If he should finally burst through that gate—"but never, never can that happen"—he would merely find himself where he began, "in the center of the world, crammed to bursting with its own sediment." And the fabulist concludes: "Nobody could fight his way through here even with a message from a dead man. But you sit at your window when evening falls and dream it to yourself."

This is surely a metaparable of Kafka's "absent-minded window gazing" as he sat in his study above the Niklasstrasse, looking out over the bridge to the green slopes on the other side of the river, as we find Georg Bendemann at the beginning of "The Judgment." At his desk, Kafka would await the *Bote* [messenger] sent him from the remotest regions of consciousness with that message of salvation—a sentence would be enough—to reassure him that the empire of his parables was still intact. Throughout his diaries, Kafka reveals that his worst writing resulted from "straining too hard after the word" while his best work took him by surprise, when he was most vulnerable. There is a parable of this in "A Fratricide," where Schmar lies in wait for Wese, the "industrious nightworker," as he pauses on his journey home to gaze into the night sky. Nothing draws together in a pattern to interpret the immediate future for him—everything stays in "its senseless, inscrutable place"—and he walks on into Schmar's naked knife. All this time Pallas, the "private citizen," observes in bemused indifference from his second-story window. Schmar shouts: "The bliss of murder! the relief, the soaring ecstasy from the shedding of another's blood!" It is, of course, the writer's own blood. Kafka's early diary entries speak of the joy of imagining a knife twisted in his heart; but it is no ordinary *Selbstmord* [suicide] that he has in mind. It is the same blade which descends on Wese and on K. at the abortive conclusion of *The Trial*—the scalpel of his writing which might make an incision between his literal and figurative existence. He admits to Brod in an early letter that he had been considering suicide until he realized by staying alive he would interrupt his writing less. In another early diary entry Kafka entered this reflection: "It is as if I were made of stone, as if I were my own tombstone . . . only a vague hope lives on, but no better than the inscriptions on tombstones. Almost every word I write jars against the next, I hear the consonants rub leadenly against each other and the vowels sing an accompaniment like Negroes in a minstrel show. My doubts stand in a circle around every word, I see them before I see the word, but what then! I do not see the word at all, I invent it."

This metaphorical association of inscription and incision looks forward to many of Kafka's parables, notably "A Dream," which puns on "engraving" and "en-graving" (*eingraben*). K. glides to a rendezvous with the artist at the cemetary down paths that are "winding, ingeniously made and unpractical," like the deeply incised letters of his epitaph which race across his monument while K. sinks, as if everything had been prepared beforehand, into the "impenetrable depths" of his grave. The epitaph of the parable comes engraved, like shards of ancient clay tablets, in a language which the author himself can scarcely understand. Kafka's struggle with the word is a *Strasskolonie* [penal colony] in which he is condemned to play the simultaneous roles of Officer, Explorer, Commandant and Prisoner, all gravitating around the *Apparat* which cuts into the victim's flesh the predetermined message "bringing enlightenment to the most dull-witted." This instrument of torture is clearly a *Schreibmaschine*—not the typewriter at Kafka's office, of course, but his own hand as it etched its way over the barren landscape of the blank page, directed by the "designer" which is regulated, in turn, by the sentence of judgment against the condemned. The guiding plans for the machine have been drawn by the Old Commandant, and are therefore beyond recognition for the explorer. When the Officer holds them up for him to read, all he can see is "a labyrinth of lines crossing and recrossing each other, which covered the black spaces between them." When the explorer protests that he cannot read the plans, although they are very ingenious, the Officer argues that they are clear enough, yet "it's no calligraphy for school children. It needs to be studied closely, I'm quite sure that in the end you would understand it too," he continues. "Of course the script can't be a simple one; it's not supposed to kill a man straight off, but only after an interval of, on an average, twelve hours; the turning point is reckoned to come at the sixth hour. So there have to be lots and lots of flourishes around the actual script; the script itself runs around the body only in a narrow girdle; the rest of the body is reserved for the embellishments." There can be little doubt that at least one model for these plans is the parable of the Penal Colony itself, or Kafka's fiction in general, with its associational flourishes surrounding a narrow girdle of actual script that torture and liberate alternatively.

During the session in which Kafka composed "The Judgment," the execution of the sentence did take the course of one evening, with the turning point coming around the sixth hour. With a mixed feeling of joy and strain, Kafka compared the writing process to the labor of childbirth and expressed the hope that all of his work might be done with such coherence and completeness. Needless to say, the verdict was against him—it was the first and last of his writings to be born with so few complications. Within this parable also, the hero is "sentenced to death" because of his writing, albeit apparently trivial letters to his erstwhile "friend" who is wasting away in the remoteness of Russia. As with Kafka, Georg's fiancée and his father come between him and the friend whose role is perhaps best associated with the estranged alter-ego of the writer. Like his father, Georg's friend is victim of his neglect, and has even "turned yellow enough to be thrown away." Of course, this metaphorical description in itself forces the reader to beware taking the tragedy of these circumstances either too literally or too seriously. The association is to "An Old Manuscript," the manuscript page of another of Kafka's parables. The enormous newspaper the father has been reading is also yellow with age and written in a language unreadable to Georg, suggesting that it also comes from the depths of Russia. As in most of Kafka's stories, these relations parallel Kafka's chronic estrangement from his father, along with his tentative engagements at this time to Felice Bauer. In both instances, Kafka attributed the alienation to his preoccupation with his writing. That there should be an alliance between the father and the friend in the parable is reminiscent of Kafka's expressed need to have his father recognize him through the medium of his art, a circumstance most graphically revealed in his hundred-page "Letter" to his father, which he wrote only when he was thirty-six. It is as if Kafka could only speak to his father in parable. Paradoxically, his fiction was at the same time an attempt to get away: "My writings were about you," he admits in the letter, "in them I merely poured out the lamentations I could not pour out on your own breast.

It was a farewell deliberately drawn out, save that, although you, it is true, imposed it, the direction it was given *I* determined."

The farewell was, of course, drawn out to the end of Kafka's life, as it would have to be, since the father had been internalized as *das Urteil* [the judgment] the son imposed on himself. The actual father merely fulfilled his wildest dreams. Needless to say, Kafka's mother intercepted the letter, in the realization that, at best, it would end up lying unread in the dust which covered the stories Kafka had given his father to read years before. If Kafka could avenge himself for such neglect in parable, it would have to take the form of self-punishment. He reveals in the letter that he was even afraid the feelings of shame and guilt he experienced in his father's presence would live on after he died. If he could commit murder in parable, he could just as well sentence himself to death by drowning. Yet again, it is impossible to take the sentence too seriously. As Georg rushes downstairs to his fate, he meets the Charwoman who exclaims "Jesus!" and covers her face with her apron. It is a scarcely subtle parody of Kafka's "passion," and it reaches the level of sardonic tour-de-force when Georg declares his love for his parents with his final breath while waiting for the noise of passing traffic to cover the sound of his splash in the river below.

In light of these associations, moreover, if one turns to Kafka's own exegesis, he risks drowning in the same river. In one of his few metacommentaries, Kafka attempts to reveal "all the relationships which have become clear to me in the story as far as I now remember them" (the entry in his *Diaries* is dated five months after the story was written). "This is necessary," he continues, "because the story came out of me like a real live birth, covered with filth and slime, and only I have the hand that can reach to the body itself and the strength of desire to do so." There follows an account of the relationships, pulled out by the hand of the midwife, that is even murkier than the live birth. Although Kafka reads his own story as a parable of the father problem, centered around the friend as "their strongest common bond," he does not reveal what the rationale for that bond may be, nor the reasons why the son's relation to the father must be mediated through this remote and ambiguous friend. Kafka does suggest, paradoxically, that the "lesser things" they share in common—love, devotion to the mother, loyalty to her memory, the father's business clientele—all permit him to "set himself up as Georg's antagonist," so that the son is left with nothing. He argues that even the bride "lives only in relation to the friend," since ultimately, "she cannot penetrate the circle of blood relationship that is drawn around father and son." He concludes that Georg takes the sentence as seriously as he does because he has "lost everything except the awareness of his father."

The question is how seriously one should take Kafka's explication of his own text when it reads like a parable itself. More revealing are some of the flourishes around the actual script, such as Kafka's explanation of the anagrammatic formation of the characters' names: "Georg has the same number of letters as Franz. In Bendemann, 'mann' is a strengthening of 'Bende' to provide for all the as yet unforeseen possibilities in the story, but 'Bende' has exactly the same number of letters as Kafka, and the vowel *e* occurs in the same places as does the vowel *a* in Kafka." It is this palimpsest of metaphoric association which gives to Kafka's stories those "unforeseen possibilities" that make them parables of narrative self-consciousness. Although all of his writings may be about the father, it is the process of figuration which provides the actual missing links in their relationship. When the father challenges the authenticity of Georg's friend, and the motives behind his engagement, Georg shrinks into a corner as far away as possible, thinking: "A long time ago he had firmly made up his mind to watch closely every least movement so that he should not be surprised by any indirect attack, a pounce from behind or above. At this moment he recalled this long-forgotten resolve and forgot it again, like a man drawing a short thread through the eye of a needle." The hidden motive for this defensiveness is no doubt Kafka's chronic fear of a surprise attack from his father—verbal rather than physical—and because of his father's "certain eloquence," as Kafka puts it in his "Letter," the son would be left feeling impotent to reply. Kafka sometimes stammered in these confrontations and felt that his only recourse was to his writing, where his own eloquence would assert itself. Yet in his narratives, the verbal contests result in the capitulation of the son. Indeed, they are represented symbolically as physical barriers, labyrinths through which the hero winds, expecting at any moment to be slaughtered by the monstrous hybrid of his own creation. No ball of thread is long enough to lead Kafka's narrators back to the entrance because they have never been outside this wall of displaced and overdetermined association. It forms, at one and the same time, their palisade and prison. Thus Kafka could never come to grips with the minotaur of his father because he could only exist in his full reality "in parable."

It is because of this ceremonialization, nevertheless, that Kafka's *Prozess* needs be taken no more seriously than he takes himself, at least in parable. Georg's conversation with his father is a jest, as they both admit. "Yes, of course I've been playing a comedy! A comedy! That's a good expression!" the father shouts. Like all comedy, it parodies the sacred text—it is full of Georg's futile attempts to sneak out through the back door of the word: " 'You comedian!' Georg could not resist the retort, realized at once the harm done and, his eyes starting in his head, bit his tongue back, only too late, till the pain made his knees give." It is as if Georg could create or destroy the father if he could only find the right verbal formula: "Now he'll lean forward, thought Georg, what if he topples and smashes himself! These words went hissing through his mind." At this point the father leans forward but does not topple. Only later, after the sentencing, does the crash of his fall behind Georg ring in his ears as he flees the room. It is a fall which resounds with the magical self-reflection of language, like the parable of Humpty Dumpty behind Lewis Carroll's *Looking Glass,* or in Joyce's *Finnegans Wake.* At one point the father exclaims, "I have your customers here in my pocket!" and Georg remarks to himself, " 'He has pockets even in his shirt!' . . . and believed that with this remark he could make him an impossible figure for all the world. Only for a moment did he think so, since he kept on forgetting everything." This nonsense parodies the "short thread" of the symbolic process which actuates the event at the turn of a phrase. Even the sentence, *das Urteil,* is pronounced as if it were a figure of speech taken literally by the son. It is only appropriate that he drops into the stream of narrative possibilities which parabolize his existence.

There is a degree of self-indulgence in Kafka's self-consciousness. Yet his vision is not circumscribed by his writing compulsion; instead he sees the world itself as a parable, an hermetic text in every passage of which is interwoven a complex matrix of signification. It is because that world may be represented only as an extension of narrative consciousness that a decodification of the text assumes a decodification of the cryptographer. As Richard Macksey has observed with regard to this narrative tradition, metaphor can only tell something about the viewer, nothing about the object. Thus not merely the characters, but the topography of the narrative text, its *Sinnenwelt,* serves as the mirror of the symbolic process. In "Advocates" the narrator argues that once you have started out on a walk you must continue it whatever happens, you have only to gain and nothing to risk, even if you fall over a precipice, for "had you turned back after the first steps and run downstairs you would have fallen at once—and not perhaps, but for certain. So if you find nothing in the corridors open the doors, if you find nothing behind these doors there are more floors, and if you find nothing up there don't worry, just leap up another flight of stairs. As long as you don't stop climbing, the stairs won't end, under your climbing feet they will go on growing upwards."

This is the same endless stairway on which the Hunter Gracchus climbs about in a parable which Wilhelm Emrich takes as "the model of all Kafka's stories and novels." It is the stairway stretched between the planes of the literal and the figurative. In this parable even the distinction between life and death is open to interpretation, since the Hunter is, in a manner of speaking, both dead and alive at the same time. His dialogue with the Burgomaster, a rhetorical debate which assumes that the question may be resolved through determination of guilt, concludes with the Hunter's lament:

> No one will read what I write here, no one will come to help me; even if all the people were commanded to help me, every door and window would remain shut, everyone would take to bed and draw the bedclothes over his head, the whole earth would become an inn for the night. And there is sense in that, for nobody knows of me, and if anyone knew, he would not know where I could be found, he would not know how to deal with me, he would not know how to help me. The thought of helping me is an illness that has to be cured by taking to one's bed.

The image is reminiscent of Dostoevsky's reflection, in *Notes from the Underground,* that to be conscious is "a thoroughgoing illness." The slightest "wrong turn of the wheel" can lead one into that region of symbolic indeterminacy characterized by the Hunter's voyage. Placing his hand on the Burgomaster's knee in order to make good the jest, the Hunter chooses to return to his ship without rudder, "blown by the winds that blow in the undermost regions of death."

It is a mood of self-conscious parody which looks forward to Kafka's last parables, such as "The Burrow," which finds the animal-narrator tunneled so deeply into the underground burrow of his text that it is impossible to tell one from the other. This labyrinth of rooms and passages, so carefully hammered into shape with the architect's forehead, and designed so carefully for his protection from the enemy outside, serves merely to make him more vulnerable because of his complete investment in the construction process. The author has designed the labyrinth so carefully, in fact, that he finds himself both exasperated and touched when, as sometimes happens, he loses himself in his own maze, as if the work of his hand were doing its best to prove its sufficiency to its maker "whose final judgment has long since been passed on it." Of course there could be no final judgment on a process of writing which could never come to completion. Threatened with doubts about the safety of his refuge, the animal resolves to fly from it forever, only to discover once outside that he is not really free from those doubts. Thus he rushes back, ready to spend his life keeping watch over the entrance, gloating perpetually on the reflection—and in that finding his happiness—

how steadfast a protection the burrow would be if he were inside it. It is a paradox created in "the impossibility of grasping, at once, all the possible consequences of one's actions." Thus he finds himself drawn ineluctably back inside the burrow of his parable, only to confront a new danger from within—those "legendary creatures of the inner earth" whose clawing and whistling, once heard, indicate "already you are lost."

Aside from the droning of "possible consequences," the unseen creature whose whistling prefigured the inevitable destruction of Kafka's burrow was tuberculosis, which had tunneled into his lungs far enough to to kill him six months after the story was written. When Kafka first learned of his illness, seven years previous, it prompted a sardonic allusion to God's providence: "I should have taken him for more of a gentleman." That sense of irony remained with Kafka until he rose up from his deathbed to criticize his companion for refusing to give him more morphine: "Kill me, otherwise you are a murderer!" It is a final paradox that looks back to Kafka's earliest parable in which the Supplicant reflects: "Are we not free to say what we want in conversation? After all, we're not aiming at any definite purpose or at the truth, but simply at making jokes and having a good time." From that moment of self-parody to "Josephine, the Singer," which was written practically on his deathbed, Kafka would be "making a ceremonial performance out of doing the usual thing." He would keep intruding into the temple of parable until he became part of the ceremony. And for the visitor to the sanctuary, cowering in the remotest corner and trying to make some sense of the litany, there remains an inevitable feeling that if in reality he has won, in parable he has lost. Thus it is perhaps only just to conclude these remarks with a final parable from Kafka's diaries on the critical *Prozess*:

> The difficulties of bringing to an end even a short essay lie not in the fact that we feel the end of the piece demands a fire which the actual content up to that point has not been able to produce out of itself, they arise rather from the fact that even the shortest essay demands of the author a degree of self-satisfaction and of being lost in himself out of which it is difficult to step into the everyday air without great determination and an external incentive, so that, before the essay is rounded to a close and one might quietly slip away, one bolts, driven by unrest, and then the end must be completed from the outside with hands which must not only do the work but hold on as well.

WALTER H. SOKEL

Language and Truth in the Two Worlds
of Franz Kafka

In Kafka's earliest extant narrative, "Description of a Struggle," a wild exhibitionist attracts the attention of the narrator in a church. Because he is ostensibly praying, while indulging in grotesque antics, the exhibitionist is called the Praying Man, while the obese narrator bears the title Fat Man. The Fat Man accuses the Praying Man of being the bearer of a disease with which he himself admits to being familiar. He calls this disease "a seasickness on dry land." The nature of the affliction is linguistic. Its symptom is the inability to remember "the truthful names of things," which leads to the compulsve effort to invent ever-new names for them. The victim of this disease cannot recall, for instance, the word "poplar," and in consequence names the tree "the Tower of Babel." Then, having forgotten that name also, he calls it "Noah in his Cups."

We encounter in the victim of such "forgetfulness" the prototype of the poet or literary man. He substitutes metaphor for straight language. The first symptom of his "seasickness" of language is a metaphor. In the word "Tower," there is still contained a recognizable element of comparison. A tall tree, the poplar, can be compared to a tower. However, in this disease, metaphor immediately degenerates into a wildly associative discourse that turns incomprehensible. For the associations which carry it are personal and lead completely away from the original referent. To be sure, the stream of associations can be reconstructed. The comparison of a tall tree to a tower leads to Babel as the place where the highest tower had been attempted. At

From *German Quarterly* 52, no. 3 (1979). Copyright ©1979 by the American Association of Teachers of German.

the same time, "Babel" exemplifies of course the very process of forgetting of a shared language and suggests the resulting confusion of human relationships which is the topic of the narrator's complaint. In *Genesis,* the building of the Tower of Babel follows closely upon man's first inebriation. The stream of associations thus leads understandably from "the Tower of Babel" to "Noah in his Cups" (literally: "Noah when drunk"). However, this sequence of signifiers for "poplar" shrouds the referent, the object signified, in obscurity for all those who are not initiated in this sequence of associations. It destroys the possibility for communication. The languages of personal and social self are sundered. The result is the speaker's imprisonment in total isolation. The Praying Man, as viewed by the narrator, and the narrator himself, are the forerunners of Gregor Samsa, who ceases to make himself understood by everyone else.

Poetic speech, insofar as its essence is metaphor, appears as the first step toward the individual's exclusion from the human species. Mankind is a community of mutually comprehensible communicators. Exclusion from it is the lot of the insane. Appropriately, the Fat Man addresses his alter ego, the Praying Man, as "a perfect lunatic" ("ein gelungener Tollhäusler"). The "perfect lunatic" remains bottled up in incommunicable subjectivity. This is not the place to go into the very interesting threads that lead from here to Kierkegaard—Abraham's inability to communicate God's demand. The poetic mode of speech, as viewed in "Description of Struggle," is born of a defect and ends in disaster. The defect is forgetfulness of the fact that the world receives meaning literally from the consensus of the community which bestows the "truthful" names on things. Metaphor signifies the individual's incapacity to retain his foothold in the community of speakers. By the same token, it signals the disintegration of the self which loss of memory entails. For the extreme individuality of metaphoric speech paradoxically results from the lack of a sense of personal identity. The sense of a coherent and continuous self depends on a functioning memory, which the practitioners of metaphor in "Description of a Struggle" lack. The Praying Man's exhibitionism results from his inability to be convinced of his own existence.

"There has never been a time," he says, "in which I have been able to convince myself of my life." Therefore, he has the need to be "looked at by people, to cast a shadow upon the altar, as it were." He "needs" to be hammered, by people's regard, into a fixed position, {at least] for the duration of a brief hour." The purpose of his "praying" is to gain a temporary feeling of identity.

The Praying Man is a direct ancestor of the existential hero, plagued as he is by the spiritual seasickness that Sartre will call "nausea." (The etymol-

ogy of Sartre's term suggests its origins in sea- or ship-sickness.) The lack of
a sense of substance in himself corresponds to the dissolution of all appearance of stability in the world. For the Praying Man things do not hold
together when he approaches them. He cannot grasp them. "I grasp the
things around me only in such debilitated imaginings, that I always believe
that they had once been alive, but are now sinking from view." And in the
second version, "things sink around [him] like falling snow, while in front of
others even a small glass of schnaps stands on the table firm like a monument." For him nothing is self-evident, nothing induces a feeling of permanence and identity. The untroubled certainty that others seem to enjoy
challenges him, as it does Roquentin, the hero of Sartre's *Nausea.*

However, the profound difference between Kafka and the exitentialists
becomes apparent here as well. In contrast to Sartre, Kafka stacks the cards
against the spokesman of his own way of being. (Kafka's identification of the
persona of the writer with his Praying Man is shown by his definition of
writing as the "form of prayer.") Sartre's Roquentin ascribes the appearance
of stability and certainty about the objective world to the conspiracy of the
"salauds," the bourgeois hypocrites who pretend that an orderly cosmos
exists in order to protect their self-importance. For Kafka, on the other
hand, the spiritual "seasickness" of his protagonists is not necessarily the
truth of human reality. Kafka's protagonist is inclined to accept a reliable
and harmonious universe which only his own unfortunate peculiarity, his
"sickness," prevents him from perceiving. He is eager to concede that it
might be *his* perspective that dissolves the calm beauty of a world in which
expectations are fulfilled as a matter of course, and no gap exists between
individual consciousness and being. Supporting this surmise, he refers to a
childhood experience which he describes as follows (in the first version of the
tale):

> When as a child, I opened my eyes after a brief afternoon nap I
> heard, still entangled in sleep, my mother, on the balcony, ask
> someone downstairs, in a natural tone: "What are you doing, my
> dear? It's so hot." A woman answered from the garden: "I am
> having high tea in the green [garden]." They said that without
> reflecting and without undue distinctness, as if everyone would
> have to expect it [their statements].

And in the second version of the story, Kafka's protagonist makes this
exchange of trivial remarks even more definitely the touchstone and test case
for the existence of a profound difference between his own uncertainty and
the certainty of all others in regard to the nature of things.

It is a shared language, a dialogue, that seems to guarantee a graspable world, a stable cosmos. This language has to be spoken in such a way "as if everyone would (and could) expect it." It is precisely this condition which the protagonist, because of his forgetfulness, i.e., his lack of a sense of identity, can never attain. His loss of communal memory, stored in the common names of objects, makes his speech radically unexpected, a monologue of capricious, purely subjective signifiers. Whereas for Sartre, meaninglessness and incoherence are the objective characteristics of Being which only the conspiratorial hypocrisy of the pillars of society and "law and order" conceals from us, Kafka leaves the overwhelming possibility open that his protagonists' (and his own) disorientation may only be a pathological deviation, and that the seeming certainties of others may indeed be the truth. If such a truth should exist, its guarantor is a language shared.

The course of the plot of Kafka's earliest tale (and there definitely is a rudimentary recognizable plot in it) shows that the "poetic" and aesthetic way of life of his protagonists leads to the "revenge of things against them" and their "obliteration." Wronged by being wrongly named, creation rebels and drowns those who cannot abide by the order of "truth." Metaphoric signifiers do not contain the communal consensus which lives in the common word "poplar." It is the presence of the "trace" of that community which makes the names of things "truthful" ("wahrhaftig"). From this vantage point, metaphoric speech is untruth. Significantly, lying begins with the Tower of Babel as the primal locus of loss of a universally shared language. Community for Kafka is lodged in the family. As the family disintegrates, community is lost. This is what the sequence of the narrator's associations alludes to. The metaphor following "Tower of Babel," "Noah in his Cups," alludes to the rebellion of son against father, reported in *Genesis*. When Noah lies in drunken stupor, his son Ham mocks him for his exposed genitals. Man's first inebriation leads to the self-exposure of the second father of mankind—Noah—and his consequent fall from authority. The first rebellion of son against father, Ham's against Noah, is in turn followed by mankind's self-assertion against God in the building of that tower that was to reach into Heaven and ended in the breakup of the human family into isolated, mutually uncomprehending groups of individuals—the atomized, strife-ridden societies of history. What is hinted at in "Description of a Struggle," in thickly veiled form and abstractness, becomes personalized and concretized eight years later in "The Judgment," Kafka's first mature work. Georg Bendemann's sanctimoniously concealed disrespect for his apparently senile father marks that self-assertion of the uprooted ego, which, as in "Description of a Struggle," ends in obliteration by drowning. Between these two works lies Kafka's decisive encounter with the Yiddish Theater and Eastern Jewish culture, the importance of which for Kafka's literary development has been pointed out by Evelyn Beck.

Under the profound influence of the Yiddish Theater and the discovery, through this exposure, of an unbroken link to a communal culture, reaching from the past into the present, Kafka was able to concretize the abstract framework of his youthful tale. For his fanciful protagonists, Fat Man and Praying Man, he now substituted the Westernized German-speaking Jew and made him his prototype for the uprooted and condemned literary individual. When he adopted German as his language, the Central European Jew falsified his relationship to the Jewish way of life, from which he sprang, in which he had his roots, and from which he could not truly extricate himself, but to which he referred in the words of, and therefore with the thoughts of, an alien tongue. In his most intimate relationships, namely those of his family, the referent of his speech remained a Jewish reality with specific emotions attached to it. However, when the signifier of this Jewish referent became German, it designated a world alien to the Jewish reality. The true link between signifier and signified, which is truth, was broken. But the effect of this situation on the individual was a severance from his roots, and the blocking of the path that should lead from words back to the experiences and memories they supposedly referred to. The Jewish speaker of German concealed this rupture from himself. His self was split. He spoke, and therefore thought, differently from the way he felt and remembered. His thoughts became estranged from his emotions, and he became a stranger to himself.

The real self remains bound up with the speaker's childhood and family. It was in diagnosing his lack of warmth toward his mother that Kafka developed the linguistic theory we have sketched. In the same year, 1911, in which the Yiddish Theater exerted its greatest influence on him, Kafka noted in his diary a coldness, a want of love toward his mother which he ascribed to the use of German in a household that was Jewish. The actual human reality of the family had been profoundly un-German, namely Jewish. But the constant use of the German idiom falsified this reality by subverting it and substituting inappropriate associations for the original ones.

> The Jewish mother is no "Mutter"; calling her "Mutter" makes her somewhat comical . . . we give the name German mother to a Jewish woman, but we forget this contradiction, and having been forgotten, it sinks all the more heavily into our emotional

life. "Mutter" is an especially German term for the Jew; below his consciousness, it contains, together with gentile splendor, also gentile coldness. The Jewish woman who is addressed as "Mutter," therefore, does not only turn comical, but alien. Mama would be a better term [name], if only one would not still imagine "Mutter" behind it. I believe that only memories of the ghetto preserve the Jewish family, for even the word father [Vater] by no means targets the Jewish father.

In his early diary passage (October 24, 1911), we find delineated a self-alienation that thereafter finds its expression in the structures of Kafka's family tales, "The Judgment" and *Metamorphosis*, and, in subtler form, but with particular relevance to the mother figure, in *The Trial*. All these works show retrogression and destruction of an adult individual by the eruption of a repressed force, a *revenant*, that finds its strongest ally, and is lodged, within the self. This force stands in a more or less obvious connection to the protagonist's family from which he had, unsuccessfully as it turns out, tried to break away. Analogously, in Kafka's diary entry about his mother, the German linguistic medium is seen as a façade which has usurped the place of the original Jewish childhood self. It alienated the adult son not only from the other members of his family, but above all from himself. This linguistic façade can never become the true expression of his self. Words are arbitrarily imposed on a reality forever different from what they convey. The result is an incurable self-alienation of the German-speaking Jew, which is at the same time an alienation from his family. The inappropriate linguistic medium falsifies his childhood memories and presents to the self a perverted and distorted image of itself. The gentile associations conveyed by the German words for "mother" and "father" can be compared to the decorative "fillers" that creep into writing when the writer's connection with his original inspiration slackens and gives out. But the socio-cultural view of truth in language goes further than the poetics of the inner self, which I have tried to delineate elsewhere, in preparing the self-condemnation of Kafka's writing. For even in those rare moments when inspiration seemed sustained, the German medium must falsify it.

For several years Kafka did not follow through this pessimistic logic of the German-Jewish writer's self-alienation from his truth, for, as I have indicated above, he drew somewhat different conclusions from his insight, which proved productive rather than inhibiting for his writing. The disruption of the self-deceiving façade of consciousness by a hidden truth, as exemplified by some of Kafka's most famous and powerful works, from "The

Judgment" of 1912 to "A Country Doctor" of 1917, counteracted the inhibitions against his work which his view of the fundamental inner fraudulence of the Western Jew necessarily entailed. But the conviction of the inherent deceitfulness of this German-Jewish literature reasserted itself and became central to Kafka's poetics in the period of his relationship to the non-Jewish Milena.

In 1921, Kafka, in a letter to Max Brod, diagnosed the whole of German-Jewish literature as hopelessly suspended between a Judaic past betrayed by these writers and a German present which they could never make their own in truth. The lack of identity which drove the Praying Man to his fraudulent praying is now presented in terms of a sociology of literature. This literature has no true substance because it does not have a language which it can call its own.

The view of language implied in this wholesale condemnation of all German-Jewish literature partakes of that strange phenomenon of Jewish self-hatred which Stölzl brought to our attention in *Kafkas böses Böhmen,* [Kafka's Evil Bohemian], and which Hartmut Binder subsequently elaborated in his *Kafka aus neuer Sicht* [Kafka in a New Light]. The Central European Jewish intellectuals imbibed a good portion of the anti-Semitic ideology of the culture in which they lived, to which they richly contributed, but from which they also received essential gifts which often proved extremely mixed blessings. As has been pointed out, even the Zionist attack on the Diaspora borrowed from that mystical Central European nationalism that had given rise to anti-Semitism. The anti-Semitic cliché of the Jew was not alien to Zionst propaganda. In this context, the astounding resemblance which Kafka's theory of language bears to the linguistic theory contained in the Bible of modern German nationalism, Fichte's *Addresses to the German Nation* (1807/1808), deserves a brief mention.

Fichte postulates the superiority of the Germans over the West and South Europeans on the premise that the German language, in which the Scandinavian tongues are included, is an original rather than a derived language. The speaker of a Germanic language can immediately see the connections between his words and the objects and concepts to which they refer. The speaker of German, who thinks in a language which makes truth transparent to him, is imbued with the truth of the original thought processes—the Transcendental Ego—from which all reality receives its being. He will therefore be creative and "truthful" in his essence. However, languages such as French, Italian and English, on the other hand, whose vocabulary largely consists of words transmitted from a dead foreign tongue—Latin—convey the thinking of a dead nation and fail to reflect the living reality of the speakers. Such speakers are alienated from their being.

The assumption common to both Fichte's and Kafka's view of language is the demand that truthful speech be the direct emanation of being. It is this view which Jacques Derrida has exposed as "metaphysical nostalgia" for the impossible presence of the referent—reality or being—in the signifying system that is language. The vast difference between the German Idealist and Kafka lies in the nature of what it is that should be present in truthful speech. For Fichte it is the divine mental activity, the Transcendental Ego, which is the ground of being. For Kafka it is the ideal community.

Language for Kafka should be the proper *adaequatio* for the activities and emotions which bind the members of the community together. Only in such a cohesive community can the speaker of the language be one with himself and with the partners of his discourse. Such wholeness is for Kafka the criterion of truth.

In the social world in which Kafka found himself, this condition was of course utopian. The true community as the basis for a truthful language was a countermodel to Kafka's actual world. It was a projection propelled by the profound lack of and need for the experience of such a community. For Kafka, the nucleus of community, whether actual or imagined, was the family. As we have seen from his diary entry of 1911, it was in his relationship to his mother that the painful lack of a truthful medium of communication emerged. Implicitly he blamed his family for having deprived him of a true language, and thus turned him into a cold son and inauthentic speaker. Social and economic ambition had made his father and his father's class and generation adopt German as their language and thus displace the true language with an alien idiom. The displacement of language was also a tragic displacement of the true self for their sons. The fathers had begun the betrayal to which the sons had fallen victim and which they completed. The Yiddish actors, on the other hand, did show the possibility of a truthful relationship to language. However, for the Westernized Jew, this homecoming to his past must remain practically unattainable.

Already in "Description of a Struggle," the idea of a stable reliable world pertains for Kafka's protagonist to a quasi-mythic, legendary past of his own imagining.

> Always, dear Sir, I am plagued by such a tormenting desire to see things as they might conduct themselves *before* they would show themselves to me. Then they are in all likelihood beautiful and calm. It must be so, for I often hear people talk about them in that way.

This calm and stable world is literally based on hearsay; it is a product of language. The speaker has never experienced it himself. It remains a utopian construct like the definitive acquittals in *The Trial,* the call for a land surveyor in *The Castle,* the free and open entrance into the Law in "Before the Law." Significantly, it is the speaker's mother who, in her dialogue with the woman in the garden, supplies what seems like the guarantee for the existence of a world without anxiety; but that world is withheld from him. Analogously it is, as we have seen, his own mother who induces in Kafka the feeling that he is left without a truthful language and thus without a truthful being.

In a recent "text linguistic" study of Kafka, Rudolf Kreis, applying the psychoanalytic theory of Jacques Lacan and René Spitz, has pointed out the importance of the mother and mother figure for Kafka's language. Spitz stresses the crucial role of the mother in giving the infant, in his pre-linguistic stage of development, the feeling of "object constancy," the expectancy of a reliable and stable world, and with that "the formation of a rudimentary self." Where the relationship between mother and infant is disturbed, as it undoubtedly was in Kafka's biography, the sense of predictability concerning the external world and of self-identity fails to develop adequately. The learning of verbal language later on in the child's development constitutes a distancing process in which the mother has to assume the role of nay-saying figure to prepare the child for the self-discipline of civilized life. The acquisition of verbal language is thus always associated with denial, withdrawal, and prohibition. The earlier absence of the ego-encouraging function of the mother in Kafka's case prevented the pre-linguistic certainties of self and world from being carried over into the language-forming stage. The basis for a trusting and unproblematical acceptance of the necessary distancing and negativity of verbal language was absent in Kafka's life, and its duplicity and "coldness" therefore became intolerable to him.

Our analysis of Kafka's earliest narrative and the diary entry about his mother tend to confirm the link between the mother figure and Kafka's view of language and truth. (The diary entry of October 24, 1911, begins significantly with his mother's constant absence from the home, necessitated by her helping Kafka's father in the business—a circumstance which repeated exactly Kafka's early childhood experience.)

The community which, through a "truthful" language, must underwrite the reliability of the world, remains only a conjecture and presupposition for Kafka's spokesmen. Because he has never known such a community as a fact, the Praying Man, like the later heroes of Kafka, must seek to acquire a sense of identity and existence by pretense, by desperate clamor and

antics. Anticipating so many of Kafka's later heroes, he frantically gropes for
a "recognition" which would confirm his existence. In the drawing room,
which represents society, he desperately seeks to gain the seat at the piano,
even though "all seemed to know that [he] was unable to play." Like his
descendants in Kafka's later work, he can only *try* to exist; but he can never
gain the conviction that he exists. When Kafka calls writing "a form of
prayer," he obviously identifies with his early protagonist. The purely religious meaning usually attributed to Kafka's statement must be profoundly
modified when we realize that "praying" refers to a desperate need to be
"looked at" in order to receive the minimum of stability and identity
necessary for existence.

In the whole view of language, as we have traced it so far, language
always remains subordinate to being. Primacy belongs to life, to acts and
feelings, not to words. Actions and feelings are the touchstone for the right
life and its truth. In such a moral universe, literature can only appear as
secondary. By spending all his time on describing life, the writer misses his
duty to live it. Kafka condemns literature as a mere substitute, a dodging, a
"putting of wreaths around the house instead of moving in." In the same
vein, in a diary entry of 1921, Kafka condemns writing for its dependence on
life, its merely referential character, which lives parasitically on the primary,
"autonomous" activities that are reality.

> The dependency of writing. Its dependence on the maid making
> the fire, on the cat warming itself by the stove, even on the poor
> old person warming himself. All these are independent, autono-
> mous activities; writing alone is helpless, does not dwell in itself,
> it is a joke and a despair.

Its referential nature convicts writing of essential insignificance—frivolity;
and for the moralist in Kafka frivolity had to spell despair.

So far, we have considered Kafka's view of language and truth from only
one of two diametrically opposed perspectives, which accompanied him
through his entire life. Kafka saw himself suffering from two mutually
exclusive perspectives on life, which he summed up in the following
statement:

> [for me] the most important or the most appealing desire has
> been this: to acquire a view of life (and . . . to be able to convince
> others of it by writing) in which life would keep its natural heavy
> falling and rising, but at the same time, with no less distinctness,
> would be understood as a nothing, a dream, a floating. A beauti-

ful wish perhaps, if I had truly wished it. . . . It is comparable to the desire to hammer together a table, with painfully exact craftsmanship, and simultaneously to be doing nothing, but not in such a way that one might say: "His hammering is nothing to him," but rather that "hammering is real hammering for him, and at the same time, nothing. . . ."

One of these contradictory views might be called the naturalist, the other the spiritualist perspective. The difficulty of doing justice to Kafka lies in the equal validity of these two perspectives which seem to vitiate every statement made about Kafka, no matter how justified, by the equal appropriateness of its exact opposite. Yet it is absolutely necessary in speaking about Kafka to insist on the applicability of each pole of this particular dichotomy, and to establish this polarity itself as the essence of his intention.

Essentially the dichotomy goes back to the equal rigor with which Kafka treated the demands of what one might call the social and the inner or spiritual self. As Kafka matured, he tended toward ever greater depersonalization and universality of each "self," extending each into a "Weltanschauung" (in the literal, nonideological sense of the term), which complemented and, at the same time, excluded the other. But even in his earliest extant work, he called this co-existence of the radically contradictory, "Proof of the Fact That It Is Impossible To Live."

The demand of the social self becomes universalized as Judaism, the communal ethos, the right action in this life. This side of Kafka corresponds essentially to the image of Kafka given to us by his friend Max Brod. Elsewhere I called this demand "the law of Jehovah," because its fundamental commandment is the procreation and correct transmission of human life in the continuous chain of the generations that Jehovah vouchsafed to Abraham in His covenant with him. The opposite pole is a profound disgust with earthly life, the yearning for transcendence and total liberation from the flesh. This yearning too becomes universalized into a view resembling Gnosticism, or Indian (and Schopenhauerian) pessimism, a view that posits spirit as sole reality, denies the sensory world as an illusion, and demands a self-destructive asceticism. The following aphorism sums it up succinctly.

There is only one spiritual world. What we call the sensory world is only the evil in the spiritual one.

This pole corresponds to the mystic whom Walter Benjamin, in sharp opposition to Brod, saw Kafka to be.

Since language only refers to the sensory world, it can never be the instrument of truth.

> For anything outside the sensory world, language can be used only allusively, but never, not even approximately, by way of analogies, since it, in correspondence to the sensory world, only deals with possession and its relationships.

Paradoxically, however, this debasement of language, from this perspective, allows a substantial elevation of the status of literature. For as the above-quoted aphorism clearly shows, there does remain one aspect of language which can be used to allude to the reality that lies beyond our senses and which is, according to the earlier-quoted aphorism of Kafka's, the only true one. This allusive use of language is obviously the kind of writing toward which Kafka aspired, when he tried to present "the enormous world in [his] head," and put down in his diary his ambition to redeem the sensory world, i.e., "to raise it" "into the pure, the true, and the unchangeable." The spiritualist perspective frees literature from the servility to which a poetics of referential mimesis reduces it. Here language does not depend on "the autonomous activities" going on in the sensory world. On the contrary, language—i.e., a very special kind of non-referential, merely allusive language—is a means by which human beings may receive an inkling of the invisible, true world.

The idea of a purely allusive language establishes the otherness of langue in regard to truth, not as a defect, but as the necessary condition for the fulfillment of a proper and essential function. To be sure, language can never hope to represent the extrasensory reality, but it can hope to point toward it and thus to sharpen human awareness for it. Here, writing does not aim at the *adaequatio* of linguistic formulation and reality. Such a "true" referentiality is completely beyond its reach. Language can only hope to capture the trace of something that has to be essentially and eternally absent from the sensory world.

The way for literature is therefore not to try to express the truth, but to hint at it by showing the undoing of untruth.

> Our art is a being blinded by the truth. The light on the retreating grimace is true, nothing else.

It is not difficult to see that this aphorism applies to a basic feature of all of Kafka's work, in which some falsehood, some self-deception or deception, is contradicted and exposed. The protagonist, who embodies this falsehood, is forced to retreat, one way or another. The official viewpoint of the work, represented by the protagonist, is found to be untrue. Since the reader does not gain access to any other consciousness in the work, and since the narrator withholds all revealing commentary, the reader first tends to be persuaded by the protagonist and to side with him. Closer reading calls this support into question. Too many indications emerge that make the protagonist's claim untenable. His defeat at the hands of his antagonist or antagonists—his "counterworld," in Martin Walser's term—is revealed as the refutation of a false claim. Beyond that the reader is not able to go. He may witness the negation of an untruth. The truth itself remains shrouded from him. The defeat of the protagonist by no means entitles him to assume that the "counterworld" represents the truth. The structural feature reflecting this withholding of the truth is the absence of a reliable and authoritative narrator.

In the poetics implied in the aphorism about art and truth, Kafka's two perspectives converge. It accommodates his community-oriented naturalism as well as his gnostic spiritualism. If truth is seen to reside in the collective, the stream of life and procreation, the totality of existence, then the defeat of the individual subjectivity, embodied in the protagonist, vindicates the collective and establishes it as the truth. If, on the other hand, truth is seen as transcending this world and residing in an extrasensory beyond, or spiritual realm, the withholding of the truth alludes to its ineffability. The only "trace" of the truth is its absence made manifest by the refutation of what the reader had thought to be true. From his naturalist perspective, it would seem that Kafka tends to equate vitality, energy, and power—characteristic of his father—with truth, and to endorse the collective in which these qualities are lodged as the repository of truth. Weak in his isolation, and impotent in his subjectivity, the individual qua individual must be wrong. The reader, having first sided with the protagonist, on second thought is tempted to rectify his mistake, and is inclined to see the counterworld (what I would prefer to call "the power figure") as being right. However, on a third "reading"—each "reading" standing for a level of meaning further removed from the surface—he would realize that not even that equation holds, and that there is no way of establishing the "truth." All that can be uncovered are successive layers of untruth. With this insight, the spiritualist perspective is approximated. For such a procedure demonstrates the inadequacy of all languages to express the truth. All language can show is the "retreat" of untruth. The process of making untruth evident is the only "light" that language can shed on truth.

In his late phase, following the Zürau period, Kafka tended to equate the spiritual world with literature. Literature, however, was not the finished work; it was the process, the act of writing, not its result. Because it was not the product, but the act that counted. Kafka could ask that his writings be burnt and yet continue to write to the last, and correct printer's proofs on his deathbed. The finished work catered to the ego and its narcissism which afflicted Kafka, but which he loathed and hated as the writer's fundamental curse. Consideration for work done was self-caressing and a sin against the law of Jehovah with its commandment to live fruitfully, to engage, to care, to procreate, to love. Vanity was the original sin against the self's duty to be part of the communal world. But living the work, not basking in it, constituted fulfillment of the law of the spirit. In the act of writing, Kafka felt closest to existing in a purely spiritual world, as a member of another universe, differently organized from the physical and social world of bodies and possessions, free of the imperfections and the cruelties built into Jehovah's realm. Living in and as literature, Kafka felt as close as anyone could be to that unity which he called truth. Writing, Kafka formulates in a late diary entry, gives supreme happiness. It enables one to step out of "murderer's row," which is this life, and gain an observation post on it. However, writing gradually evolves from a point of observation into a pure autonomous realm, a universe of its own, operating in complete heterogeneity from life, according to its own laws and needs.

The impression that one of the two "laws" ever superseded the other would be wrong. To the end of Kafka's life, the demand of "Jehovah's law" persisted as inexorably as the demand of absolute spirituality. Kafka's "double bind," to use Bateson's term, could never be truly resolved.

DAVID I. GROSSVOGEL

The Trial: *Structure as Mystery*

The fate of Oedipus hinges on a misreading. The oracle speaks unambiguously but through force of conditioning. Oedipus tries to read *into* the signs traced out by the gods. The gods know that, one way or another, Oedipus is fated not to understand. His quick wit and impetuousness notwithstanding, Oedipus is turned into a plodding and awkward interpreter. His exacerbated attempt upon the limits of human understanding is reduced, like any other such attempt, to a questioning of the impediment. As in a fluoroscopic process, what cannot be penetrated contrives the only possible picture of the impenetrable. For Oedipus, the veil that hides the unknown is a *text*.

It is the possibility for his text to be this kind of veil that causes Borges to turn his text into a *reflecting* surface, a mirror that keeps his reader out even as it talks to that reader about him and his problematic world. The reader's desire to penetrate the Borgesian surface makes of him a different kind of reader—a reader conscious of reading. And when the fiction, within whose surface text the reader is birdlimed (the text as labyrinth, as palimpsest), also speaks about the efforts of a man (as often as not a reader) to progress beyond metaphysical entrapments, the story makes its appeal to the self-conscious part of the reader created by the text; the fiction of Borges is then transubstantiated as it reawakens the reader in a moment of his metaphysical dilemma.

Through an interesting coincidence, the surface of the text happens to be already the special province of a particular sort of critic who is less likely to be engaged by the author's purpose than by the way in which the author went about achieving that purpose. The superficial eye of this kind of critic

From *Mystery and its Fictions: From Oedipus to Agatha Christie.* Copyright © 1979 by The Johns Hopkins University Press. Originally entitled "Kafka: Structure as Mystery."

(like that of a tailor for whom the cowl does not make the monk, or the painter for whom pigment does not turn into a landscape) has the virtue of making its object *real* which, at a greater depth, would be only a semblance: all surfaces, whatever intent is vouchsafed them, have in common this substantiality. When the critic has been encouraged by authors like Borges to look for the substance of the work within its surface, he is the more likely to read the surface of other texts as intention, as Lacan in the case of Poe. But the deciphering of a textual surface that is intentionally indistinct from other phenomenological evidence returns the reader/critic to the existential perplexity of Oedipus. At the ultimate extension of this process, the critic is a psychoanalyst questioning the man (the author) through the utterance of his fiction. When that has happened, the unaffected mystery is located once again, after its avatars as fiction, at its nonfictional source.

A century after Poe, what might have been his private nightmares have become considerably less private. Much of the century's writing assumes that the reader feels less comfortable in a world that seems more alien even as it is better known. When Kafka takes his turn as chronicler, he does not describe the aberration of a single consciousness; rather, he describes the aberration of a world that mocks the obdurate sanity of a single consciousness. The reader recognizes Kafka's strange world in his own familiar malaise, but that very familiarity is strange—it is unable to allay the reader's sense of estrangement. Evolution from the private world of Poe to the public world of Kafka suggests that the specialized probing of the psychoanalyst has become less necessary for an understanding of the author behind his text: Kafka is closer to his reader by virtue of what has happened to that reader since Poe. The affinities between author and private awareness, which the fiction of Poe may well mask for the lay reader, appear on the surface of Kafka's text. Kafka has no story to tell; he conveys a mood, an anxiety—*his* anxiety. He does not comment on the mystery: he and his book are a part of it. In the deceptive hints given him, Oedipus reads a text that alludes to the unknown only through such hints as preserve that unknown. When, for once, the god of the oblique speaks straight, he demonstrates that the impossibility of knowing is in Oedipus: Oedipus, the fumbling reader, is seen fumbling before an obliging text. When Kafka contrives a text that discloses Kafka rather than a fiction, he shows again that the impossibility of knowing is within the one who wants to know. And, like Apollo, he does it for a captive reader. Without the benefit of Borges's mirrors or Poe's psychoanalyst, the reader reads himself in the man writing because even after the veil of Kafka's fiction has been thinned into evanescence, the mystery is still not disclosed—only the author stands revealed as another kind of text to be deciphered within the unending process of reading.

Blanchot, who is not necessarily in disagreement with this "reading" of Kafka, begins nevertheless with a challenge: since the art of writing creates at best a surrogate self, are we not indulging in loose talk when we substitute the man writing for his text? How can I write "I am unhappy," asks Blanchot, without turning misery into *calculation* through the contrivance of a text that *states* my misery? An answer (though not quite the one Blanchot proposes) is that a wholly impersonal contrivance by the author is just as impossible. The least personal statement—the most fictional—is an idiosyncrasy: the voice of the writer is in his words whatever those words say. Blanchot, who concludes that writing can only sham life, also concludes that writing is impossible: the writer's voice, as that voice, cannot sham. And Kafka writes stories whose only subject is Kafka.

The paradox begs the question of Kafka's intent; Kafka is not just an anxious man transcribing an anxiety: no act of transcription is innocent. However much the man Kafka is caught up in his act of transcription, that transcription remains a conscious strategy that is distinct from the intimate sense that impels it. That strategy is affected by the strange persistence of the reader's hope—the reader's desire for his text to have a meaning (that is to say an *end*) that corresponds to his need for his world to have a meaning, to *signify*. The modern reader appears to remain as thralled by his expectation as did previous readers who could assume more legitimately that the book might finally be *closed* and its truth contained, though so much of modern fiction subverts the possibility of closure, resists the possibility of a metaphysical assertion even within the boundaries provided by the physical space of the text.

The success of that strategy can be seen in *The Trial*, a text about the confusion of critics and other readers that adroitly confuses critics and other readers. *The Trial's* story (before Kafka finally wears out the veil of the story) looks like those of the most fraudulent, and hence the most comforting, of fictional appropriations of mystery—the mystery story. Even when his predicament cries out for K. to ask "why?" he insists on asking, as any ordinary detective might, "where?" or "who?": condemned by a perverse metaphysics, the victim argues all aspects of his case except the metaphysical. We recall from our discussion of Freud that this refusal to internalize is necessary for the dissemination of the "unheimliche": Kafka is conjuring not a metaphysics, but its climate.

That climate results from a world described as a surface (the resistance to interiorization begins in this kind of description): it is a staged, artificial,

but generally nonsymbolic world; it has the partially comic, partially fright-
ening rigidity of any nonhuman imitation of life. The staged artificiality
suggests a self-consciousness, the felt presence of an observer. "One fine
morning," when the day begins as innocuously as any other for K., he notes
among many familiar reminders "the old lady opposite, who seemed to be
peering at him with a curiosity unusual even for her." K.'s angered exclamation at the presence of the warders confirms their being and their presence as
a dominative intrusion: "It occurred to him at once that he should not have
said this aloud and that by doing so he had in a way admitted the stranger's
right to superintend his actions." The strangeness of K.'s circumstances
results from his attempt to enact everyday gestures on what is becoming
more and more definitely a stage: "The old woman, who with truly senile
inquisitiveness had moved along the window exactly opposite, in order to go
on seeing all that could be seen." "At the other side of the street he could still
see the old woman, who had now dragged to the window an even older man,
whom she was holding round the waist." "In the window over the way the
two old creatures were again stationed, but they had enlarged their party, for
behind them, towering head and shoulders above them, stood a man."

K.'s sense that the gaze of another is on him represents largely his
altered perception of the world around him; he now subjects what would be
otherwise an unperceived continuation of his existence to the disjunction of
analysis so that what should seem natural appears to be contrived, as when he
hears the intimate talk between Leni and Block: "K. had the feeling that he
was listening to a well-rehearsed dialogue which had been often repeated and
would be often repeated." Only very occasionally does the strangeness of this
staging derive from an actual alteration of K.'s world, as when the warders
first appear in his bedroom, or when, walking along a hall in his bank, K.
discovers those same warders being whipped in a closet.

Because the event is staged, it *contains* the actor and limits him. The
metaphysical constraint is forever being echoed in the comic reductiveness of
functional gestures that have become problematic—as when K. tries to
hurry his loud and indiscreet uncle out of the bank: " 'I thought,' said K.,
taking his uncle's arm to keep him from standing still, 'that you attach even
less importance to this business than I do, and now you are taking it so
seriously.' 'Joseph!' cried his uncle, trying to get his arm free so as to be able
to stand still, only K. would not let him, 'you're quite changed.' " But the
implications of this comic constraint extend into the implication of a
menace: any attempt at a disengagement from this constraint, however
successful the attempt appears to be, leads only to further constraint. Direct
confrontation of the impediment may cause it to recede, not to disappear:

"Here's a fine crowd of spectators!" cried K. in a loud voice to the Inspector, pointing at them with his finger. "Go away," he shouted across. The three of them immediately retreated a few steps, the two ancients actually took cover behind the younger man, who shielded them with his massive body and to judge from the movements of his lips was saying something which, owing to the distance, could not be distinguished. Yet they did not remove themselves altogether, but seemed to be waiting for the chance to return to the window again unobserved.

The futility of even modest gestures to achieve an intended purpose demonstrates through comic reduction the metaphysical verdict of the Court that Titorelli spells out for K.: he is "provisionally free"; definite acquittal is out of the question; only the possibilities of ostensible acquittal and indefinite postponement can sustain the balance of hope and frustration that define the victim once he has begun to question his circumstances.

The comic quality of this artificial world eventually turns into what it was all along—the horror of inhuman motion, a supreme illogicality resulting from the only logic that is possible: somewhat in the manner of Munch's cry frozen within the silence of his canvas, Kafka arrests within the frieze of his denouement K. moving at an ever accelerated pace, and finally at a run, to his own death. What accounts for the comic and the horror is the man at the center, K., not simply an initial but an anthropocentric obduracy, the persistent belief in a world that cannot be subverted "one fine morning" by agents of the unknown; a world in which a sense of boundaries and control makes the question "where?" possible and gives it meaning—along with all other aspects of existence. K. is more than the evidence that Kafka assumes the same expectations in his readers: K. is the encouragement for them to persist, as does K., in those expectations. Kafka's whole strategy of disquietude depends on his ability to counterstate the obdurate normalcy of K. and of a reader who, like K., obdurately requires that normalcy. Kafka thus presents and subverts simultaneously the reassuring surfaces of a familiar world. Henry Sussman notes that this duality reaches the heights of irony in K. himself, whose everyday existence absorbs within its unvarying pattern the magnitude of the abnormalcy that has invaded it: K. goes as far as to abet the conspiracy of which he is a victim whenever he can. K.'s outburst to Frau Grubach (an exclamation later reinterpreted by Groucho Marx) is a comic synopsis of the duality that acknowledges his victimization even as he makes an attempt at self-assertion by assuming the point of view of the victimizers: " 'Respectable!' cried K., through the chink in the door; 'if you want to keep your house respectable you'll have to begin by giving me notice.' "

The power of any self-assertion is ultimately sexual. For K., sex represents, like the rest of his life, the evidence of both a process that continues and its subversion. His desperate need for the familiar, normative world is, in part, libidinal—this is one way of reading K.'s assault on Fräulein Bürstner: " 'I'm just coming,' K. said, rushed out, seized her, and kissed her first on the lips, then all over the face, like some thirsty animal lapping greedily at a spring of long-sought water." His staged world stresses both the reality of closure and the possibility of transcending it, and as a part of him intuits that both the definition and the desire are located within him, he is desperately attracted towards others; communication is a way of transcending, and sex is a way of communicating. But on the unnatural stage, that truth becomes, like all others, constrained and misshapen. When the Court usher's wife leads K. to a part of the Law's library, he discovers obscene books instead of the revelatory texts he had hoped for—and they themselves are emblematically marred, artificialized out of even their erotic meaning:

> He opened the first of them and found an indecent picture. A man and a woman were sitting naked on a sofa, the obscene intention of the draftsman was evident enough, yet his skill was so small that nothing emerged from the picture save the all-too-solid figures of a man and a woman sitting rigidly upright, and because of the bad perspective, apparently finding the utmost difficulty even in turning toward each other.

This stage stunts its actors: when she thrusts herself on K., the usher's wife cannot of course allay the malaise to which her ministrations contribute. She is a part of the circumstances that invert K.'s libidinal assertion: the females around K. turn into hungry, uterine mouths. Montag, Leni, the girls in Titorelli's studio, are sexually aggressive, and the threat of the aggression is magnified by the flawed quality of the pleasure they promise: all have more or less startling physical deformities; Fräulein Bürstner's second incarnation—Fräulein Montag—limps; Leni's two middle fingers are webbed; the girl at Titorelli's who pursues K. most closely is hunchbacked, though "scarcely thirteen years old." The womb that is the promise of selfhood recovered, the ultimate possession of self through possession of another, but that becomes instead a threatening vortex, corresponds to a necessary law of gravity that replaces on this stage the lost possibilities of a motion that might have been willed and effective. The Law is the central evidence of such a process; instead of being a dialectical object contained within the mind, it functions as a kind of monstrous tropism—another form of the vortex: "Our officials," the warder explains, "never go hunting for crime in the populace, but, as the Law decrees, are drawn towards the guilty and must then send out us warders." Its mode describes the sort of process that draws K. into its working from the moment he begins dressing for his part even as he refuses to play his role:

> "What are you thinking of?" [the warders] cried. "Do you imagine you can appear before the Inspector in your shirt? He'll have you well thrashed, and us too." "Let me alone, damn you," cried K., who by now had been forced back to his wardrobe. "If you grab me out of bed, you can't expect to find me all dressed up in my best suit." "That can't be helped," said the warders, who as soon as K. raised his voice always grew quite calm, indeed almost melancholy, and thus contrived either to confuse him or to some extent bring him to his senses. "Silly formalities!" he growled, but immediately lifted a coat from a chair and held it up for a little while in both hands, as if displaying it to the warders for their approval. They shook their heads. "It must be a black coat," they said. Thereupon K. flung the coat on the floor and said—he did not himself know in what sense he meant the words—"But this isn't the capital charge yet." The warders smiled, but stuck to their: "It must be a black coat."

In the force of this strange gravitational pull, the reader senses the presence of an alien world—however familiar its surfaces might be. But Kafka is not satisfied with such reminders. What marks him as a modern author is his refusal to let the reader find refuge within that last perimeter of his control—the book. Like Borges or Poe, Kafka replaces the *idea* of an alien world with the objective *evidence* of a text. This inhibiting and contrived world is, after all, a real book that rehearses, within the one who wants to know, the impossibility of fully knowing. The reader cannot *contain* Kafka's text even though it presents itself as the form (the mystery story) that most readily contains mystery.

The evidence of the text is confirmed by the central image: the Law is a world of books; K. is convinced that if he could read them, he would win his case—possession of the Word being, perhaps, less problematic than possession of an other: K. responds to the sexual blandishments of the Court usher's wife in order to possess the books that are in the library of the Law (only to find in their stead, as we have seen, further instances of an unappealing and frustrating sexuality). These books are not, of course, available to K.: those behind whom the Law hides are the sole repositories of a textual secret. The Examining Magistrate has, as his only distinguishing prop, a single notebook:

> But the Examining Magistrate did not seem to worry, he sat quite comfortably in his chair and after a few final words to the man behind him took up a small notebook, the only object lying on the table. It was like an ancient school exercise-book, grown dog-eared from much thumbing. "Well then," said the Examining Magistrate turning over the leaves and addressing K. with an air of authority, "you are a house painter?"

Writing is a lingering activity, even within the deserted Court offices: "Some of the offices were not properly boarded off from the passage but had an open frontage of wooden rails, reaching, however, to the roof, through which a little light penetrated and through which one could see a few officials as well, some writing at their desks." Because he is a part of the Court, Titorelli is the scribe of a tradition, even though he is a painter. Because he uses a different language, he *paints* Court legends:

> [W]e have only legendary accounts of ancient cases. These legends certainly provide instances of acquittal; actually the majority of them are about acquittals, they can be believed, but they cannot be proved. All the same, they shouldn't be entirely left out of account, they must have an element of truth in them, and besides they are very beautiful. I myself have painted several pictures founded on such legends.

What Titorelli's paintings have in common with other texts that represent the Law is that they cannot be grasped, that they possess no efficacy, no firm or reliable substance; like the very text given the reader, the texts of the Law are adequate only to sustain for a while the hope of the one who inquires of them, not to reward that hope.

But texts persist in the persistence of the decipherer's hope of possessing his text: one of the many ways K. is tempted to join the world of his persecutors is by turning into a writer of his own script—creating the arcane document that will *stand for him*:

> The thought of his case never left him now. He had often considered whether it would not be better to draw up a written defense and hand it in to the Court. In this defense he would give a short account of his life, and when he came to an event of any importance explain for what reasons he had acted as he did,

intimate whether he approved or condemned his way of action in retrospect, and adduce grounds for the condemnation or approval. The advantages of such a written defense, as compared with the mere advocacy of a lawyer who himself was not impeccable, were undoubted.

Writing would represent a new aspect of the same quest for K.: it would be a way for the patient reader, which the victim—K. or Block—has already become, to seize his text, instead of being reduced, like Kafka's own reader, to read those reading (writing), unable as he is to read the text those readers read (or write).

Whatever object the quest may posit, through whatever subterfuge, that object remains elusive. The word *God* is absent from Kafka's fiction, but the Jewish mystical tradition (upon which Borges also draws) equates for Kafka the impossible revelation and the revelatory letter: it is within scripting signs that the unknowable shows and conceals itself. The word, as mystical mediator, as initiate, is caught up in the dialectical process that affects the way in which all initiates are perceived: it can only state its failure to reveal but in so doing is suffused with intimations of the mystery it has attempted. The Kabbalah believes in the occult meaning of the letter, the presence of God in the sign of His word: instead of making God apprehensible, this presence makes the letter awesome. We have noted in our reading of Borges how, in time, this awesome signifier becomes little more than an amulet, a container suggesting a reversal of the original denial by offering as *possible* the appropriation of a final and absolute mystery. But a sacredness attaches to even the ineffectual amulet (it is for that reason that no amulet is wholly ineffectual).

In Kafka's fiction, the missing term *God* is replaced by His letter, the Law, an ironically scripted form of the absolute, in the same way as the letter of this text is informed by the presence of its own *deus absconditus*—Kafka. "Everyone strives to attain the Law": K.'s hope, and the reader's, are sustained by an awareness—the importance of the part of themselves that is concealed by the fiction of their text. For both, the integument of the mystery that cannot be uttered (as cannot be uttered the name of God) will be the *parable,* the traditional reduction of that mystery as allegorical fiction.

The parable, a mode in which Kafka showed an abiding interest, acknowledges intellectual slippage, a failure of the mind to apprehend its object. The parable is a *substitute,* a simile. The German word *Gleichnis* also means simile; its root, *gleich,* evidences the perplexity of knowing: it means both *same* and *resembling*—that is to say, identical and different. It is not improbable that Kafka favored the parable because he was most intent on demonstrating this slippage, on making the reader experience the impossibility of locating his world anywhere else but in this slippage. In his *Parables and Paradoxes,* he says, "All these parables really set out to say is merely that the incomprehensible is incomprehensible." The parable also contains the tone, the tradition, and the manner of the failure of the hidden god to become manifest. And when the parable comments on the failure of the parable, it merely returns to literature a traditional concealment of god as text.

Long before Kafka turns formally to the parable, he has already constructed a fiction that proves, in the multiple instances of its own slippage, to be more than a mere fiction. And in this endeavor, he is seconded by an ironic fate: none of his major fiction is complete in the form we have of it; in *The Trial,* the very ordering of the chapters is not necessarily Kafka's. It is on this shifting ground that contrives the deceptive revelation of a parable whose magnitude is equal to the totality of the fiction that Kafka establishes a central parable that his fiction treats as a problematic text—a parable whose lesson is the doubtful nature of parables.

Since the parable is a *likeness* that discloses and disguises a more distant truth, what will be the central parable of *The Trial* does not disturb the innocuousness of other events: the self-consciously moral fiction develops within the continuation of an apparently conventional fiction. An influential Italian customer of the bank where K. still works is visiting town and K. is appointed to squire him. Like all other episodic and trivial events within K.'s life, this one contains in germ the mood of, and what might be read as emblems for, something more than the story that those episodes contrive. K's encounter with the Italian visitor in the office of the Manager suggests the inevitable continuation of the perverse law proclaiming that everything that can go wrong will. K.'s knowledge of Italian is tenuous, the Italian speaks fast and lapses frequently into a southern dialect, a bushy moustache conceals the motion of his lips: the problem of understanding signs, of trying to solve the unintelligible, becomes once again a preoccupation of K., within the similar but overriding preoccupations that already perplex him. Once more, K. is outside an event that concerns him but that he cannot penetrate.

The visitor wants to visit the town's Cathedral, where K. agrees to meet him later in the morning. While waiting for that meeting, K. continues within a life whose normalcy has already become an annoying irrelevance. Now, additionally, that normalcy mocks the urgency of an event: a new puzzlement has thrust itself into a pattern whose ordinariness has long since been subverted by K.'s other predicaments. K. is now three times baffled:

the routine at the bank prevents him from refreshing his Italian, which he will need for his encounter with the incomprehensible visitor; and the visitor, for whom he must perfect his Italian, provides an additional distraction from K.'s obsessive need to give all his time to his "case." This tiered frustration leads him to believe that "they're goading me": as usual, K. creates an otherness in which to place his dilemma.

K. arrives punctually for his appointment at the Cathedral, but his visitor is of course not there. Since the central question revolves around the possibility of *understanding,* K. wonders whether he is in possession of the correct facts: was the visitor supposed to be there at all? The day is rainy, the Cathedral dark. A few candles have been lit, emblematic objects that do not cast sufficient light to see clearly by; their own true clarity is in their emblematic significance. To their half-light, K. adds the inadequate light of his own pocket lamp. It picks out of the gloom the strange figure of a knight in a canvas against one of the walls. For a moment, the incongruity of the figure holds K.'s attention. When he moves his light over the rest of the canvas, it discloses a conventional Sepulture of Christ and he loses interest. In this rare instance, the normative world dissipates the question, and K. is no longer able to be held by a normative world.

K. catches sight of a verger who is making signs to him that he cannot understand: the verger is enacting a role for the benefit of K. but it is one that K., once again, cannot fathom. The Cathedral is full of such signs, among them a light over a small side pulpit that is hardly larger than a niche for a statue. K. is drawn to the pulpit: the light over it would be "the usual sign that a sermon was going to be preached." Is a sermon going to be preached there—will there be a religious discourse delivered for the sake of instruction? The answer is that a religious discourse will be delivered indeed: the pulpit has the attributes of height and sanctity from which an absolute truth is traditionally handed down. But whether instruction will be handed down as well, or what exactly the form of that instruction will be, is problematic: instead of the sermon's instruction, Kafka will insert here the ambiguity of the parable.

In the house of God, and in the accepted manner of any solemn handing-down, a voice calls K. from the pulpit: the ultimate mystery, like lesser ones, states clearly its relation to its object and little more. The voice acquires its resonance not only from the spiritual acoustics of the Cathedral but because it belongs to a young priest who knows K.: he is connected with the Court. Intuiting the ambiguity of what will follow, K. responds only when he has been able to make the unequivocal summons seem ambiguous:

But if he were to turn round he would be caught, for that would
amount to an admission that he had understood it very well, that
he was really the person addressed, and that he was ready to obey.
Had the priest called his name a second time K. would certainly
have gone on, but as everything remained silent, though he stood
waiting a long time, he could not help turning his head a little
just to see what the priest was doing.

With comic obduracy, and true to his mode, K. tries to reduce the
intrusion of a transcendental revelation to the mundane level of his everyday
life: "I came here to show an Italian round the Cathedral." So K. must be
told what the reader knows already, that this normalcy is "beside the point."
The point is that K. is presumed guilty. For one of the few times in his life,
K. rebels: if he is guilty, then no man is innocent: "If it comes to that, how
can any man be called guilty? We are all simply men here, one as much as
the other." The priest acknowledges this similarity but reminds K. that this
is nevertheless the talk of guilty men; the condition is not circumstantial and
is therefore not subject to rational rejection. The *trial* (in German, *der
Prozess*), which is never a trial but simply a *process,* turns into guilt as part of
the process: "The verdict is not suddenly arrived at, the proceedings only
gradually merge into the verdict." In the *process* of our existence, our *arrest* is
nothing more than our awareness, our *trial* the result of that awareness.

This concomitance denies the possibility of melioristic gestures and
human contact. The priest is supposed to bring comfort, but however good
his intentions, he is likely to harm K. Still, K. is drawn to this figure of
good: "With you I can speak openly." The priest's answer is ambiguous:
"Don't be deluded"; it may refer to what K. was saying previously, it may
refer to what K. has just said. K. attempts to clarify the ambiguity; in
response, the priest delivers Kafka's parable, the similitude that instances an
otherness, the periphrase whose elaboration confuses.

The parable reinforces within this context notions of mystery, elevation, and final revelation. In a story about the impossibility of passing
beyond, the Door (the traditional gateway to a supernatural realm) and the
Law loom (like the word of God) before the man from the country. For the
reader, the parable also borrows biblical cadences in order to tell about the
Door—the uttermost extension of the human possibility, informed with the
terribly mystery that it proclaims and protects.

The doorkeeper is the traditional intercessor similarly haloed (though
here in a comic mode) by his proximity to the unknown and, in the manner
of all intercessors, utterly ineffectual. The doorkeeper, like the Door itself,

like the priest who tells the story, like the very story of which that story is a part, is on *this side* of the impenetrability: he can only be a distracting focal point. Moreover, he does not keep out the man from the country, and the door is always open; the inability to enter is in the one seeking admission. The priest's critical analyses may be confusing in their catholicity, but they are not necessarily wrong:

> He allows the man to curse loudly in his presence the fate for which he himself is responsible.

> The man from the country is really free, he can go where he likes, it is only the Law that is closed to him, and access to the Law is forbidden him by only one individual.

> There is no lack of agreement that the doorkeeper will not be able to shut the door.

It is the necessary ineffectiveness of the intercessor that allows him even to be kind: "The doorkeeper gives him a stool and lets him sit down at the side of the door"; "The doorkeeper often engages him in brief conversations, asking him about his home and about other matters." The kindness of the door-keeper, like the consolation of the priest, is of the same order as the impediment that may be forced temporarily to recede, but not to disappear, or the human gesture that achieves an immediate end mocked by the metaphysical dilemma that constrains it.

The man from the country can do only what man has always done before the unknowable: fasten on the figure of the intercessor. Like Oedipus, like Block, like K. himself, the man becomes a close reader of the surface of an impenetrable text: "In his prolonged study of the doorkeeper he has learned to know even the fleas in his fur collar." As the mystery asserts its impenetrability, man acknowledges his failure to know by deifying the unknown: in an ultimate and self-deriding attempt to contain what cannot be contained, he makes of the mystery God: "In the darkness he can now perceive a radiance that streams inextinguishably from the door of the Law."

But Kafka is concerned, of course, with an entirely different text— there is no man before the Door: there is only a reader, Kafka's, before *his* text. The parable that complicates the complex fiction within which it is set will now be turned into an object lesson—literally, a parafictional object on which the reader will perform the exercise suggested by the fictional charac-ters. The priest, who belongs to the Court, has charitably entertained all of K.'s unanswerable questions; the priest, as critic of the text, will entertain sufficiently numerous and contradictory interpretations to show the impossibility of reading.

The "scripture" related by the priest is both holy and full of holes: it is given as the comfort of a truth recaptured, an absolute that can be comprehended. But modern fiction, perhaps starting with Kafka, opens fiction unto the unknown deliberately, offering itself as experience rather than imitation. The priest is not content to set forth a parable about the impossibility of knowing; he will not lose the reader within the diverse and contradictory possibilities afforded by the genre. Though he is the only speaker of the parable, he cautions K. against hasty interpretations: "Don't take over someone else's opinion without testing it." But there is no "someone else": K. has only the priest's text, just as the reader has only Kafka's; the suggestion is inescapable: though the priest has told "the story in the very words of the scriptures," the very text as text is suspect.

Once doubt has been cast on the body of orthodoxy, its absolute assertion is no longer commensurate with absolute revelation. Any interpretation is possible: "The commentators note in this connection: 'The right perception of any matter and a misunderstanding of the same matter do not wholly exclude each other.' " The scripture therefore invites a gloss that is supposed to provide further steps towards the unknown. But as the gloss is the intercessor of an intercessory text, it represents in fact a step back, a greater distance from the inaccessible truth. Even though K. was admonished by the priest because he had "not enough respect for the written word," that "disrespect" comes from the only posture that is possible before the text: utmost respect; through overly close scrutiny, K. has analyzed the only surface allowed him into meaninglessness. It is through this same kind of gloss-making that the priest now leads Kafka's reader. As the reader is drawn though the maze of the text, he is drawn through another part of his awareness; forced to proceed tentatively through the text, he rehearses the tentative nature of his being, the tentative nature of an existential process of which the book he is reading is now only a part.

For neither K. nor the reader can there be any ultimate revelation. There is only description, necessity: "I don't agree with that point of view," said K., shaking his head, "for if one accepts it, one must accept as true everything the doorkeeper says. But you yourself have sufficiently proved how impossible it is to do that." "No," said the priest, "it is not necessary to accept everything as true, one must only accept it as necessary." "A melancholy conclusion," concludes K., "It turns lying into a universal principle." But such "lying" results only from a confrontation with the absolute; the priest is more philosophical and relativistic—he is, after all, only a part of the shifting boundaries that defeat the possibility of any human grasp.

K.'s light, which the priest gave him to hold, has long since gone out; small loss: it was more limiting than revelatory. Kafka snuffs it out three times: in the cathedral, in the death of K. (our confused eye within this particular text), in the text itself. Like K., and for the duration of the fiction we share, we have been kept at arm's length from something that is important to us and that we can sense only by circling around it. But in our circling we have become K., and we also have been reading about ourselves reading—hopelessly. Starobinski notes a similarity between Dostoevsky and Kafka in that the characters of each no longer have a "chez soi"—they have been expelled from their rightful home, they are in exile from themselves. Kafka's purpose is to make us aware of our own exile, but in the process we have entered his book, we have entered into his sense of the unenterable: *we* now inform the pale surfaces of his story as he first did.

DAVID EGGENSCHWILER

"The Metamorphosis," *Freud,* and the Chains of Odysseus

For nearly half a century, since Hellmuth Kaiser's 1931 essay in *Imago,* Kafka's *Metamorphosis* has been an obviously rich subject for psychoanalytic critics, from the most casual, who merely note its dreamlike qualities and Oedipal tussles, to the most persistent, who translate all of its symbolic odds and ids. Such inevitable interpretations have called for the equally inevitable reactions from the opponents of psychoanalytic criticism, who charge reductionism and the neglect of aesthetic values. So Gregor has become a test case, forced to carry on his spindly legs an increasing burden of controversy. I would hesitate to add another straw except in the hope of resolving some of the controversy and showing that the concerns of Freudian and formalist must converge in this story, that they are not merely equal but also inseparable. It will not do to keep an aloof toleration of various critical methods or even to combine approaches in a loose mixture, moving back and forth from manifest to latent content, trying to satisfy both Apollo and Dionysus in a mad rush from temple to temple. In this story the two gods consort in a most disturbing and amusing way.

The origin of "The Metamorphosis" came almost two months before its conception, in another literary "birth," as Kafka described it. On the night of September 22–23, 1912, in one eight-hour sitting, he wrote "The Judgment," the most important story he had written to that time, and the next day he rejoiced in his diary:

From *Modern Language Quarterly* 39, no. 4 (December 1978). Copyright ©1979 by the University of Washington. Originally entitled " 'Die Verwandlung', Freud, and the Chains of Odysseus". Original quotations in German. The editor has substituted published translations from several works, which are noted in the text.

[The fearful strain and joy, how the story developed before me, as if I were advancing over water. Several times during this night I heaved my own weight on my back. How everything can be said, how for everything, for the strangest fancies, there waits a great fire in which they perish and rise up again . . . Only *in this way* can writing be done, only with such coherence, with such a complete opening out of the body and the soul. (*The Diaries of Franz Kafka 1910–1913,* ed. Max Brod, trans. Joseph Kresh. New York: Schocken, 1949. All further references will be to *Diaries.*)]

It is quite understandable that he felt such a release in this rush of composition and that months later, while reading the proofs, he described the story as having been born covered with filth and slime (*Diaries*). "The Judgment" is the most obviously confessional piece of fiction he ever wrote. Georg Bendemann's ambivalent feelings about his father—aggression, fear, disgust, guilt, love, competition—correspond exactly to the feelings Kafka claims to have had about his own father, and the story reads like a transparent Oedipal fantasy. Kafka himself realized the obvious psychological qualities, for he wrote in his diary: "[Many emotions carried along in the writing, joy, for example, that I shall have something beautiful for Max's *Arkadia,* thoughts about Freud, of course . . . (*Diaries*)]." Unlike Kafka's later works, "The Judgment" seems less a parable than a psychological fable with overt and straightforward themes. As Erich Heller has written, "Never before or after, it seems, has Freud ruled so supremely over a piece of literature." But the revolution was already at hand, for within two months Kafka would begin *The Metamorphosis,* in which he would treat similar psychological themes in ways that examine and debate what the earlier story naïvely represented. Freud's supreme reign was soon followed by a democratic republic.

Kafka's jottings about psychology form a useful background for *The Metamorphosis.* Opponents of psychoanalytic criticism too readily seize on his brief outbursts in his octavo notebooks ([""Never again psychology!"] or [""Nausea after too much psychology." (*Dearest Father: Stories and Other Writings,* trans. Ernst Kaiser and Eithne Wilkens. New York: Schocken Books, 1954. All further references will be to *Dearest Father.*)]) to show that he soon rejected the whole business. But some of his comments show a more balanced, and at times brilliant, view of contemporary psychology. His most perceptive statements are entered in his notebooks for October 19, 1917:

[There is no such thing as observation of the inner world, as there is of the outer world. At least descriptive psychology is probably, taken as a whole, a form of anthropomorphism, a nibbling at our own limits. The inner world can only be experienced, not described.—Psychology is the description of the reflection of the terrestrial world in the heavenly plane, or, more correctly, the description of a reflection such as we, soaked as we are in our terrestrial nature, imagine it, for no reflection actually occurs, only we see the earth wherever we turn.

Psychology is impatience.

All human errors are impatience, the premature breaking off of what is methodical, an apparent fencing in of the apparent thing.
                    ("Wedding Preparations," *Dearest Father*)]

If we were to understand "Psychologie" to refer to an older Lockean, instead of Freudian, theory, would this not sound, in style and content, like something from Blake's notebooks? So history turns upon itself as poets challenge scientists. But even as Blake eventually found a necessary, if largely antagonistic, role for Newton and Locke in his visionary apocalypse, so Kafka found a useful and carefully limited role for Freud in his own experience of the inner world. In the last part of the passage from the notebooks, he accuses psychology of what we now call reductionism, of too strong a desire to formulate, simplify, explain in terms of basic concepts. But in saying that it prematurely breaks off, he says, not that it is on the wrong path, but that it is too impatient to reach the goal and so mistakenly accepts partial answers for complete ones. Of course for Kafka (as for Blake) one can never reach final insight—["There is a goal, but no way" ("Wedding Preparations")]—but one must journey; one must not worship false gods by mistaking a part for the whole, a stage of the journey for its end. And a proper view of psychology can help to show the way and to reveal the limits at which we nibble in our search.

If this last part of Kafka's entry is intelligent and explicit, the first part is brilliant, suggestive, and even more to our purposes. By calling psychology a form of anthropomorphism, Kafka claims that through it the conscious mind projects its own image onto the inner world; while thinking that it is describing the entire self, that mind is actually describing its own features. The subsequent analogy of the terrestrial falsely reflected in the heavenly extends the religious connotations of anthropomorphism and implies that the inner world is sacred. Thus psychology pretends to describe in rational and observably human images an inner world that is indescribable, irrational, and inhuman; it profanes the sacred and makes the mysterious seem knowable. It lies to us, but it might tell us, soaked as we are in our terrestrial nature, what we want to hear, perhaps what we need to hear if we are to carry on our human commerce in a world that otherwise would be full of terrors. What, though, if one were to awaken from uneasy dreams to find that one no longer had a human form? How could the rational mind deal with that failure of anthropomorphism? And how could we, reading an account of such a thing, explain that impossible metamorphosis in terms that make it comprehensible, that apparently fence in the apparent thing and give the story, if not the creature, a human form? And how might an author who is wise and skeptical about an anthropomorphic psychology lead us to examine our own needs and illusions? We have, it seems, good cause to be wary in our assumptions about Kafka and psychology.

So, Gregor Samsa, hard-working salesman, dutiful son, quiet home-body, awakes one morning to find that he has been transformed into a gigantic insect (or a monstrous vermin or a monstrous bug or, in any case, "einem ungeheueren Ungeziefer"). If the rest of the story sustained this potential element of fairy tale or surrealistic fantasy, we could easily accept this opening incident as part of a genre in which such suspensions of natural law are everyday occurrences, requiring a ready suspension of disbelief so that we could enter the fabulous province. But, as most readers and critics have testified, the realistic form of the story after the opening sentence will not allow us to adjust our expectations so comfortably. Because the humdrum world that Gregor inhabits is not an appropriate setting for such nocturnal metamorphoses, we (if not the characters) cast about for an explanation, and literature as well as literary criticism has taught us that such incidents might well be considered symbolic, especially when they so emphatically interrupt a realistic surface and thus imply special significances, figurative meanings when literal ones seem so inadequate.

Kafka, writing this story only two months after "The Judgment," invites us to turn psychological as, in passage after passage, he supplies the most obvious grist for the Freudian mill. Why else does he give such a prominent place in his second paragraph to the picture of a woman in furs that Gregor has cut out of a magazine and put in a special frame he has spent his evenings making? And why does Kafka stylistically mark that passage with the odd comment that the woman's whole forearm had vanished ("verschwunden war") into her muff, as though such a disappearance were uncanny rather than commonplace? Since we are indirectly given Gregor's point of view here as he looks about his room, apparently the attention to, and impressions of, the furry woman are his, and she is the first thing to which he turns his attention after seeing his insect's body. Soon, of course, he thinks of his tiring job, his demanding schedule, his sacrifices for his parents, his employer who sits on high and talks down intimidatingly to his employees. When one combines these initial thoughts with Gregor's strong appetite this morning, his preference for garbage over fresh food, and the pleasure and relief he feels in abandoning an upright posture to crawl, even over ceiling and walls with extraordinary agility, one may well conclude—as many critics have—that the metamorphosis symbolizes a rebellious assertion of unconscious desires and energies, the primitive and infantile demands of the id. Gregor soon implies as much and also provides a complementary interpretation when he suggests that he has been driven mad and made unable to leave his bed because he is conscience-stricken over wasting even an hour of his firm's time. Thus one might conclude that the transformation symbolizes both a libidinous rebellion and a condemnation of such rebellion, even of unconscious desires to rebel. Simultaneously, Gregor, poor bewildered simpleton, is caught between psychological forces that are either too immoral or too moral. Fortunately psychoanalytic theory, with its condensations and reversals, can accommodate such contradictory meanings of a symbol: that dexterity is one of its most charming means of making perplexing things coherent, as Kafka knew when he wrote ironically in his notebooks: ["as regards the always correct result, it is richly informative" ("Wedding Preparations")]. It is always correct because it is a self-validating system with its own means of explaining away objections that are not derived from its premises. That is why it is such a useful and reassuring method for explaining the monstrous transformation of Gregor into vermin. It can accommodate such a multeity of significances into its unity. If we allow the context of "The Judgment" into our speculations, it can even explain that, like Georg Bendemann's sentence of death, the metamorphosis signifies guilt and the desire for punishment for having usurped the father's role (as well as signifying guilt for wanting to abandon that tiresome role). And, for a final reversal, it can demonstrate a desire for aggression against the supplanted father and the other figures of authority associated with his primal power.

A patient reading of Stanley Corngold's summary of articles and chapters on the story will show that all of these interpretations have been offered by commentators, although not often in such profusion. And there are good reasons why such explanations should be common: the obtrusively obvious images and actions, the patent juxtaposition of symbols with descriptions of Gregor's longings, frustrations, and guilt, even the coy asides that suggest a psychological possibility while pretending to deny it—these techniques coax from the reader a psychological interpretation. And if the reader were to consider Kafka's personal writings (including a contemporaneous letter to

Max Brod in which he told of a near suicide to escape a conflict analogous to Gregor's) and preceding fiction (including "The Judgment" and "Wedding Preparations in the Country" in which a character desires to send his clothed body into the world while he remains in bed as a large beetle), if, that is, the reader were to consider contexts likely to determine intention and validate interpretation, why then he might well have ["thoughts about Freud, of course" (*Diaries*)]. About this story, however, those thoughts should be complicated with irony.

Throughout the first two parts of the story Kafka repeatedly and brilliantly confounds our responses by first encouraging a symbolic interpretation and then dropping us uncomfortably into literal fact. By a sophisticated form of romantic irony he dislocates our critical point of view. For example, when Gregor's sister and mother are removing his furniture in order to give him more crawling space, he suddenly realizes that he is losing his human past, and, as a gesture of opposition, he places himself over the picture of the woman described so obtrusively in the opening paragraphs. His choice of human object seems inevitable for a psychological reading; he is momentarily trying to preserve a symbol of his sexually repressed and socially acceptable past in order to resist further surrender to the primitive instincts that are controlling him. But what are we then to make of the comment that the glass of the picture ["was a good surface to hold on to and comforted his hot belly (*Bauch*)" (*Franz Kafka: The Complete Stories*, ed. Nahum N. Glatzer, trans. Willa and Edwin Muir. New York: Schocken Books, 1971. All further references will be to *The Complete Stories*.)]? This comment does not thematically contradict the psychological reading; if we were tactlessly persistent, we could even mutter something about sublimations cooling the overheated id. But these tactile images do something more effective; they jar us out of the symbolic mode and into the world of the literal vermin. They make us imagine in an awful moment what it would be like to have human sensations (is a bug comforted by being cooled?) through the body of a gigantic insect conceived in partly human terms (does a bug have a belly, *Bauch,* rather than the entomological *Hinterleib?*). Of course a symbolic reading should not try to account for every description in the text, but, if it is to remain confident, it cannot afford to be challenged so strikingly by incongruous, juxtaposed details. And Kafka challenges it often in this manner. He sends Gregor across the walls to hang from the ceiling in almost blissful absorption; and we recognize in these acrobatics a new freedom even in Gregor's confinement, a feeling of release and pleasure in his inhuman agility, a rising above the plane of his old, routine life. (And Kafka, to his shame, was such a poor gymnast, whereas his father was proudly athletic.) Then we are shown the sticky traces Gregor leaves behind, traces that do not come from the subconscious: they are repulsively entomological, not psychological. They befoul our symbols as well as Gregor's once-human room.

Not all of the shifts in perspective are so gruesome: some even contribute to the humor of the tale. Has not every reader noted the amusingly strange nonchalance with which Gregor at first accepts his metamorphosis? That strangeness corresponds to the incongruities I have been discussing. On the one hand, we have Gregor's reasonable attempts to explain his new state as nonsense or as fantasy or as delusion caused by the hyperactive conscience of a dutiful employee. We could add other explanations, but even if we consider the metamorphosis as literary symbolism rather than delusion, we would still be imitating Gregor's attempts to explain the literal change as somehow unreal, as metaphorical. On the other hand, Gregor also applies his calm reason to problems of manipulating this unfamiliar body in which his consciousness is encased. This switching of hands causes comic non sequiturs when Gregor first decides that after he has gotten out of bed the fantasy will disappear, then spends much mental and physical effort trying to operate the unknown mechanisms of this supposedly unreal body in order to get up so that the body will prove unreal. And around he goes, from a detached perspective (this body does not literally exist) to an immanent one (how does one work these writhing little legs?). Because Kafka gives us vivid accounts of the body and Gregor's frustrating attempts to manipulate it, we too are wrenched from one perspective to another, from symbol to fact, with what should be amused perplexity. How else could we at one moment consider solemn psychological interpretations and at the next witness a scene of awful and amusing slapstick in which Gregor muddles on with the same kind of deadpan stoicism with which Buster Keaton and Charlie Chaplin endure the intolerably inhuman obstacles that surround them? Psychoanalytic theory might explain such humor as defensive screening, but it would thereby trivialize the problem with its self-validating formula; it would supply an unconscious cause for the comic incongruities without considering their strong and subtle effects, their literary value and complex purposes. It would be reductive.

A still more obvious example of such double perspective is the scene in which Gregor first confronts his father, a confrontation that seems inescapably and intentionally Freudian. After Gregor has first emerged from his room and has caused the office manager to flee, he is set upon by his father, who grabs the manager's cane (symbol of authority and, if you will, a phallic flayer) and a newspaper, which Kimberly Sparks has convincingly shown to be also a symbol of authority (they who rule the house—Gregor, Mr. Samsa, the three boarders—sit at the head of the table and read the newspaper). The father drives Gregor before him, hissing like a savage ("wie ein Wilder"), and as Gregor nears his room, the sound becomes so loud that it no longer seems to him the voice of only one father ("gar nicht mehr wie die Stimme bloss eines einzigen Vaters"). A brandished cane, a savage, a multiplied father—the scene pushes irresistibly into a primal conflict, representing the unconscious infantile fears that Freud had already described in the famous and then highly controversial *Three Essays on the Theory of Sexuality*, published in 1905. But at the same time we have another emotionally incongruous scene superimposed on this elemental struggle; we have a man chasing away a large bug in the way in which bugs and other unpleasant creatures are usually chased, by waving a newspaper, prodding with a stick, and hissing (shooing). This incongruity challenges us by refusing to allow an adequate response. Are we not to sympathize with Gregor in his confusion and fear, and are we not also to recognize the allusions that associate that fear with what Freud claimed to be a most elemental source of anxiety? We respond to the plight of the loathly son and understand that it symbolically represents the plight of all sons. But our compassion and our understanding seem mocked by the opposing image of a man shooing away a bug. Can we be sure that we do not have a grotesque joke? And at whose expense would it be? And how much would it undercut the psychological themes? If, intellectually, the latent content is made almost too obvious by the manifest content, is it not, affectively, subverted by the manifest? In corresponding terms of literary analysis, the figurative meanings stated or implied in the scene that broaden its references (like a savage, like many fathers) are opposed in tone by some of the literal meanings. The symbolic collides with the matter-of-fact.

Kafka repeats this technique in the second confrontation between father and son, but this time makes the psychological symbolism so obvious that it approaches caricature. The mother has fainted in Gregor's room upon seeing her son; Gregor has rushed into the living room to help the sister secure aid; the sister has locked Gregor out of his room in which the mother still lies; and the father returns, finding the son interposed between him and his wife, pressed against the bedroom door. A pat tableau for the psychological climax, especially since we are now told that, in the times of Gregor's dominance in the family, the feeble father used to walk between mother and son in their daily strolls. As the physical positions are now reversed, so are the biological and psychological, for the dominant father is revitalized; he stands erect, his eyes dart under bushy eyebrows, and he wears a uniform with gold buttons (we might recall the photograph of Gregor from his army days: he stands there confident, smiling, with his hand on his sword, of all things). As the father approaches, Gregor is appropriately astonished at the enormous size of the soles of the father's shoes. While they circle the room, the father begins his deadly assault on his son: he begins throwing apples at him. As horrified as Gregor feels, as symbolic as this confrontation may be, the scene is a bit silly: the father filling his pockets from the fruit bowl and pitching the apples at his verminous son, the little red apples rolling about the floor as if magnetized and knocking into each other. The description suggests some kind of children's game. And if we are to take the apples as particularly symbolic, as some commentators have done without irony, the scene becomes even more ridiculous. If these apples have been imported from Eden and if they symbolize the instrument by which the original Father expelled his son from paradise, then Kafka has turned *Moses and Monotheism* into a travesty a quarter of a century before it was written. But one need not seek so obscurely for parody of Freud. No sooner is Gregor wounded and made to feel nailed ("festgenagelt") to the spot (perhaps making him Christ as well as Adam in this biblical collage) than his mother, dressed in her chemise, breaks from his bedroom, embraces the father in complete union with him ("in gänzlicher Vereinigung mit ihm"), and begs for her son's life. That is a primal scene with a vengeance. It is no wonder that the son's sight fails at this point. Commentators who write only of Gregor's exclusion here from the complete union of the family group seem willfully unpsychological, but those who merely point out its Oedipal character without considering its tone and parodic nature seem willfully unliterary. As Gregor reaches the climax of his Freudian drama, Kafka pulls out all stops and plays a wonderfully loud and heavy-handed variation on the Oedipal themes he has used throughout. Here, no more indirection, no more allusion, no more symbol, but the veritable primal scene *an sich*.

The brassy crescendo that ends section 2 all but ends Kafka's use of Freudian themes in his treatment of Gregor; as we shall soon see, these themes will be redistributed in the Samsa family to different effects. Necessarily, then, except for a brief reappearance in section 3, it also ends the ironic use he has made of Gregor's verminous body to suggest and to undercut psychoanalytic themes. That technique of playing the literal against the symbolic corresponds generally to what Corngold has explained as Kafka's development of ["gigantic insect"] as a distorted metaphor that is neither entirely figurative nor entirely literal (*The Commentators' Despair*). But whereas Corngold sees the subject of *The Metamorphosis* as language itself, I am concerned with that use of language to suggest the values and limits of psychology. Kafka's allusions and patterns do imply that psychology helps to specify the desires and fears of the inner life. And his use of inexplicable brute and brutal fact marks limits, implies that the inner life cannot be entirely known, entirely fenced in by anthropomorphic theories. Either to spell out a set of psychoanalytic patterns or to assert that Gregor's metamorphosis is entirely and intentionally incomprehensible is to miss the further pleasure of recognizing both and appreciating their interplay. In part 3 Kafka pointedly interrupts that interplay and by doing so clarifies his tale and further develops its power and its humor.

The changes of structure in the final part and the corresponding adjustments in symbolic method are acts of great intelligence. Kafka himself thought that the story should have been better constructed and should have had a more consistent style; but *The Metamorphosis,* with its multiple climaxes and changing structure, has a far more sophisticated and interesting form than "The Judgment," which Kafka seemed to prefer. And the basic change in structure that occurs in section 3 makes possible a still more interesting critique of psychology than had been achieved in the first two sections.

Because Gregor has been decisively defeated and seriously wounded in his struggle, even the father is now reminded that Gregor is a member of the family ("ein Familienmitglied"); so the Samsas leave the son's door open in the evening. On the hinges of this opened door the story turns about thematically and structurally. By admitting that Gregor is one of them—although separated, in darkness, on the other side of the doorway—the Samsas begin to assume some of the burdens that have been symbolized by Gregor's metamorphosis. Throughout sections 1 and 2 the Samsas usually act singly or in pairs and almost always in direct relation to Gregor: the sister feeds Gregor and cleans his room; the sister and mother remove his furniture; the father struggles with him. At the beginning the three Samsas address Gregor in three different tones of voice (one gentle, one harsh, one imploratory) through three different doors. But in section 3 they always act as a group and seldom in direct relation to Gregor (except at their own psychological climax). These changes are revealing, for the three Samsas, acting now as the closely related parts of one unit, of one psychologically symbolic character, assume and struggle with many of the problems that Gregor once had. They become the central actors, or composite actor, in the Freudian drama. And because Gregor now becomes, in a psychological sense, the main symbol of what they experience in economic, social, and domestic relationships, they do not deal with him directly until their crisis, until they must confront all of their problems as represented by him. Until then, they turn their attention outward, enduring the symptoms of their essential problems, not facing and acting on the causes.

Meanwhile, Gregor waits and watches. His door, which has opened symbolically onto the family group, has opened literally as well. In a concise gesture, Kafka has combined symbol and fact to great narrative advantage. Because, until Gregor's death, the narrator's physical (if not always intellectual) point of view is limited to Gregor's, we need that open door so that we can observe the other Samsas for the first time as they deal with and endure the world in which they have become the main actors. What we see through that doorway is not the revitalized family that some commentators have too casually described as emerging once Gregor has been removed from his prematurely dominant position in the household. That revitalization will come, but not so directly, not so easily. We see a family that is exhausted and depressed from laboring at menial jobs— messenger, seamstress, salesgirl. They live much as Gregor did before his metamorphosis. Like him each of them could say ["Oh God . . . what an exhausting job I've picked on" (*The Complete Stories*)], like him they spend weary evenings at home in a spiritless routine; like him they labor under an economic and psychological debt, which the father incurred and the son later returned: and like him they feel only a distant possibility of release. How appropriate that Gregor, transformed into a monster under such circumstances, should now serve as a symbol of their frustration, servility, and sacrifice. In a passage of subtle and precise juxtapositions Kafka makes it clear that the monstrous vermin is more a representation than a literal cause of their state:

[But what they lamented most was the fact that they could not leave the flat which was much too big for their present circumstances, because they could not think of any way to shift Gregor. Yet Gregor saw well enough that consideration for him was not the main difficulty preventing the removal, for they could have easily shifted him in some suitable box with a few air holes in it; what really kept them from moving into another flat was rather their own complete hopelessness and the belief that they had been singled out for a misfortune such as had never happened to any of their relations or acquaintances. They fulfilled to the uttermost all that the world demands of poor people, the father fetched breakfast for the small clerks in the bank, the mother devoted her energy to making underwear for strangers, the sister trotted to

and fro behind the counter at the behest of customers, but more
than this they had not the strength to do.

(*The Complete Stories*)]

Although the passage may be indirectly limited to Gregor's point of view
["Yet Gregor saw well enough . . ."], the narrative tone makes it seem quite
reliable, and it prepares us well to understand later changes in the family.
The three Samsas blame their condition most of all on Gregor, although they
emphasize the practical problem of moving the monster. We are immediately told, however, that the practical concern is mainly a pretense and that
their hopelessness and sense of unusual misfortune keep them from trying to
improve their lot. Does not the reader at this point assume that the great
[misfortune] that has imprisoned them is Gregor's metamorphosis, which
makes them feel shame, victimization, and powerlessness? And certainly the
metamorphosis itself is one of their misfortunes. But the next sentence tells
not of Gregor's debilitating presence, but of the family's servile jobs. Ruled
by small clerks, strangers, and customers, this petty bourgeois family that
once had its own business has fallen into the laboring class, where its
strength, pride, and independence are lost. As a composite character the
Samsas are now dominated, as Gregor once was, by authorities who correspond in the social world to the father in the infantile (and later the repressed)
world of the Freudian Oedipal drama.

Appropriately, the center of this fallen family is Mr. Samsa. As he had
risen to savage, gigantic, and even uniformed power in vanquishing the
apparently rebellious son, so now he has declined into the most pathetic of
the three Samsas. Even his uniform, which was once a sign of power and
authority in the battle of father and son, has become a sign of servility. As he
sleeps exhausted in his armchair at home, he continues to wear that uniform,
not as if he were the proud patriarch, but ["as if he were ready for service at
any moment and even here only at the beck and call of his superior" (*The
Complete Stories*)]. The uniform undergoes its own metamorphosis as the old
father nods in his chair and the women form a chorus of gentle lamentation.

To balance these scenes of naturalistic pathos and to prepare for the
second reversal of the story, Kafka introduces three stylized boarders. If the
plight of the three Samsas has not seemed clearly enough psychological to
this point, the appearance of the [three boarders] should change that, for
they turn this part of the story into a Freudian comedy, both in its structure
and in its tone. The three gentlemen are explicitly figures of authority, harsh
judgment, and hostile power. They dominate the Samsas, sitting arrogantly
at the dinner table, reading the newspaper (that sign of dominance), haugh-

tily judging the food and the sister's violin playing, and demanding strict neatness in the household, especially in the kitchen (that source of primal pleasure). They live together in one bedroom, wear full beards, dress alike, and move together like Siamese triplets, with the middle boarder always acting as the leader and the two side men of this little troupe always acting and speaking in unison. It is no wonder that the more persistent psychoanalytic critics have identified this aggressive hairy trinity, especially considering its isosceles arrangement, as a symbol of the paternal genitals. But if we indulge in such specific naming of parts, we ought to do so playfully. If Kafka is consciously or unconsciously representing the dread father's phallus, we must credit him, at whatever psychic level he resides, with a sense of humor. Yet we need not talk of phallic symbols or superegos to understand the function of the boarders. Intimidating this servile family, the boarders represent all forms of authority, both internal and external, that dominate such poor and ashamed people. And they pointedly *represent* such powers, for they are such stylized puppets, acting out a caricature of social and psychological forces. Because they are so stylized, representative, and ridiculous, they can focus the Samsas' anxieties on limited and well-defined antagonists, and by clearly defining the problems they make possible rebellion and reversal.

The condition of the three Samsas has become very schematized. Superimposed upon, and representing, their general anxiety is a pair of contrasting symbols. In the dark bedroom, in the jumble of discarded furniture and filth, is the monstrous vermin, a grotesque, hidden part of the family, a sign of their shame and unworthiness. Controlling the well-cleaned living room are the boarders, who insist that the Samsas are shameful and inferior. The pattern, which reproduces in simplified form the conflicts of Gregor's earlier life, is quite obvious, and the climax of the Samsas' story makes it even more so since it brings together the symbols of shame and judgment, forcing the Samsas to act decisively if they are to survive.

When the boarders first see Gregor, they mock the Samsas, then angrily demand explanations, and finally give notice, refusing to pay for their lodging and threatening legal action. Now the Samsas reach the bottom of their despair, for they face still more financial hardship and a public recognition of their shame. In desperation Grete, the youngest and pluckiest of the three, exclaims that the thing must go, that they must stop thinking that it is Gregor. Her outcry is climactic; it changes the Samsas' situation as decisively as the thrown apples had changed Gregor's. During the night Gregor dies. In the morning the Samsas discover the death, retire to the parents' room where they weep, then emerge to confront and banish the peevish boarders. The psychological pattern is again obvious: by a desperate act of will the Samsas have refused to believe any longer that the vermin is part of themselves; they have disclaimed their guilt and unworthiness by reversing the gesture of acceptance with which section 3 and the account of their suffering began. When they have refused to be overwhelmed by shame and hopelessness, the symbol of those feelings disappears, and they can banish the figures who have judged them.

If this were all there were to it, the climax of the story would be as thin and uninteresting as the above summary. But the psychological scheme is realized so well in ways that give interesting perspectives on the scheme itself. We must put aside for a moment the effects of juxtaposing Gregor's pathetic death with the family's comic rebirth: that issue is crucial and needs its own frame of reference. But we need only to consider the amusing way in which Kafka describes the family's triumph in order to realize how artful the artless psychology becomes in the telling. When the boarders enter in the morning, they are still arrogant, but as they stand looking at Gregor's corpse, they put their hands in the pockets of their somewhat shabby coats ("etwas abgenützten Röckchen"). Their shabbiness, of which we had no indication before and which might remind us of Mr. Samsa's stained, used messenger's coat, becomes apparent with Gregor's death and announces the imminent defeat of the powers of intimidation. At this moment, as if on cue, the Samsas emerge from the parents' bedroom, the father walking in the middle in his uniform, the two women flanking him, their arms linked with his. Now that there is no more son to complicate the father's possession of the women and no more symbol of the family's unworthiness, this united primal horde advances directly upon the middle lodger, whom the father orders from the house. Confronting each other like mirror images, triad faces triad in mock-heroic battle (each with its champion) over the corpse of yesterday's battle. The middle boarder submits and leaves humbly; the other boarders hurry after their fallen leader. Actually those two ridiculous figures hop away ("hüpften"); and, because they had been standing by, rubbing their hands behind their backs, they seem to have acquired their own insectlike mannerisms. If one cares to turn entomological, one might suggest that this hopping and dorsal rubbing of limbs suggest not the sacred and excremental dung beetle, to which the charwoman and Vladimir Nabokov liken Gregor, but the locust. Yet if one wishes to think of plagues and Pharoahs and patriarchs (again, some twenty-five years before *Moses and Monotheism*), one must also remember the comic tone of the description; if any such allusions are present, they lighten as well as deepen the text.

Feeling a burden lifted, the Samsas decide to celebrate by taking a day off from work, first writing excuses to their employers. How wonderfully important and trivial this gesture is. They assert the freedom and rebellion that Gregor had never asserted in his five years as dutiful salesman; they play hooky. The women are still discomforted by the coarse charwoman who wants to tell them boisterously how she got rid of the dead bug, and Mr. Samsa is again irritated by the upright feather in the aggressive woman's hat (apparently the phallic father still resents competition), but they decide to fire that reminder of their past. So, they take a trolley ride into the country, in the warm sunshine, where they realize that their jobs are really advantageous and their prospects good. Noticing that their daughter has blossomed ("aufgeblüht") into a beautiful young girl, the parents think it soon time to find her a husband (no magazine pin-ups for her), and she seems to respond by stretching her young body in a new beginning. Furthermore, this happens at the end of March, which is surely not the cruelest month for this family, whose rebirth happens suddenly and fairly painlessly.

There has been much disagreement about this ending; in fact, Kafka himself was not satisfied with it. Should we see it as a triumphant assertion of health and happiness, or as the family's obtuse assertion of bourgeois values without their realizing what higher values might have been learned from their drama, or as something more ambivalent? First of all, we must assume that the final description of the family does imply a desirable state. The biographical evidence, including Max Brod's testimonies and the letters to Felice at this time (before the painful vacillations over marriage had begun), indicates that, despite any fears and misgivings, Kafka considered marriage and family life to be a great achievement, one that he later claimed had been denied by his father. Furthermore, the weight of almost the entire story supports this assumption. One must not make too much—although I shall make much—of a bit of violin music or of external parallels between Gregor as a verminous recluse and Kafka as a solitary writer. It is too clever by far to make brief scenes or general analogies determine the entire story, to find keys that open hidden doors, which, when entered, show us the mirror image of the tale, making all ironic and reversing apparent values. Still, the entire presentation of the Samsas' triumph and rebirth must give us more than pause. Their problems become so narrowly focused, their triumph so swift, and their reversal so apparently complete. Also, the psychological symbolism by which these terms are figured is too pat, too schematic, even to the point of caricature. The methods of presentation become an ironic commentary on the Samsas' development.

Despite the psychological caricatures in sections 1 and 2, the representations of Gregor's condition are complex, illusive, and puzzling: the anthropomorphic imge of the inner life is not adequate. Yet in section 3, when the Freudian pattern is tranferred to the other Samsas, who replace Gregor in the world, the psychoanalytic theory is quite adequate to the situation. Indeed, if the desires, fears, and conflicts of the inner world could be reduced to the terms in which they are expressed in the Samsas' case, then they might be grasped and governed by the simple gestures whereby Grete rejects the monster and Mr. Samsa kicks out the boarders. If, that is, they could be so reduced; if one could become as naïve as the Samsas. But their problems are not Gregor's: they have not been changed into a monstrous vermin, either literally or symbolically. They have shallower problems to confront, comprehend, and solve—at least the problems are shallower as they are presented by the detached narrator and perceived by the characters. Perhaps the Samsas' ability to see their condition so simply—or their inability to see it more complexly—enables them to change that condition, to formulate it in manageable terms and then to take care of it. The authorial perspective is quite complex and subtle in its admiration for, and condescension to, the naïveté of this middle-class family.

This perspective is clarified by a brilliant parable that Kafka wrote in his octavo notebooks on October 23, 1917; he called it "The Silence of the Sirens," and began it with the statement, ["Evidence that even inadequate, indeed childish means may serve to save one." ("Wedding Preparations")]. He explains that the fatal song of the sirens could not be withstood by Odysseus' simple devices of wax to plug the ears and chains to secure himself to the ship's mast; the song could penetrate anything, and the passion in the hearer would snap chains and mast. But even more terrible is the silence of the Sirens from which nothing could ever escape. Attempting to resist the singing with his little stratagems, Odysseus sailed toward the Sirens in innocent delight, and they, seeing the reflected glory in his eyes as he thought confidently of his wax and chains, stood aghast, unsinging, their mouths agape. Odysseus, thinking that they had sung and that he had outwitted them, did not hear their silence and so sailed on as they stared in longing. (Kafka adds in a cunning afterthought that the wily Odysseus may have noticed that the Sirens were silent and may have confounded them and the gods with a trick. But he says that this possibility is beyond comprehension by the mind of man. It surely is beyond the minds of the Samsas, who seem truly naïve, not wily.) So the Samsas with their wax and chains, their inadequate, childish means, their family bug and boarders, confound the Sirens by their simplicity and escape temptations to despair and death. In doing so they are not even aware of the most terrible weapon, the silence of the sirens. But Gregor does not have their little stratagems; he hears the song, and perhaps at the last the silence.

After Gregor has been defeated by his father and has seen his mother embrace the victorious father in an all-out Oedipal scenario, he progressively withdraws from such conflicts, carrying with him the festering wound that is both a literal and symbolic cause of his withdrawal. As the Samsas assume the psychological burden of worry, labor, and shame, Gregor loses it. At first he waits hours for the door to be opened onto the living room where the others sit in the evening; he worries about them and sometimes thinks that he ought to take charge of their affairs as he once had done. But in time, with neglect and weakness, he loses his concern and often does not even heed the open door. Many of the traits that had given specific psychological significance to his metamorphosis disappear: his ravenous hunger, his pleasure in acrobatic crawling, his repressed feelings of aggression. He even becomes indifferent to his filth, no longer feeling the guilt or shame that was associated with his metamorphosis.

It is fully appropriate that the scene that takes Gregor most beyond Freudian concerns and then returns him to them for a last flicker should involve the Samsas, the three boarders, and the living room into which Gregor emerges for a third time. Having realized that he was hungry but not for such food as the boarders are glutting themselves with, Gregor hears his sister's violin playing, finds it beautiful for the first time, and thinks that he is finding the way to the unknown nourishment he craves ("der ersehnten unbekannten Nahrung"). Whatever religious, mystical, or aesthetic significance we might find in this music and Gregor's response to it, we can be sure that the significance is not Freudian; that unknown nourishment is not made by a mother's breast, and it is not desired by a pleasure-seeking id. It is beyond not only the pleasure principle, but the Freudian principles as well. Yet, in horrible irony, this music of whatever remote spheres draws Gregor into the family's living room, that psychological arena that he has come to ignore. As he approaches Grete, entering further into the room, his attention slips from the music to the musician to the sister whom he will keep in his room as his own and finally to the girl whose bare neck he will kiss. Within a few sentences Gregor slides down the scale from spiritual quester to the monster guarding the hidden lady to lewd vermin. And as he is again drawn into the psychological scheme, we are again confronted with the contrast between symbolic meaning and grotesque fact. Psychologically we have Gregor's lapse into erotic, incestuous desire. We might even be tempted to recall something Kafka jotted in his diary two months before he wrote *The Metamorphosis*: ["Love between brother and sister—the repeating of the love between mother and father" (*Diaries*)]. And we might note that the image of Gregor guarding his bedroom door in which his sister is hidden repeats the image in section 2 of Gregor pressed against that door, which then separated his mother from his father. But we also must contend with the literal image of the vermin pressing its jaws against the girl's soft neck. Here again is the jarring double perspective: the human character whose impulses we can explain so well and the creature whose appearance mocks our explanations with a revulsion that no theory can dispel.

It is appropriate for the psychological perspective that precisely at this point in the story the middle boarder calls out and points at Gregor, first in scorn, then in anger. Having reentered the Samsas' room and experienced forbidden erotic longings, Gregor automatically calls forth the accuser that has been judging the Samsas. After the sister then disowns the creature, another psychological defeat to another incestuous assertion, Gregor returns to his room where he dies, thus ending the long decline that began when his father had injured him during the last emergence.

As Gregor lies in the darkness of his locked room, unable to move, he seems mentally remote from the verminous body to which he had once accustomed himself: ["It seemed unnatural to him that he should ever actually been able to move on these feeble little legs" (*The Complete Stories*)]. And as he dies we are given no more reminders of his verminous body or of anything suggesting psychological symbolism:

> [He thought of his family with tenderness and love. The decision that he must disappear was one that he held to even more strongly than his sister, if that were possible. In this state of vacant and peaceful meditation he remained until the tower clock struck three in the morning. The first broadening of light in the world outside the window entered his consciousness once more. Then his head sank to the floor of its own accord and from his nostrils came the last faint flicker of his breath.
>
> (*The Complete Stories*)]

Gregor dies here not as a monstrous vermin (do bugs have nostrils through which a dying breath passes?) and not as an Oedipal son (that tenderness and love are not erotic), but as a human being with affection, acceptance, and peace. The scene is moving in its quiet, understated gentleness, and we should not obscure its emotional effects with talk of religious symbolism or claims that, in thinking of his family, Gregor has slipped back into his old preoccupations. The morning light is quite effective without being a beatific radiance, and the love that Gregor feels is hardly the same as his former feelings of duty, responsibility, and possessiveness. The tone of the passage denies such abstract equations.

Indeed, we should not try to explain the account of Gregor's death in terms of mysticism, religious allegory (no Christ images, please), or psychological theory (no death wishes either). It should abide our questions, as death often does in Kafka's works. By recognizing its lyrical beauty, its lack of irony or symbols, we can see how strongly it contrasts both with the broad naturalistic humor that enters immediately afterwards with the charwoman and with the intellectual humor that follows in the confrontation between the Samsas and the boarders. Gregor's death, to a large extent the culmination of his increasing withdrawal throughout most of section 3, is accessible neither to gruff common sense nor to abstract explanations, both of which project their anthropomorphic images onto a state that recedes into stubborn silence.

In sum, then, *The Metamorphosis* has a forked structure. In the first two sections Gregor dominates, representing psychological themes but also acting out incongruities and parodies that question the adequacy of those themes. In section 3 the story splits, and our attention moves back and forth between complementary sets of characters. The Samsas, having received Gregor's duties and frustrations, also receive his Freudian themes, but in such an apparently unchallenged way that the themes adequately explain the Samsas' condition and provide pat, somewhat comic solutions. Gregor, by contrast, withdraws more and more from his "human" concerns of father, mother, prohibitions, and pleasures; thus he is separated from the Freudian themes that an anthropomorphic psychology describes as the content of the inner world. Only at the eleventh hour does Gregor temporarily join his family in its "human" psychological world, and that brief scene emphasizes how far he has withdrawn and how futile it is for him to look back; it enables him to complete his withdrawal into a quiet, mysterious death through which he enters a realm of pure parable, leaving the Samsas to live in daily life, to struggle with and overcome the cares of everyday.

These last contrasts come from one of Kafka's writings, "On Parables," which can furnish a final commentary on the ending of the story and on the relationship between the reader and the entire work:

> [Many complain that the words of the wise are always merely parables and of no use in daily life, which is the only life we have. When the sage says: "Go over," he does not mean that we should cross to some actual place, which we could do anyhow if the labor were worth it; he means some fabulous yonder, something unknown to us, something that he cannot designate more precisely either, and therefore cannot help us here in the very least. All

these parables really set out to say merely that the incomprehensible is incomprehensible, and we know that already. But the
cares we have to struggle with every day: that is a different
matter.

Concerning this a man once said: Why such reluctance? If
you only followed the parables you yourselves would become
parables and with that rid of all your daily cares.

Another said: I bet that is also a parable.

The first said: You have won.

The second said: But unfortunately only in parable.

The first said: No, in reality: in parable you have lost.

                                                    (*The Complete Stories*)]

The first two paragraphs of this extraordinary passage describe Gregor's
progress in the story as he goes over to some fabulous yonder, becomes
parables, and loses his daily cares; whether it is a yonder to which a wise man
would bid one go is a matter of much critical dispute and will have to be
settled by a wiser man than I. The dialogue in the passage then distinguishes
between parable, which is incomprehensible even though it might be experienced (like the inner world), and interpretation, which is valid only in the
everyday world, the world that is comprehensible because we accept its
limits, its categories and conventions. (["I bet that is also a parable"] is, in
fact, an instance of genre criticism; the second speaker may have studied at
Toronto.) Interpretation accommodates parable to life, perhaps making it
useful ["You have won"], but it cannot completely describe it, for interpretation is reductive ["in parable you have lost"]. Within *The Metamorphosis*
Kafka dramatizes a contrast similar to that described above: Gregor's
metamorphosis is a form of parable; in section 3 the Samsa family acts out an
interpretation of that parable, both clarifying and reducing it in the world of
everyday. In that world they win, both in the validity of their interpretation
(psychology always has correct results) and in its practical consequences. In
parable, of course, they have lost. Correspondingly, the reader is encouraged
to interpret the metamorphosis psychologically, although with far more
intellectual understanding than the Samsas, who merely dramatize an interpretation they could not express. Perhaps the reader may also win in the
world as he reduces a disturbing and frustratingly elusive story to a manageable pattern, an anthropomorphic form. Of course, he too loses in parable.

But Kafka, whose autobiographical accounts show how much he
wrestled with the experiences he represented, had such sensitivity and
intelligence that he could not accept these interpretations of man, of the

inner world, as adequate; yet he had enough honesty to admire those who did not see life as mysterious, who could see it in their own terms and so, like Odysseus, still live. Milena Jesenská explains as much in a letter written in 1920 to Max Brod, who quotes it in his biography of Kafka:

> [There are very intelligent people who also do not wish to make any compromises. But these put on rose-colored glasses and see everything in a different light. For that reason they do not need to make compromises. For that reason they can type rapidly and have women. He stands beside them and looks at them in astonishment, looks at everything, including the typewriter and the women, in equal amazement. He will never understand it. . . . For, obviously, we are capable of living because at some time or other we took refuge in lies, in blindness, in enthusiasm, in optimism, in some conviction or others, in pessimism or something of that sort. But he has never escaped to any such sheltering refuge, none at all. He is absolutely incapable of living, just as he is incapable of getting drunk.
>
> (Max Brod, *Franz Kafka: A Biography,* trans. G. Humphreys Roberts and Richard Winston. New York: Schocken Books, 1960)]

How impressive that this man could incorporate into his fiction the demands of mystery and terror and the promises of refuge, and that he could do it so well that readers still argue the relative demands of each. But the squirming fiction exceeds the squamous mind. As we interpret *The Metamorphosis* (and as readers we must, to some extent), we should remember that, no matter how flexible and comprehensive we are, we shall lose in parable. We can hope to win more completely, more interestingly, only in life.

LAURA QUINNEY

More Remote Than the Abyss

*January 21 {1922}. As yet, it is not too calm. In the theater suddenly, when I
see Florestan's prison, the abyss opens. Everything—singers, music,
audience, neighbors, everything—more remote than the abyss.*

"It would be very unjust to say that you deserted me; but that I *was*
deserted, and sometimes terribly so, is true." In this late journal entry
(1922), Kafka observes the inadequacy of the logic of cause and effect, action
and reaction; between what the unspecified "you" has done and what Kafka
experiences "you" as doing lies a void of non-correspondence, for there is
desertion without the act of deserting. This void appears even in the formulas with which such a truth can be expressed. "It would be very unjust to
say that you deserted me; but that I *was* deserted . . . is true"; these
illogically juxtaposed statements only circumscribe the "desertion" that has
illogically taken place. The two halves of this sentence are as estranged as
"you" and Kafka; their "truths" turn away from one another in "blindness
and separation." This estrangement of truths remains characteristic of those
passages in Kafka's writing which have been too glibly classed as "paradoxes." In "The Next Village," his shortest of sketches, Kafka distilled the
affect of such non-correspondence: "My grandfather used to say: 'Life is
astoundingly short. To me, looking back over it, life seems so foreshortened
that I scarcely understand, for instance, how a young man can decide to ride
over to the next village without being afraid that—not to mention acci-

---

dents—even the span of a normal happy life may fall far short of the time needed for such a journey.' "

The sense of time lived does not match the sense of time as it is lived, so much so that, when this "foreshortened" past is taken as the measure of time, the future seems vertiginously brief. The shock of such foreshortening appears in "Before the Law," when the man from the country, who has been interacting with the law in a bureaucratic mode during all the long years of his vigil at the gate, discovers as he is dying that the law has made way for him individually, or as the doorkeeper puts it, "No one else could ever be admitted here, since this gate was made only for you. I am now going to shut it." The dying man feels "all his experiences in these long years gather themselves in his head to one point, a question he has not yet asked the doorkeeper," and this, the doorkeeper's answer, in turn gathers those "long years" into one instant of error. Kafka found the same dynamic of foreshortening in a parable not his own, and the journal entry about this parable can serve as a gloss on "Before the Law":

> October 19 [1921]. The essence of the Wandering in the Wilderness. A man who leads his people along this way with a shred (more is unthinkable) of consciousness of what is happening. He is on the track of Canaan all his life; it is incredible that he should see the land only when on the verge of death. This dying vision of it can only be intended to illustrate how incomplete a moment is human life, incomplete because a life like this could last forever and still be nothing but a moment. Moses fails to enter Canaan not because his life is too short but because it is a human life.

Here Moses appears as a peripheralized and residualized subject (his is "a shred" of consciousness). It is this residualization that renders his life "incomplete," disproportionately slight by comparison with its length. The parable figures this residualization as a wandering, a perpetual estrangement between Canaan and the Wilderness, which can only asymptotically approach intersection. In his "Letter to His Father," Kafka mourned the asymptotic approach to the truth which, from the start, doomed the project of his letter to incompleteness:

> You asked me recently why I maintain that I am afraid of you. As usual, I was unable to think of any answer to your question, partly for the very reason that I am afraid of you, and partly because an explanation of the grounds for this fear would mean going into far more details than I could even approximately keep

in mind while talking. And if I now try to give you an answer in
writing, it will still be very incomplete, because, even in writing, this fear and its consequences hamper me in relation to you
and because the magnitude of the subject goes far beyond the
scope of my memory and power of reasoning.

His subject is of such a "magnitude" that it generates a supra-cognitive
excess, inundating and evading articulation. Together with the distorting
effects of his fear, this supra-cognitive excess prohibits any analysis of the fear
from corresponding with its truth. The fear, the excess, and the flawed
transcription of them join to create and to occupy the zone of estrangement
between Kafka and his father, who remain faint to each other, banished as
they are to the peripheries. After sixty-odd pages, Kafka surrenders his
effort, closing with contradictory statements that, laid side by side, circumscribe the supra-cognitive excess that cannot be formulated because, as he
writes here, "life is more than a Chinese puzzle." He ventriloquizes his
father's "rejoinder," and allows that, with this "correction" subverting his
own account, "something has been achieved which . . . closely approximates
the truth."

Kafka's longer works, and short stories such as "The Great Wall of
China," bear witness to his belief in the exigency of "approximation";
obsessive and circular, these works play variations on the impasses they begin
with, and never come to a climax or conclusion. For all their discursive
plenitude, they grind to a halt in quite literal incompleteness. Their endless
subtlety Kafka would have attributed to what he called (rather more modestly than he meant it) his emotional "pedantry." In these writings, "resolutions" of plot, like K.'s summary execution in *The Trial,* or the miraculous
interposition of "The Nature Theater of Oklahoma" in *Amerika,* have a
comical precipitancy which calls attention to their arbitrariness. Karl is
embraced by the exuberant "Nature Theater," while K. is dispatched by two
men in frock coats and top hats, whom he calls "Tenth-rate actors"; the
introduction of theater to resolve plot suggests that these "resolutions" are
illusory. But if these works seem repetitive and endless in their "action" (or,
as we might say of *The Trial* and *The Castle,* in their "episodes of discourse"),
they are all the time pursuing development in another sphere; against a
background of impasse, iteration, and reiteration, the subject deteriorates.
The bulk of discursive material, and the bulge of supra-cognitive excess,
succeed in residualizing the subject, who begins as solid and complacent,
but ends as insecure and shadowy. This move in Kafka's work reverses that of
more conventional fiction; instead of constructing and "realizing" characters,

Kafka seeks to dematerialize them. A model for this inverted "development" appears in "The Bucket Rider": a poor man who needs coal jumps onto a bucket, flies into the sky, and so becomes a ghostly night rider, only to find, when the coal-dealer's wife waves him off with a flutter of her apron, that he is indeed apparitional, and fast fading at that; when he evaporates completely, he is ejected from the story and it abruptly ceases; "And with that I ascend into the regions of the ice mountains and am lost forever."

Kafka exploits the uncanniness of the residualized subject in his sketches about eerie hybrids ("The Bridge," "A Crossbreed," and "The Cares of a Family Man"). In "The Cares of a Family Man" and "A Crossbreed," Odradek and the Cat-Lamb are literally residual—obsolete and singular; the Cat-Lamb is a "legacy" of the narrator's father, while Odradek, the flat star-shaped spool with dangling threads, makes one think of "a broken-down remnant." Without origin or relation, these solitary creatures are vulnerable and yet oppressively persistent. Both stories begin with off-hand, matter-of-fact narrative, but come to be dominated by a burdened sense of uneasiness at the creatures' opacity, for these hybrids seem to fluctuate in the degrees of their remoteness and prescience. The narrator of "A Crossbreed" can see his Cat-Lamb as a fond household pet, but then again, can behold in it a quasi-human consciousness, capable of identification, telepathy, even fortitude in the face of martyrdom. Odradek's is a still more unsettling case of instability. When "the family man" condescends to address him conventionally, Odradek retorts with a sinister wit:

> Many a time when you go out of the door and he happens to be leaning directly beneath you against the banisters you feel inclined to speak to him. Of course, you put no difficult questions to him, you treat him—he is so diminutive that you cannot help it—rather like a child. "Well, what's your name," you ask him. "Odradek," he says. "And where do you live?" "No fixed abode," he says and laughs; but it is only the kind of laughter that has no lungs behind it. It sounds rather like the rustling of fallen leaves.

His liminal existence is characterized by his disembodied laugh, which seems inanimate and arbitrary, "like the rustling of fallen leaves." He can even retreat back across the threshold of inanimation: "these answers are not always forthcoming; often he stays mute for a long time, as wooden as his appearance." Both Odradek and the Cat-Lamb are shadowy remnants of consciousness, wavering presences that become uncanny because their residualized subjectivity appears as otherness, an otherness which resists codification and assimilation. Their opacity succeeds in dematerializing the solid "family men" who oversee them; as the narrator of "The Cares of a Family Man" acknowledges in the story's concluding paragraph, Odradek's presence has brought him to feel, himself, volatile and marginalized.

It is the confrontation with bureaucracy that makes characters like K. feel their residualization. In Kafka's work, the bureaucracy itself is the locus of the residualized subject, as it appears in its *heimlich,* rather than *unheimlich* form. Kafka's petty bureaucrats have curiously thinned-out inner lives; their "thoughts" eddy in anxieties and complaints about work, schemes of evasion and advancement, and obsessional analyses of their status and their superiors. Their interior monologues often have an impersonality which makes it difficult to distinguish them as "interior." "Blumfeld, An Elderly Bachelor" begins with such an interior monologue:

> One evening Blumfeld, an elderly bachelor, was climbing up to his apartment—a laborious undertaking, for he lived on the sixth floor. While climbing up he thought, as he had so often recently, how unpleasant this utterly lonely life was: to reach his empty rooms he had to climb these six floors almost in secret, there put on his dressing gown, again almost in secret, light his pipe, read a little of the French magazine to which he had been subscribing for years, at the same time sip at a homemade kirsch, and finally, after half an hour, go to bed, but not before having completely rearranged his bedclothes which the unteachable charwoman would insist on arranging in her own way.

Here Kafka wittily has his stale protagonist "think" the establishment of the story's scene. This description of Blumfeld's evening activities apparently belongs to his own musings, yet it almost has the bland objectivity of a third-person narrative. The faint echoing of interiority dramatizes his residualization as a subject. Blumfeld desires some companionship, "someone to witness these activities," as if to enact the deflection of his own consciousness into objectivity. When he reaches his apartment, he finds that some companionship has mysteriously introduced itself, in the form of "two small white celluloid balls with blue stripes jumping up and down side by side on the parquet." These bouncing balls follow Blumfeld everywhere, and even take up a station under his bed as he tries to sleep; thinking as he does in a bureaucratic vocabulary, he begins to attribute to them a dutiful perseverance and a pragmatic intelligence. He is more right than he knows in applying these bureaucratic standards, for the senselessly bouncing balls reify the monotony of his own existence. These "witnesses" of his activities have his blank diligence and impersonality, while their strangeness mirrors the residuum of his life as a subject. The familiar form of residualization seems to call forth its uncanny double.

Kafka locates bureaucracy as the place of the residualized subject in "Poseidon" and "The New Advocate," where he opposes the attenuations of bureaucracy to the mythology of a "full" life. In "The New Advocate," the narrator and his kind imagine that the scope of existence has diminished with the fall into modernity. "Nowadays—it cannot be denied—there is no Alexander the Great." Once Alexander's battle charger, the new advocate is an anachronism, a residue from an age which the "people" in this story mythologize as simpler, bolder, and richer than their own. Dr. Buchephalus now earns respect for his resigned adaptation to a shrunken world:

> Today the gates have receded to remoter and loftier places; no one points the way; many carry swords, but only to brandish them, and the eye that tries to follow them is confused. So perhaps it is really best to do as Buchephalus has done and absorb oneself in law books. In the quiet lamplight, his flanks unhampered by the thighs of a rider, free and far from the clamor of battle, he reads and turns the pages of our ancient tomes.

Dr. Buchephalus' newly bureaucratized existence seems as textual—recessed and monotonous—as the law books he reads. Yet with this final sentence of the story comes a suggestion of serenity and disinterest on his part, a suggestion which makes it clear that hysterical complaints about a diminished age reflect only the projections of "people." This is the irony that energizes the sketch: the marginalization of the subject implies (and mythologizers eagerly seize upon this implication) that the subject has been or could be unmarginalized, but at the same time it exposes that possibility as a mirage.

Bureaucracy figures the ineluctable residualization of the subject even more vividly in "Poseidon." Here we find the great water-god, wielder of wrath and destruction, sitting quietly at his desk, "going over the accounts." His recessed, if not buried existence makes a joke of the active life that mythology imagines for him (and note that in this sketch Kafka exploits the conventional meaning of the word "mythology"); instead of "cruising through the waves with his trident . . . here he was sitting in the depths of the world's ocean endlessly going over the accounts, an occasional journey to Jupiter being the only interruption of the monotony." It is funny and touching that Poseidon himself looks forward to the deferred emanation of his mythologized self, but casts even this hope in the vocabulary of the bureaucracy that represents his residualization to him: ". . . he had hardly seen the oceans, save fleetingly during his hasty ascent to Olympus, and had never really sailed upon them. He used to say that he was postponing this until the end of the world, for then there might come a quiet moment when, just before the end and having gone through the last account, he could still make a quick little tour."

These witty renditions of the residualized subject issue from a strain in Kafka's work that becomes more influential and more grave in the writing he did after 1921. In his last novel, *The Castle*, and in his last stories, "Investigations of a Dog," "A Little Woman," "The Burrow," and "Josephine, the Singer," Kafka chronicles the ebbs and flows of affect, fluctuating and mutating in isolation. These late works chart the vicissitudes of investment (*Bezetsung*). As Henry Sussman has written of *The Castle*, "K.'s critical detachment from the world-order subsuming the villagers degenerates into a subservience more pronounced than the orthodoxy of any insider." The novel portrays the evolution of K.'s tenacious Oedipal cathexis of the Castle, from which he sees himself as more and more estranged, the more he becomes convinced of its power and greatness. The point at which he comes to believe in the majesty of Klamm, and so of the Castle (by a metonymy which the mythology of the Castle insists upon), is simultaneously the point at which he must come to suffer its infinite distance from him:

> The landlady's threats did not daunt K.; of the hopes with which she tried to catch him he was weary. Klamm was far away. Once the landlady had compared Klamm to an eagle, and that had seemed absurd in K.'s eyes, but it did not seem absurd now; he thought of Klamm's remoteness, of his impregnable dwelling, of his silence, broken perhaps only by cries such as K. had never yet heard, of his downward-pressing gaze, which could never be proved or disproved, of his wheelings, which could never be disturbed by anything that K. did down below, which far above he followed at the behest of incomprehensible laws and which only for instants were visible—all these things Klamm and the eagle had in common.

In this figure of Klamm as the inaccessible, oblivious eagle, K. acknowledges the non-correspondence of investment with the object invested, although it is part of his newly-won naïveté to attribute this gap to the distance of the object itself. From the gap which investment opens up springs the inevitability of its own frustration (so that even the Messiah, as Kafka wrote, "will come only when he is no longer necessary"). That Kafka never completed *The Castle,* nor for that matter "The Great Wall of China,"

"The Hunter Gracchus," etc., signals the essential endlessness of these works which thematize endless nonfulfillment. The gap between investment and the invested object frees the investment to operate independently, its wheels spinning in isolation, residualizing the desired object even while it seems to aggrandize it, and residualizing the desiring subject as well. The "infinite remoteness" in this passage from *The Castle,* and in its persistent appearance throughout Kafka's work, arises from the freedom and alienation of desire. As pure excess, it intervenes between subject and object, appropriating each to its own uses and producing estrangement as a consequence of its own buoyant tyranny. Kafka described to Milena Jesenská this autonomous movement of excess, which seemed to render him helpless and prey to annihilation at the same time that, wrapping him in its flight, it freed (and banished) him from its distant, dwindling origin; if she were to leave him, he wrote, "I would have nothing, not even a name, this too I gave you. . . . And this is why I, in a sense, am independent of you, just because the dependency reaches beyond all bounds."

Kafka refined the pure movement of investment to its purest in "The Burrow." In the perfect solitude of subterranean isolation, the animal narrator details the intricate patterns of its feeling for its life's work. It begins with a professional, but nonetheless loving, appraisal of the burrow's strengths and flaws, then describes the ambiguous pleasures of its foray into "the external world," from which it can contemplate the peace and safety of its burrow, but from which it can return only by imperiling the burrow; this return, which it both longs for and is content to do without, it accomplishes at last with incompetent haste, yielding in turn to the joyousness of reunion. Anxiety eddies in all of these changes, but it starts to make great sweeps when the animal hears a whistling which disturbs the beloved silence of its home; it coolly assesses the whistling, but soon collapses in panic and despair, mutilating the burrow, ignoring it, mistrusting it, hating it, fearing and mourning for it. The burrow is the center of the animal's affective life, and that around which, like the Castle for K., all its desires and anxieties accumulate. The whistling that sounds in the burrow strikes the creature to the heart, for it is the refutation of that sign by which the animal had judged the burrow's harmony with it. It had addressed the burrow with the passion and devotion of an erotic love: "What do I care for danger now that I am with you? You belong to me, I to you, we are united: what can harm us? What if my foes should be assemblimg even now up above there and their muzzles be preparing to break through the moss? And with its silence and emptiness the burrow answers me, confirming my words."

In an affirmation of its own solitude, the creature makes of "silence and emptiness" a source of warmth and joy. But "the whistling in the walls" destroys this delicate illusion of mutual care, and the animal flees from the burrow as from an adversary. Retreating to the entrance, the creature now regards the "external world" with tender affection, as the desirable "place of tranquillity" that it has organized: "Deep stillness; how lovely it is here, outside there nobody troubles about my burrow, everybody has his own affairs, which have no connection with me; how have I managed to achieve this?" The animal can sustain only briefly this effort to re-create the conditions of its desire; it accelerates into anxiety and paranoia when it recollects that "even here there is no peace in reality, here nothing has changed." The whistling sets into operation a new series of emotions and investments, including awe of the "great beast" who the creature comes to believe has produced it. But as an originless, eerily persistent and yet remote emanation, it seems aligned with the burrow, which the animal has treated sometimes as a thing, sometimes as almost a being. Still, to call it "the voice of the burrow" would be to fall into the creature's own literalizing interpretive habits. We might just as well consider the whistling as an emanation from the creature itself—in Blanchot's terms, as the sound of the animal's solitude returned as an unrecognizable alterity. Either way, the whistling appears as an unanticipated effluence of the animal's investment, by which it is literally cornered, as well as unsettled and diminished. This unanticipated effluence is the sign of its estrangement from its own production, investment, and self. That "it" has, in this paragraph, referred to the animal, the burrow, the whistling, and the animal's investment reflects the move in the story itself to volatilize these things into spectrally residualized presences. This process spins itself out in the isolation and invisibility of affective life, and the last line of the story aptly seals it off with the words, "But all remained unchanged."

In "Josephine, the Singer," Kafka portrayed the circumscription and figuralization of the invested object, which finally succeeds in residualizing it as pure figure (so the Castle became for K.). The narrator sets out to explain the appeal of Josephine's singing, which, despite her conceited airs, seems to be no more than a frail version of the Mouse Folk's ordinary "piping." He describes his people's relationship to Josephine as, variously, devoted (but not unconditionally), indifferent (but not unmoved), and paternalistic (but also submissive); his explanations shuttle between affirming and denying Josephine's power, venerating and slighting her. This inconclusive analysis, which circumscribes the power of her song without defining it, can come to rest only in accounts of its figurative capacity: it is "piping set free from the fetters of daily life," or it has "[s]omething of our poor brief childhood" in it, or it is "like our people's precarious existence amidst the tumult of a hostile world." Her song is, the narrator insists, a nothing, yet it exercises a sway, which he must attribute to its resonance with actualities beyond and outside of it. Josephine herself is in a similarly disarticulated, ambiguous relationship both to her song and her people; an ordinary mouse who claims transcendent value for what might be ordinary piping, she is at once a snotty prima donna, a brave isolate, and a mean-minded artist lost to the grandeur of her own art. In the story, she is a wavering presence, sometimes salient as an individual, sometimes as a relational index, a finger indicating the boundaries of the Mouse Folk's life. Her people are most affected by her song when it residualizes her as an individual, that is, when it so wholly absorbs her that only a faint presence of Josephine lingers behind:

> So there she stands, the delicate creature, shaken by vibrations especially below the breastbone, so that one feels anxious for her, it is as if she has concentrated all her strength on her song, as if from everything in her that does not directly subserve her singing all strength has been withdrawn, almost all power of life, as if she were laid bare, abandoned, committed merely to the care of good angels, as if while she is so wholly withdrawn and living only in her song a cold breath blowing upon her might kill her.

In an ironic confirmation of her claims for her song, she is at last completely residualized by it, as it is residualized into an evanescent memory. Prompted by Josephine's sudden disappearance in a fit of pique, the narrator anticipates her final disappearance, and as soon as he imagines her death, it is as if that death had already happened and she, identified with the pure figurality of her song, were already fading into oblivion:

> Josephine's road, however, must go downhill. The time will soon come when her last notes sound and die into silence. She is a small episode in the eternal history of our people, and the people will get over the loss of her. Not that it will be easy for us; how can our gatherings take place in utter silence? Still, were they not silent even when Josephine was present? Was her actual piping notably louder and more alive than the memory of it will be? Was it even in her lifetime more than a simple memory? Was it not rather because Josephine's singing was

already past losing in this way that our people in their wisdom prized it so highly?

In the course of this paragraph, Josephine dies into her song, and both die into silence, as the distinction between her song and the memory of it dissolves, and the song becomes the memory of itself that it has yet to be. When it is volatilized into "a simple memory," it reaches a purely relational, or figurative, status; it stands at one remove from itself, as a figure, not (any longer) for actualities beyond it, but for its own existence. The epitaphic tone of this paragraph draws on the epitaphic role of figurality; the song recedes into a memorial, a residue of itself, as if it had the prior or other existence that it does not. Because of this vacuum, it cannot be lost, but is "already past losing."

It was in the terms of figure and residue that Kafka described what he called "my isolation from life." In two long journal entries, written in 1922 at the Spindelmuhle sanatorium, he traced the forms of his residualized engagement with "this world.") Blanchot cites these two passages as the most imposing moments in Kafka's journal. As a citizen of the other world, Kafka looks back at this "like a foreigner"—"though in this other world as well—it is the paternal heritage I carry with me—I am the most insignificant and timid of all creatures and am able to keep alive thanks only to the special nature of its arrangements." Marginalized in the other world, as in this, he maintains here an illusory presence, illusory first of all to himself:

> It is indeed a kind of Wandering in the Wilderness in reverse that I am undergoing: I think that I am continually skirting the wilderness and am full of childish hopes (particularly as regards women) that 'perhaps I shall keep in Canaan after all'—when all the while I have been decades in the wilderness and these hopes are merely mirages born of despair, especially at those times when I am the wretchedest of creatures in the desert too, and Canaan is perforce my only Promised Land, for no third place exists for mankind.

In a sort of spectral superimposition, he imagines himself to keep a tenuous hold on the world from which he has already been exluded, and to which he must be as much of a mirage as it is to him. His "exile" does not take the form of simple absence but—as it would have to be, since a certain Franz Kafka still walked the streets—of an infinite remoteness which leaves behind its lingering residue. In the entry that he wrote a day later, Kafka added a more precise account of that residualization which was both the means and the product of his estrangement. I must quote at length here, so as to reproduce both the atmosphere of Kafka's reflections and the atmosphere in which he made them, as he evokes it himself:

> January 29. Suffered some attacks on the road through the snow in the evening. There are conflicting thoughts always in my head, something like this: My situation in this world would seem to be a dreadful one, alone here in Spindelmuhle, on a forsaken road, moreover, where one keeps slipping in the snow in the dark, a senseless road, moreover, without an earthly goal . . . I too forsaken in this place . . . incapable of striking up a friendship with anyone, incapable of tolerating a friendship, at bottom full of endless astonishment when I see a group of people cheerfully assembled together . . . or especially when I see parents with their children; forsaken, moreover, not only here but in general, even in Prague, my "home," and what is more, forsaken not by people (that would not be the worst thing, I could run after them as long as I was alive), but rather by myself vis-à-vis people, by my strength vis-à-vis people; I am fond of lovers but I cannot love, I am too far away, am banished, have—since I am human after all and my roots want nourishment—my proxies "down" (or up) there too, sorry, unsatisfactory comedians who can satisfy me (though indeed they don't satisfy me at all and it is for this reason that I am so forsaken) only because I get my principal nourishment from other roots in other climes, these roots too are sorry ones, but nevertheless better able to sustain life.

When Kafka writes of his "proxies," it becomes clear that he sees himself as figured in this world, but figured by dispersed and illusory representatives from whom he is also far away. These spectral emanations could prove to assert their own power and to produce their own alienating effects; within a year or so of this journal entry, Kafka had expressed regret for this in a letter to Milena: "The reason I ask whether you won't be afraid is that the person of whom you write doesn't exist and never existed, the one in Vienna didn't exist, nor did the one in Gmund, though the latter one more so and he shall be cursed." ("Kafka" had met with Milena in Vienna and Gmund.) Yet this figuralized existence had its own beauty, both for Kafka, as a measure of his ambivalence, and for others, as a residue, signalling "possibilities" (to use one of Kafka's privileged words) in an inaccessible region: "I live elsewhere; it is only that the attraction of the human world is so immense, in an instant it can make one forget everything. Yet the attraction of my world too is strong; those who love me love me because I am 'forsaken' . . . because they sense that in happy moments I enjoy on another plane the freedom of movement completely lacking to me here." This passage has a strangely epitaphic tone, as if Kafka's estrangement allowed him to view his "dead" relics from "elsewhere." But this distant and mediated engagement was also, as he put it in a slightly different context, his "way of participating in life."

Kafka saw his appearance in this world as frail and tenuous, so frail that it could disappear without trauma: "So the thought of death frightens you? I'm terribly afraid only of pains. This is a bad sign. To want death but not the pains is a bad sign. But otherwise one can risk death. One has just been sent out as a biblical dove, has found nothing green, and slips back into the darkness of the ark." The dove which is the envoy but not the power of an exiled source fades unnoticed out of the barren field which is hardly its home. As an avatar of Kafka, this slight emanation is not to be confused either with the "proxies" of this world nor the demons of the other. It is at the mercy of these forces, but is also that through which they work, and which allows them to manifest themselves. For Kafka, it was the measure of self-estrangement, since this remnant continued uncomprehending, but helpless to resist, the demands of its moving powers. Kafka figured this self-estrangement as a sort of uncoordinated bureaucratic structure, much like that surrounding the Law and the Castle. He asked that, in his "case," one imagine three circles, the innermost A and the outermost C: "To C, the active man, no explanations are given, he is merely terribly ordered about by B; C acts under the most severe pressure, but more in fear than in understanding, he trusts, he believes, that A explains everything to B and that B has understood everything rightly." Stranded on the outskirts, C is the most contingent and benighted avatar, but also the only one free to give an account of itself. It speaks as the vestigial "I" of Kafka's diaries and letters (and here, though we should not identify the two, it shares the fragility and porousness of the ego, as Freud describes it). "I" is imperiled but acquiescent, depending for its marginal existence on the regressive pressures to which it has resigned all its vitality:

> You can't properly understand, Milena, what it's all about, or what in part it was about. I don't even understand it myself, I just tremble under the attack, torment myself to the point of madness, but what it is and what it wants in the long run I don't know. Only what it wants at the moment: Quiet, darkness, creeping into a hiding place, this I know and must obey, I can't do otherwise.

It's an outbreak and it passes and partly has passed, but the powers that call it forth are trembling within me all the time, before and after—indeed, my life, my existence consists of this subterranean threat. If it ceases I also cease, it's my way of participating in life; if it ceases I abandon life, as easily and naturally as one closes one's eyes. Hasn't it been there ever since we've known one another, and would you have glanced at me even furtively had it not been there?

Of course one can't just turn it this way and say: Now it has passed and I'm nothing but calm and happy and grateful in the new being-together. One dare not say it although it's almost true (the gratitude is thoroughly true—the happiness only in a certain sense—the calm is never true) for I will always be frightened, above all by myself.

As in "The Burrow," this "subterranean threat" is the ground of "I's" epiphenomenal existence; it ebbs only to leave "I" shadowed and uncertain moments of peace. Yet Kafka takes an oddly forbearing and protective stance towards this animal- or child-like "threat," which is nonetheless brutal for all the solicitude it exacts. It is the commanding and obscure otherness of this "threat," as "I" trails it in loyalty and bewilderment, that aligns it with "the other world." Its buoyant tyranny, unpredictably ebbing and flowing, condemns its host to eternal anxiety, or as Kafka termed it, "fear." Nor was there room to fly, for this region could assert its own tenacious and oppressive vitality, in "the attraction of the human world" which is "so immense," and in the imposing reality of others: "Just now A. was here, do you know him? If only the visits would cease! Everyone is so eternally alive, really immortal, perhaps not in the direction of real immortality but down to the depths of their immediate life. I'm so afraid of them." The volatile "I" sways back and forth between these opposing summons, as Kafka revealed in his shifting degrees of alliance with "this" world and the "other."

But this topographical metaphor, which shows "I" as overlapping and mediating between worlds, could yield to an even more minimalist scheme of the dynamics involved; here, this world acts in unknowing complicity with the other to banish the subject into "infinite remoteness." Writing, which for Kafka had always been an offspring of the other world, remains faithful to its lineage when it is superimposed on this world, for it generates "proxies" which, in figuring it, residualize and so isolate the subject. In inclining toward "the attraction of the human world," the subject seeks to represent itself, but because of the slippage inherent in representation, only the estranging "mirages" of the other world come to light:

All the misfortune of my life—I don't wish to complain, but to make a generally instructive remark—derives, one could say, from letters or from the possibility of writing letters. People have hardly ever deceived me, but letters always—and as a matter of fact not only those of other people, but my own. In my case this is a special misfortune of which I won't say more, but at the same time also a general one. The easy possibility of letter-writing must—seen merely theoretically—have brought into the world a terrible disintegration of souls. It is, in fact, an intercourse with ghosts, and not only with the ghost of the recipient but also with one's own ghost which develops between the lines of the letter one is writing. . . . Writing letters . . . means to denude oneself before the ghosts, something for which they greedily wait. Written kisses don't reach their destination, rather they are drunk on the way by the ghosts. It is on this ample nourishment that they multiply so enormously. . . . The ghosts won't starve, but we will perish.

Chronology

1883	Born in Prague on July 3rd.
1889–93	Attends German elementary school.
1893–1901	Attends German Staatsgymnasium.
1901–1906	Studies law at the German Karl-Ferdinand University in Prague.
1902	Meets Max Brod.
1904	Begins *Description of a Struggle*.
1906	Starts working in a law office as a secretary. Receives law degree. Embarks on his year of practical training in Prague law courts.
1907	Writes "Wedding Preparations in the Country." Takes temporary position with Assurazioni Generali.
1908	Eight prose pieces published under the title *Betrachtung (Meditation)*. Accepts position with Workers' Accident Insurance Institute.
1909	Two sketches (originally part of *Description of a Struggle*) published. Trip to Riva and Brescia (with Max and Otto Brod). "Die Aeroplane in Brescia" published.
1910	Five prose pieces published under the title *Betrachtung (Meditation)*. Starts diary. Trip to Paris (with Max and Otto Brod). Visit to Berlin.

1911   Official trip to Bohemia. Trip (with Max Brod) to Switzerland, Italy, and France, writing travelogues. Becomes interested in Yiddish theatre and literature.

1912   Starts working on *Amerika*. Visits Leipzig and Weimar (with Max Brod). Meets Felice Bauer. Writes "The Judgment." Writes *The Metamorphosis*. *Meditation* published.

1913   "The Stoker" published. Visits Felice Bauer in Berlin. "The Judgment" published. Travels to Vienna and Italy.

1914   Engagement to Felice Bauer. Breaks off engagement. Visit to Germany. Starts *The Trial*. Writes "In the Penal Colony."

1915   Reconciliation with Felice Bauer. *The Metamorphosis* published.

1916   Resumes writing after two years' silence: the fragments of "The Hunter Gracchus," "A Country Doctor," and other stories later included in *A Country Doctor*.

1917   Writing stories, among others "A Report to an Academy," "The Cares of a Family Man," and "The Great Wall of China." Re-engagement to Felice Bauer. Tuberculosis diagnosed. Takes extended sick leave. Engagement to Felice Bauer broken off again.

1918   Continued ill health. Intermittent stays at sanatoria.

1919   Brief engagement to Julie Wohryzek. "In the Penal Colony" and *A Country Doctor* published. Writes "Letter to His Father."

1920   Begins correspondence with Milena Jesenská. Intermittent stays at sanatoria.

1921   Goes back to work with the Workers' Accident Insurance Institute. "The Bucket Rider" published.

1922   Writes *The Castle,* "A Hunger Artist," "Investigations of a Dog." Breaks off relations with Milena Jesenská. Retires from Workers' Accident Insurance Institute. "A Hunger Artist" published.

1923   Meets Dora Dymant. Goes to live with Dora Dymant in
        Berlin. Writes "The Burrow."

1924   Moves back to Prague and writes "Josephine the Singer."
        Moves to Sanatorium Wiener Wald near Vienna. Dies at
        Sanatorium Kierling also near Vienna. Buried in Prague.
        Collection *A Hunger Artist* published shortly after his
        death.

Contributors

HAROLD BLOOM, Sterling Professor of the Humanities at Yale University, is the author of *The Anxiety of Influence, Poetry and Repression,* and many other volumes of literary criticism. His forthcoming study, *Freud: Transference and Authority,* attempts a full-scale reading of all of Freud's major writings. A MacArthur Prize Fellow, he is general editor of five series of literary criticism published by Chelsea House.

WALTER BENJAMIN was a journalist and literary critic, and the author of *The Origin of German Tragic Drama, Charles Baudelaire,* and two collections of essays, *Illuminations* and *Reflections.*

HEINZ POLITZER taught German literature at Bryn Mawr, Oberlin, Cornell University, and the University of California at Berkeley.

MARK SPILKA is Professor of English at Brown University, and is the author of *The Love Ethic of D. H. Lawrence* and *Virginia Woolf's Quarrel with Grieving.*

MARTIN GREENBERG is Professor of English at Long Island University; he has written extensively on science fiction and is the author of *Coming Attractions* and a number of science-fiction anthologies.

PETER HELLER is Professor of German Literature at the State University of New York in Buffalo and the author of *Studies on Nietzsche* and *Von der ersten und letzten Dingen: Studien und Kommentar zu einen Aphorismenreihe von Friedrich Nietzsche.*

THEODOR W. ADORNO, a German philosopher and music historian, is the author of *Prisms, Against Epistemology: A Meta-Critique, The Authoritarian Personality,* and *Aesthetic Theory.*

DORRIT COHN is Professor of Comparative Literature at Radcliffe University and Professor of German at Harvard University. Her work includes *The Sleepwalkers: Elucidations of Hermann Broch's Trilogy* and *Transparent Minds: Narrative Modes for Presenting Consciousness in Fiction.*

HEINRICH HENEL is Professor Emeritus of German Literature at Yale University; he is the author of *The Poetry of Conrad Ferdinand Meyer.*

ERICH HELLER is Avalon Professor Emeritus in the Humanities at Northwestern University. He is the author of *The Disinherited Mind, Thomas Mann: The Ironic German,* and *In The Age of Prose: Literary and Philosophical Essays.*

ALWIN L. BAUM teaches literature at the State University of New York in Buffalo.

WALTER H. SOKEL is Professor of German Language and Literature at the University of Virginia. In addition to many books and articles on Franz Kafka, he has published *The Writer in Extremis: Expressionism in Twentieth Century German Literature.*

DAVID I. GROSSVOGEL is Goldwin Smith Professor of Comparative Literature and Romance Studies at Cornell University, and founding editor of *Diacritics.* His books include *Divided We Stand, Twentieth Century French Drama, Limits of the Novel,* and *Mystery and Its Fictions.*

DAVID EGGENSCHWILER teaches English at the University of Southern California, and is the author of *The Christian Humanism of Flannery O'Connor.*

LAURA QUINNEY teaches English Literature at Cornell University and is working on a study of Samuel Johnson.

Bibliography

Adams, Robert M. *Strains of Discord: Studies in Literary Openness.* Ithaca: Cornell University Press, 1958.

Amann, Jürg. *Franz Kafka.* Munich: Piper, 1983.

Anders, Günther. *Franz Kafka.* New York: Hillary House, 1960.

Arendt, Hannah. "Franz Kafka: A Revaluation." *Partisan Review* 11, no. 3 (1944): 412-22.

Barthes, Roland. *Critical Essays.* Evanston, Ill.: Northwestern University Press, 1972.

Bataille, Georges. *Literature and Evil.* London: Caldor and Boyars, 1973.

Beck, Evelyn Tornton. *Kafka and the Yiddish Theatre.* Madison, Wis.: University of Wisconsin Press, 1971.

Benjamin, Walter. *Illuminations.* New York: Harcourt, Brace & World, 1960.

Bernheimer, Charles. *Flaubert and Kafka: Studies in Psychopoetic Structure.* New Haven: Yale University Press, 1982.

Blanchot, Maurice. *The Space of Literature.* Lincoln, Neb.: University of Nebraska Press, 1982.

Borges, Jorge Luis. "Kafka and His Precursors." In *Labyrinths.* New York: New Directions, 1964.

Bridgwater, Patrick. *Kafka and Nietzsche.* Bonn: Bouvier, 1974.

Brod, Max. *Franz Kafka.* New York: Schocken Books, 1960.

Camus, Albert. *The Myth of Sisyphus.* New York: Knopf, 1955.

Canetti, Elias. *Kafka's Other Trial.* New York: Schocken Books, 1982.

Caputo-Mayr, Marie Luise, ed. *Kafka-Symposium.* Berlin: Agora, 1978.

Corngold, Stanley. *The Commentator's Despair: The Interpretation of Kafka's Metamorphosis.* Port Washington, N.Y.: Kennikat Press, 1973.

Cohn, Dorrit. *Transparent Minds: Narrative Modes for Presenting Consciousness in Fiction.* Princeton, N.J.: Princeton University Press, 1978.

Emrich, Wilhelm. *Franz Kafka: A Critical Study of His Writings.* New York: Ungar, 1968.

Flores, Angel, ed. *The Kafka Debate.* New York: Gordian Press, 1977.

———, ed. *The Kafka Problem.* New York: Octagon, 1963.

Flores, Angel, and Homer Swander, eds. *Franz Kafka Today.* Madison, Wis.: University of Wisconsin Press, 1958.

Goodman, Paul. *Kafka's Prayer.* New York: Vanguard Press, 1947.

Gray, Ronald. *Kafka's Castle.* Cambridge: Cambridge University Press, 1956.

———, ed. *Kafka: A Collection of Critical Essays.* Englewood Cliffs, N.J.: Prentice-Hall, 1962.

Greenberg, Clement. *Art and Culture.* Boston: Beacon Press, 1961.

Greenberg, Martin. *The Terror of Art: Kafka and Modern Literature.* New York: Basic Books, 1968.

Hall, Calvin I., and Richard E. Lind. *Dreams, Life and Literature: A Study of Franz Kafka.* Chapel Hill: University of North Carolina Press, 1970.

Hamalian, Leo, ed. *Franz Kafka: A Collection of Criticism.* New York: McGraw-Hill, 1974.

Heller, Erich. *Franz Kafka.* London: Fontana/Collins, 1974.

———. *The Disinherited Mind.* New York: Harcourt Brace Jovanovich, 1975.

Heller, Peter. *Dialectics and Nihilism.* Amherst, Mass.: University of Massachusetts Press, 1966.

Holland, Norman. "Realism and Unrealism: Kafka's *Metamorphosis.*" *Modern Fiction Studies* 4 (Summer 1958): 143–50.

Hughes, Kenneth, ed. *Franz Kafka: An Anthology of Marxist Criticism.* Hanover and London: New England University Press, 1981.

Janouch, Gustav. *Conversations with Kafka.* New York: Praeger, 1953.

Kuna, Franz. *Franz Kafka: Literature As Corrective Punishment.* London: Elek Books, 1974.

———, ed. *On Kafka: Semi-Centenary Perspectives.* London: Elek Books, 1974.

Lukács, Georg. *Realism In Our Time: Literature and the Class Struggle.* New York: Harper & Row, 1971.

Modern Australian Literature 11, nos. 3/4 (Autumn 1978). Special issue on Kafka.

Mosaic 3, no. 4 (Summer 1970). Special issue on Kafka.

Nagel, Bert. *Franz Kafka.* Berlin: Schmidt, 1974.

Neider, Charles. *The Frozen Sea.* New York: Russell & Russell, 1962.

Neumeyer, Peter F. *Twentieth Century Interpretations of* The Castle*: A Collec-*

tion of Critical Essays. Englewood Cliffs, N.J.: Prentice-Hall, 1969.

Norris, Margot. *Beasts of the Modern Imagination*. Baltimore: Johns Hopkins University Press, 1985.

Pascal, Roy. *Kafka's Narrators: A Study of His Stories and Sketches*. Cambridge: Cambridge University Press, 1982.

Pawel, Ernst. *The Nightmare of Reason: A Life of Franz Kafka*. New York: Farrar, Straus, and Giroux, 1984.

Politzer, Heinz. *Franz Kafka: Parable and Paradox*. Ithaca: Cornell University Press, 1966.

Robert, Marthe. *The Old and the New: From Kafka to Don Quixote*. Berkeley and Los Angeles: University of California Press, 1977.

Rolleston, James. *Kafka's Narrative Theater*. University Park, Penn.: Pennsylvania State University Press, 1974.

————, ed. *Twentieth Century Interpretations of* The Trial: *A Collection of Critical Essays*. Englewood Cliffs, N.J.: Prentice-Hall, 1976.

Slochower, Harry. *A Franz Kafka Miscellany*. New York: Twice a Year Press, 1946.

Sokel, Walter. *Franz Kafka*. New York: Columbia University Press, 1966.

Spann, Meno. *Franz Kafka*. Boston: Twayne, 1976.

Spilka, Mark. *Dickens and Kafka: A Mutual Interpretation*. Bloomington: Indiana University Press, 1963.

Stern, J. P., ed. *The World of Franz Kafka*. New York: Holt, Rinehart & Winston, 1980.

Sussman, Henry. *Franz Kafka: Geometrician of Metaphor*. Madison, Wis.: Coda Press, 1979.

Thorlby, Anthony. *Kafka: A Study*. London: Heinemann, 1972.

Tiefenbrun, Ruth. *Moment of Torment*. Carbondale, Ill.: Southern Illinois University Press, 1973.

Urzidil, Johannes. *There Goes Kafka*. Detroit: Wayne State University Press, 1968.

Weinberg, Helen. *The New Novel in America: The Kafkan Mode in Contemporary Fiction*. Ithaca: Cornell University Press, 1970.

Wilson, Edmund. "A Dissenting Opinion on Franz Kafka." In *Classics and Commercials*. New York: Farrar, Straus, 1950.

Acknowledgments

"Some Reflections on Kafka" (originally entitled "Franz Kafka: On the Tenth Anniversary of His Death" and "Some Reflections on Kafka") by Walter Benjamin from *Illuminations* by Walter Benjamin, copyright © 1955 by Suhrkamp Verlag, Frankfurt A.M., English translation copyright © 1968 by Harcourt Brace Jovanovich, Inc. Reprinted by permission of Harcourt Brace Jovanovich, Inc.

"The Wall of Secrecy: Kafka's *Castle*" (originally entitled "The Bitter Herb: *The Castle*") by Heinz Politzer from *Franz Kafka: Parable and Paradox* by Heinz Politzer, copyright © 1966 by Cornell University Press. Reprinted by permission.

"*Amerika*: Sinful Innocence" (originally entitled "Sinful Innocence") by Mark Spilka from *Dickens and Kafka: A Mutual Interpretation* by Mark Spilka, copyright © 1963 by Indiana University Press. Reprinted by permission.

"Art and Dreams" by Martin Greenberg from *The Terror of Art: Kafka and Modern Literature* by Martin Greenberg, copyright © 1968 by Martin Greenberg. Reprinted by permission of Basic Books, Inc.

" 'Up in the Gallery': Incongruity and Alienation" (originally entitled "Franz Kafka: Incongruity and Alienation") by Peter Heller from *Dialectics and Nihilism: Essays on Lessing, Nietzsche, Mann and Kafka* by Peter Heller, copyright © 1966 by the University of Massachusetts Press. Reprinted by permission.

"Notes on Kafka" by Theodor W. Adorno from *Prisms* by Theodor W. Adorno, copyright © 1967 by Theodor W. Adorno. Reprinted by permission of The MIT Press.

"Kafka's Eternal Present: Narrative Tense in 'A Country Doctor' " (original-ly entitled "Kafka's Eternal Present: Narrative Tense in 'Ein Landarzt' and Other First-Person Stories") by Dorrit Cohn. Reprinted by permis-sion of the Modern Language Association of America from *PMLA* 83 (1968). © 1968 by the Modern Language Association of America.

" 'The Burrow,' or How to Escape from a Maze" (originally entitled "Kafka's 'Der Bau', or How to Escape from a Maze") by Heinrich Henel from *The Discontinuous Tradition* by Heinrich Henel, copyright © 1971 by Oxford University Press. Reprinted by permission.

"*The Castle*" by Erich Heller from *Kafka* by Erich Heller, copyright © 1974 by Erich Heller. Reprinted by permission of Fontana/Collins Paper-backs.

"Parable as Paradox in Kafka's Stories" (originally entitled "Parable as Para-dox in Kafka's 'Erzählungen' ") by Alwin L. Baum from *Modern Language Notes* 91 (6), copyright © 1976 by The Johns Hopkins Univer-sity Press. Reprinted by permission.

"Language and Truth in the Two Worlds of Franz Kafka" by Walter H. Sokel from *German Quarterly* 52, no. 3 (1979), copyright © 1979 by the American Association of Teachers of German. Reprinted by per-mission.

"*The Trial*: Structure as Mystery" (originally entitled "Kafka: Structure as Mystery") by David I. Grossvogel from *Mystery and its Fictions: From Oedipus to Agatha Christie* by David I. Grossvogel, copyright © 1979 by The Johns Hopkins University Press. Reprinted by permission.

"*The Metamorphosis*, Freud, and the Chains of Odysseus" (originally entitled " 'Die Verwandlung,' Freud, and the Chains of Odysseus") by David Eggenschwiler from *Modern Language Quarterly* 39 (1978), copyright © 1979 by the University of Washington. Reprinted by permission.

"More Remote than the Abyss" by Laura Quinney, copyright © 1985 by Laura Quinney. Published for the first time in this volume. Printed by permission.

Index